LIVING FRENCH

BEYOND THE BASICS

Written by
JENNY BARRIOL

Edited by
CHRISTOPHER A. WARNASCH

LIVING LANGUAGE®

Copyright © 2005 by Living Language, A Random House Company

Living Language is a member of the Random House Information Group

Living Language and colophon are registered trademarks of Random House, Inc.

Published in the United States by Living Language, A Random House Company

www.livinglanguage.com

Editor: Christopher A. Warnasch
Production Editor: John Whitman
Production Manager: Heather Lanigan
Interior Design: Sophie Ye Chin

ISBN 1-4000-2165-0

This book is available for special discounts for bulk purchases for sales promotions or premiums. Special editions, including personalized covers, excerpts of existing books, and corporate imprints, can be created in large quantities for special needs. For more information, write to Special Markets/Premium Sales, 1745 Broadway, MD 6-2, New York, New York 10019 or e-mail specialmarkets@randomhouse.com.

PRINTED IN THE UNITED STATES OF AMERICA

10 9 8 7 6 5 4 3 2

ACKNOWLEDGMENTS

Thanks to the Living Language staff: Tom Russell, Sanam Zubli, Christopher Warnasch, Zviezdana Verzich, Suzanne McQuade, Suzanne Podhurst, Sophie Chin, Denise De Gennaro, Linda Schmidt, Alison Skrabek, John Whitman, Helen Kilcullen, and Heather Lanigan. Special thanks to Brigitte de Wever.

CONTENTS

INTRODUCTION

Living Language® *French: Beyond the Basics* is a perfect
follow-up to any beginner-level French course. It focuses
on the specific needs of the intermediate student: vocabulary expansion, review of basic grammar, introduction of
more challenging grammatical constructions, and natural
conversational and idiomatic speech. If you've recently
completed a beginner-level course in French, or if you're
looking for a way to reactivate the French that you may
have studied years ago, *French: Beyond the Basics* is a
great course for you.

The complete program includes this course book, four
hours of recordings, and a reference dictionary. The
recordings include the dialogues and other material from
the course book; they're an essential tool for perfecting
pronunciation and intonation as well as building listening
comprehension. The book may also be used on its own if
you're confident of your pronunciation.

COURSE MATERIALS

There are twenty lessons in *French: Beyond the Basics*.
Each lesson begins with a dialogue that focuses on a particular setting designed to highlight certain vocabulary or
grammatical constructions. These settings will also give
you a good idea of various cultural issues and put the language you're learning into a realistic context. In addition
to the dialogues, each of the twenty lessons also contains
language notes, grammar and usage explanations and
examples, and several exercises. There is also a reference
section at the end of the book containing a grammar summary, a section on letter writing, and e-mail and internet
resources.

DIALOGUE: The dialogue in each lesson features standard, idiomatic French and presents a realistic situation that demonstrates natural language use in a real context. The idiomatic English translation is provided below each line of dialogue.

NOTES: The notes refer to specific words, expressions, or cultural items used in the dialogue that are worthy of further comment. A note may clarify a translation, expand on a grammatical construction, or provide a cultural context. The notes are numbered to refer back to particular lines of dialogue for easy reference.

GRAMMAR AND USAGE: This section focuses on a few key grammatical or structural points. There is a clear and simple explanation first, followed by examples to further illustrate the point. Many of the grammar points are included as a review of key basic structures, but the overall scope of this course also includes more challenging and higher level grammar.

EXERCISES: The final section of each lesson gives you an opportunity to practice the material covered in that lesson. There are several different types of exercises, including fill-in-the-blanks, multiple choice, translation exercises, and more.

GRAMMAR SUMMARY: The grammar summary contains a concise and comprehensive summary of French grammar. This section is an invaluable tool for use either with the course or on its own for independent reference.

LETTER WRITING: This section includes examples of business, formal, and personal letters. There are also forms of salutations and closings, as well as sample envelopes.

E-MAIL AND INTERNET RESOURCES: This section includes sample e-mail correspondence with vocabulary and expressions related to the internet. There is also a list of internet resources of interest to the student of French.

THE RECORDINGS

The recordings include the complete dialogues from all twenty lessons in the course book, as well as a number of example sentences taken from the grammar and usage sections. Each dialogue is first read at conversational speed without interruption, and then a second time with pauses inserted, allowing you to repeat after the native speakers. By listening to and imitating the native speakers, you'll improve your pronunciation and build your listening comprehension while you reinforce the new vocabulary and structures that you've learned in the book.

HOW TO USE THIS COURSE

Take as much time as you need to work through each lesson. Do not be afraid to look over material that you've already covered if you don't feel confident enough to move ahead. The course is organized so that you can move through it at a pace that is exactly right for you.

Start each lesson by reading through it once to get a sense of what it includes. Don't try to memorize the vocabulary from the dialogue or master the grammar items, and don't attempt to do any of the exercises. Simply familiarize yourself with the lesson in a general sense.

Then start again by reading through the dialogue a first time to get a general sense of it. Then look over the notes to help clarify points that may be confusing. Next, read the dialogue more carefully, focusing on each line and its translation. If you come across new or unfamiliar vocabulary, write it down in a notebook or somewhere else you can return to for practice. Re-read the dialogue until you're comfortable with it.

After you've carefully read the dialogue a few times, turn on the recordings and listen as you read along. The dialogue is first read at normal conversational speed, and then again with pauses inserted for you to repeat. Follow along in your book as you listen, and then again as you repeat, in order to activate two senses—sight and hearing. After you've listened while reading along, close your book and try to follow without any written material. See how much of each sentence and phrase you can successfully repeat. Again, feel free to repeat these steps as many times as you'd like.

After you've finished reading and listening to the dialogue, turn to the Grammar and Usage section. Read each point carefully until it makes sense to you, and take a close look at the example sentences to see how they relate to the point at hand. If you're using a notebook, it's a good idea to take notes on the grammar and try to restate each point in your own words. Try to come up with other examples if you can. After you've completed each point in a similar way, turn on your recordings and listen through the section in the same way as you did for the dialogue. Listening and repeating will serve as an excellent review.

The exercises at the end of each lesson will help you review the material and check your overall progress. If you're unsure of a particular exercise, go back and cover the grammar again. If you're not comfortable moving ahead, make sure you take the time you need.

Turn to the Grammar Summary while you're working through the course to remind yourself of a grammar point you may have forgotten, or to provide yourself with another way of explaining a point you're working on. Also, take a look at the Internet Resources for suggestions of how you can use the internet as a reference tool or as a way to enhance your studies.

Now, you're ready to begin.

LESSON 1

RENDEZ-VOUS AU CAFÉ
MEETING AT A CAFÉ

A. DIALOGUE

0. *Charles et Jane viennent juste d' arriver à Paris. À l'hôtel, Charles décide de téléphoner à son ami parisien, Michel. Ils fixent un rendez-vous.*
   Charles and Jane have just arrived in Paris. At the hotel, Charles decides to call his Parisian friend, Michel. They schedule a meeting.

1. Michel: **Allô?**
   Hello?

2. Charles: **Allô, Michel? Bonjour, c'est Charles Lewis, de New York. Ça va bien?**
   Hello, Michel? Good morning, it's Charles Lewis from New York. Are you well?

3. Michel: **Charles! Quel plaisir de t'entendre! Oui, ça va et toi? Où te trouves-tu en ce moment?**
   Charles! What a pleasure to hear from you! Yes, everything is well and what about you? Where are you right now?

4. Charles: **À l'Hôtel Merceau. On vient d'arriver, Jane et moi.**
   At the Hotel Merceau. Jane and I have just gotten here.

5. Michel: **Cela me fera plaisir de vous voir, après tout ce temps. Si vous êtes libres cet après-midi, nous pourrions boire un verre ensemble. À deux heures?**

I'll be glad to see you after all this time. If you're free this afternoon, we could have a drink together. At two o'clock?

6. Charles: **C'est parfait. Où peut-on se retrouver?**
Perfect. Where can we meet?

7. Michel: **Au Café des Deux Magots, Place Saint-Germain. Ce n'est pas très loin de votre hôtel, je crois. Mais prenez un taxi, ce sera plus simple.**
At the Café des Deux Magots, Place Saint-Germain. I think it's not too far from your hotel. But take a taxi, it'll be easier.

8. Charles: **D'accord. Est-ce qu'on trouvera une table libre à cette heure-là?**
Okay. Will we get a table at that time?

9. Michel: **Oui, sans doute. Alors, à tout à l'heure.**
Yes, probably. So, see you in a little while.

10. Charles: **Entendu. À plus tard.**
All right. See you later.

11. *On se retrouve au café.*
Meeting at the café.

12. Michel: **Bienvenue à Paris, Charles!**
Charles, welcome to Paris!

13. Charles: **Merci, Michel. Quelle joie d'être de nouveau à Paris!**
Thank you, Michel. It's so great to be in Paris again.

14. Michel: **Au fait, où est Jane?**
By the way, where's Jane?

15. Charles: **Elle va arriver. Elle avait envie de voir une expo d'art angolais qui finit aujourd'hui.**

J'ai préféré me reposer à l'hôtel. Ces voyages en avion sont tellement longs.

She'll be right here. She felt like going to see an Angolan art exhibition which ends today. I preferred to rest at the hotel. These flights are so long.

16. Michel: **Préfères-tu t'asseoir à l'intérieur ou à la terrasse?**
Do you prefer to sit inside or out on the terrace?

17. Charles: **À la terrasse, bien sûr!**
On the terrace, of course.

18. Michel: **Ah! Voilà une table libre, tout au bout.**
Ah! There's an available table, all the way at the end.

19. *Charles et Michel s'installent. Un serveur ne tarde pas à arriver.*
Charles and Michel sit down and settle in. Not long after, a waiter comes.

20. Serveur: **Bonjour, Messieurs. Qu'est-ce que vous désirez?**
Waiter: Hello gentlemen. What will you have?

21. Charles: **Un citron pressé, s'il vous plaît. Il fait si chaud!**
A lemonade, please. It's so warm!

22. Michel: **Et pour moi, un demi.**
And for me a draft beer.

23. Charles: **Ah, voilà enfin ma femme! Jane, on est là!**
Finally, here's my wife! Jane, here we are!

24. Jane: **Bonjour! Michel, quel plaisir!**
Hello! Michel, so nice to see you!

25. Michel: **Je suis ravi de te revoir aussi. On vient juste de commander. Que voudrais-tu boire?**
I'm so glad to see you as well. We've just ordered. What would you like to drink?

26. Jane: **Hmm. Je vais prendre un Pastis!**
Huh. I'm going to have a Pastis!

27. Charles: **Ah! La boisson préférée de Jane en France.**
Ha! Jane's favorite drink in France.

28. Serveur: **Tout de suite.**
Right away.

29. Charles: **On n'oublie jamais l'agréable initiation à la vie française! Tiens! Voici déjà le serveur qui nous apporte les boissons! À votre santé!**
You never forget the pleasant reintroduction to French life! Look! Here's the waiter bringing our drinks already! Cheers!

30. Michel: **À la vôtre! Et bon séjour à Paris!**
Cheers! Here's to an enjoyable stay in Paris!

31. Jane: **Tchin, tchin! On est vraiment bien ici. On aurait envie d'y rester toute la journée.**
Cheers! It's really nice here. One could stay here the whole day.

32. Michel: **Et ici, tu peux passer toute l'après-midi au café.**
And here, you can spend all afternoon at the café.

33. Charles: **On ne demande jamais aux clients de partir?**
They never ask the customers to leave?

34. Michel: **Non, pas du tout! Tu peux lire le journal, écrire ton courrier, bavarder avec des amis ou, tout simplement, regarder passer les gens aussi longtemps que tu le désires.**
Not at all! You can read a newspaper, write letters, chat with friends, or simply watch the people passing by as long as you wish.

35. Jane: **Quand on habite New York, on oublie bien vite l'art de se détendre.**
When you live in New York, you quickly forget the art of relaxing.

36. Michel: **À part cela, j'espère que vous avez fait quand même bon voyage.**
I hope you've still had a good trip otherwise.

37. Jane: **Oui, en plus, nous étions assis à côté d'un couple hollandais très sympathique. Ils m'ont recommandé l'exposition que je viens de voir.**
Yes, and we were sitting next to a very nice Dutch couple. They recommended the exhibit that I just saw.

38. Charles: **Oui, mais malheureusement, le vol avait du retard et il y avait des turbulences.**
Yes, but unfortunately, the flight was delayed, and there was some turbulence.

39. Michel: **Bon, tu vas pouvoir te reposer. Autrement, si vous n'avez pas de projets pour demain soir, vous pourriez peut-être dîner à la maison. Je tiens à vous présenter ma compagne, Éliane.**
Well, you'll be able to rest. By the way, if you don't have any plans for tomorrow, maybe you could have dinner at my house. I'm eager to introduce my girlfriend, Éliane, to you.

40. Jane: **Quelle bonne idée!**
    What a good idea!

41. Michel: **Très bien, alors à demain soir. Je règle et je file car j'ai un rendez-vous à 15h 30. Mais non, Charles, je vous invite pour fêter votre arrivée à Paris. Je t'en prie. L'addition, s'il vous plaît.**
    Very well, until tomorrow evening then. I'll take care of the bill and I'll quickly get going because I have an appointment at 3:30. No, Charles, I'm treating you to celebrate your arrival in Paris. Please. The check, please.

B. NOTES

0. *fixer* or *prendre un rendez-vous*: to make an appointment.

1. *Allô!*: What to say when answering the telephone.

3. *Quel plaisir de t'entendre!* Note the use of *quel* to express "What a . . . !" (See Lesson 5 for a full explanation.) *Quel plaisir* (masculine*)* with *de* is followed by an infinitive. Below is the synonymous *Quelle joie d'être . . . ! Quelle* is feminine because *joie* is feminine.
    Où vous trouvez-vous?: Form of *se trouver*, a reflexive verb, lit.: to find oneself, *vous vous trouvez*. This is often used in place of *être* (to be) to express location. Other reflexive verbs in this lesson are *se retrouver, s'asseoir, se détendre*. Reflexive verbs are discussed in detail in Lesson 5.

4. *On vient juste d'arriver*: We've just arrived.
    on corresponds to we, they, people. (See Lesson 4 for a full explanation.)

5. *Cela me fait très plaisir de* + infinitive: I'm very glad to + infinitive.

   nous pourrions: we could. The conditional is used in most expressions of courtesy. (See Irregular Verb Charts for conditional forms of *pouvoir* and Lesson 6 for the conditional of courtesy.)

7. *(le) Café des Deux Magots*: A famous café on the Left Bank in Paris.

8. *D'accord*: Agreed, okay. A synonymous phrase is *Entendu*, in line 10.

9. *À tout à l'heure*: See you in a little while

11. *se retrouver* and *se rencontrer* both mean to meet. Note that *se retrouver* means to get together or to meet up, and *se rencontrer* means to meet for the first time, or to meet someone unexpectedly.

12. *Bienvenue*: Welcome. A common courtesy formula.

13. *de nouveau*: again

14. *au fait*: by the way

15. *Elle va arriver*: She's on her way

    elle avait envie de + infinitive. she felt like + -ing verb (See Lesson 4.)

    préférer + infinitive verb: to prefer + verb. (See Lesson 6.)

    tellement or *si* : so

17. *Voilà une table libre*: Here's an available table. (For *voilà*, see Lesson 3.)

    désirer: to wish; to like

    messieurs: plural of *monsieur* (similarly: *mesdames, mesdemoiselles*).

21. *un citron pressé*: lemonade (lit.: a squeezed lemon). There is another drink called *la limonade*, which is a lemon flavored carbonated drink.

    il fait si chaud: the verb *faire* is used in weather expressions.

22. *pour moi*: for me. Note the use of the disjunctive pronoun after the preposition *pour*. (See Lesson 5 for explanation of disjunctive pronoun forms and uses.)

    un demi: short for *un demi-litre* (a half-liter). A liter is approximately equal to a quart.

25. *être ravi de* means *être content de*, that is to be glad to. Both expressions are followed by an infinitive.

26. *prendre un verre, prendre le petit déjeuner*: to have a drink, to have breakfast

28. *tout de suite*: immediately, right away

29. *la vie française*: the definite article is used with nouns that express a general concept or idea, such as: *La vie est belle*. Life is beautiful. *La santé est importante*. Health is important.

    Tiens!: Look! This is a colloquial exclamation.

    déjà: already. Notice its position in the sentence immediately after *voici*.

    le serveur qui nous apporte: (lit.) the waiter who is bringing us.

    des boissons (fem.): from the verb *boire*, to drink.

30. *À la vôtre, à votre santé*: a familiar toast. Lit.: to yours, to your health.

    bon séjour: lit. "good sojourn, stay."

31. *tchin tchin*: cheers.

    On aurait envie de is equivalent to *on voudrait, on aimerait*: we'd like to, we'd feel like. (See Lesson 4.)

y rester: to stay there. *y* is an adverbial pronoun that precedes the verb and replaces phrases introduced by *à, vers, dans* that refer to location. *Je vais à Paris* or *J'y vais*.

la journée. This feminine form of *jour* is used to indicate duration or extension of time. Note also *toute la matinée*: all morning, *toute la soirée*: the entire evening. Contrast with the masculine forms, such as *tous les jour* (every day), *tous les matins* (every morning), *tous les soirs* (every evening).

32. *passer*: to spend (time); *dépenser*: to spend (money).

33. *ne jamais*: never.

34. Two phrases with *tout*, *pas du tout*: not at all and *tout simplement*: simply.
    écrire son courrier: to write one's mail.
    aussi longtemps que: as long as.

35. *bien vite, très vite*: very quickly. *bien* is used to intensify the word it precedes.

36. *j'espère que*: I hope that. In verbs like *espérer* which have *é* as the last vowel of the stem, the *é* changes to *è* before the silent endings *-e, -es,* and *-ent*. However, the *é* remains throughout the future and conditional tenses. Other verbs similarly conjugated: *préférer*: to prefer, *répéter*: to repeat, *s'inquiéter*: to worry, *posséder*: to possess, *protéger*: to protect.
    quand même or *au moins*: at least, still.
    faire bon voyage: to have a nice trip.

37. *en plus*: in addition.
    hollandais, hollandaise: Dutch. *La Hollande* or *les Pays-Bas* is the country the Netherlands. Note that the nationality adjectives are not capitalized in French.

recommander: to recommend, to suggest.
une expo, short for *une exposition*: an exhibition.

38. *avoir du retard*: to be delayed and *être en retard*: to be late.

39. *reposer*: to rest.

   pas de projets: no plans. The preposition *de* is used instead of *des* because of the negative partitive construction. (See Lesson 8 for detailed explanation of the partitive.)

   Je tiens à vous présenter: I'm eager to introduce to you.

40. *Quelle bonne idée!*: What a good idea!

41. *régler l'addition*: to settle, to take care of the bill (in a restaurant or café)

   filer: to leave quickly

C. GRAMMAR AND USAGE

1. The expression *venir de*, literally "to come from" can be translated as "to have just done something." Note that it is followed directly by an infinitive, with or without an object pronoun.

Je viens de lui parler.
   I have just spoken to him.

Il venait de l'acheter.
   He had just bought it.

L'exposition qu'elle vient de voir.
   The exhibition she's just seen.

2. *Tenir à* can be translated as "to want very much to" or "to be eager to." Its structure is similar to *venir de*.

Il tient à vous parler.
> He really wants to speak to you.

Nous tenions à voir Michel.
> We were eager to see Michel.

Je tenais à vous présenter Éliane.
> I was eager to introduce Éliane to you.

3. Traditionally, *voici* meant "here" or "here is" and *voilà* meant "there" or "there is." If this expression is used with a pronoun, the pronoun comes first. If it is used with a noun, the noun follows.

Me voici.
> Here I am.

Les voilà.
> There they are.

Voilà mon nouvel ordinateur.
> Here's my new computer.

In modern usage, *voilà* is often used instead of *voici*.

Me voici.	Here I am.
Te voici.	Here you are.
Le voici.	Here he/it is.
La voici.	Here she/it is.
Nous voici.	Here we are.
Vous voici.	Here you are.
Les voici.	Here they are.

4. The expression *avoir envie de* means "to feel like" or "to want to" and is used primarily in the present, imperfect, and future tenses.

J'ai envie de dormir.
> I feel like sleeping.

Il avait envie de voir cette exposition.
> He wanted to see this exhibition.

Elle aura envie d'acheter le livre.
> She will want to buy the book.

5. In French, infinitives must often follow either the preposition *de* or the preposition *à*. There are some general guidelines, but it's best simply to memorize whether *de* or *à* must be used.

De is used after certain nouns that describe emotion, doubt or feeling:

J'ai envie de partir.
> I feel like leaving.

Quel plaisir de revoir Paris!
> What a pleasure to see Paris again!

Il a le droit de rester.
> He has the right to stay. / He is allowed to stay.

It is also used after certain adjectives that describe emotion, doubt, or feeling:

Nous sommes contents de partir.
> We are happy to leave.

Je suis ravie de faire votre connaissance.
> I am pleased to make your acquaintance.

Quelle joie d'être de nouveau ici!
> What a joy to be here again!

De is also used after certain verbs, among which:

Il refuse de venir.
> He refuses to come.

Vous avez décidé de téléphoner à vos amis.
> You've decided to call your friends.

On essaie de parler tous les jours.
> We try to speak every day.

Elle ne demande pas aux clients de partir.
    She doesn't ask the clients to leave.

The preposition *à* is used after nouns when the infinitive expresses the purpose or outcome of that noun:

Avez-vous une chambre à louer?
    Do you have a room to rent?

C'est une histoire à dormir debout.
    It's an unbelievable story.

J'ai entendu un bruit à rendre sourd.
    I heard a deafening noise.

The preposition *à* is also used after certain adjectives when the infinitive qualifies the adjective:

Nous sommes prêts à partir.
    We are ready to go.

C'est facile à faire.
    It's easy to do.

And *à* is also used after certain verbs, such as:

Je commence à parler français.
    I am beginning to speak French.

Nous nous attendons à partir en retard.
    We are expecting to leave late.

Il tient à régler l'addition.
    He insists on settling the bill.

6. Many verbs are followed directly by the infinitive, with no preposition at all. The following are the most common:

aller: Je vais téléphoner.
    I'm going to phone.

préférer: Nous préférons partir tôt.
    We prefer to leave early.

vouloir: Je voudrais laisser un pourboire.
   I'd like to leave a tip.

falloir: Il faut faire une réservation.
   One must make a reservation.

pouvoir: Vous pouvez lire le journal.
   You can read the paper.

savoir: Nous savons prendre le métro.
   We know how to take the subway.

EXERCISES

A. Substitute one of the words or expressions in parentheses for the underlined synonymous word or expression in the pattern sentence. Write the new sentence and say it aloud.

   1. Example: *Il fait <u>beau</u>.*
      (chaud, froid, frais, doux, bon, mauvais).

      Answer: *Il fait <u>chaud</u>.*

   2. *<u>C'est moi qui</u> l'invite.*
      (son ami, lui, tu, sa sœur, je)

   3. *<u>Quel plaisir de</u> vous voir!*
      (je suis ravi de, je suis en retard, quel problème, à la vôtre)

   4. *On peut <u>se rencontrer</u> ce soir.*
      (discuter, se voir, tenir à, voyager, rencontrer)

   5. *Nous avons <u>fixé</u> un rendez-vous.*
      (venu, tenu, parlé de, prépare, pris)

B. Replace the subject pronoun *je* with the other subject pronouns *(tu, il, elle, nous, vous, ils, elles)*. Make the appropriate changes to the verb. (Study the verb forms in the Irregular Verb Charts if necessary.)

1. *Je viens de l'acheter.*

2. *Je tiens à le voir.*

3. *J'ai envie de lui parler.*

C. Replace the underlined object pronoun with the other appropriate pronouns (*me, te, le, la, nous, vous, les*), and translate.

1. *Me voici.*

2. *Te voilà.*

D. Say the following sentences aloud, and then translate them into English.

1. *Je vais retrouver Charles.*

2. *Où pourrions-nous nous rencontrer?*

3. *Est-ce qu'on trouvera une table libre à cette heure-là?*

4. *Je voudrais téléphoner à mon ami.*

5. *Je viens juste d'arriver à l'hôtel.*

6. *Elle veut fixer un rendez-vous.*

7. *Il faut s'asseoir à l'intérieur.*

8. *Il faut payer l'addition.*

9. *Elle a envie d'aller voir une expo.*

10. *Nous allons fêter votre arrivée.*

E. Translate the following sentences into French. Then say them aloud.

1. I know how to read a French newspaper.

2. We're going there by subway.

3. I'm beginning to unpack.

4. Did they recommend that you go there?

5. She wants very much to see him.

6. I simply refuse to stay here.

7. He has asked them if they had a good trip.

8. I'm so happy to be in Paris.

9. It's time to meet Michel.

10. You have the right to stay on the terrace all day long.

F. From among the three choices given, choose the best translation for the word or phrase given at the beginning of each sentence. Write the complete sentence and translate.

1. (have just) *Je* _____ *arriver.*
   tiens à / ai envie d' / viens d'

2. (right away) _____, *messieurs.*
   À la vôtre / Heureusement / Tout de suite

3. (drinks) *Tiens, voici déjà le serveur qui nous apporte les* _____.
   Verres / boissons / pourboires

4. (never) *Et on ne demande* _____ *aux clients de partir?*
   Jamais / plus / rien

5. (of course) *À la terrasse,* _____.
   pas du tout / bien entendu / tout à fait

6. (It's) _____ *chaud aujourd' hui.*
   Il est / C'est / Il fait

7. (I feel like) _____ *marcher.*
   Je me sens / Je demande / J'ai envie de

8. (pay) *Je vais* _____ *l'addition et laisser un pourboire.*
   Rejoindre / retrouver / régler

Answer Key

A. 1. *Il fait <u>chaud</u>.* 2. *<u>Je</u> l' invite.* 3. *<u>Je suis ravi de</u> vous voir!*
4. *On peut <u>se voir</u> ce soir.* 5. *Nous avons <u>pris</u> un rendez-vous.*

B. 1. *Je viens de l'acheter. Tu viens de l'acheter. Il vient de l'acheter. Elle vient de l'acheter. Nous venons de l'acheter. Vous venez de l'acheter. Ils viennent de l'acheter. Elles viennent de l'acheter.*

2. *Je tiens à le voir. Tu tiens à le voir. Il tient à le voir. Elle tient à le voir. Nous tenons à le voir. Vous tenez à le voir. Ils tiennent à le voir. Elles tiennent à le voir.*

3. *J'ai envie de lui parler. Tu as envie de lui parler. Il a envie de lui parler. Elle a envie de lui parler. Nous avons envie de lui parler. Vous avez envie de lui parler. Ils ont envie de lui parler. Elles ont envie de lui parler.*

C. 1. *Me voici.* Here I am. *Te voici.* Here you are. *Le voici.* Here he is. *La voici.* Here she is. *Nous voici.* Here we are. *Vous voici.* Here you are. *Les voici.* Here they are. (m. & f.)

2. *Me voilà.* There I am. *Te voilà.* There you are. *Le voilà.* There he is. *La voilà.* There she is. *Nous voilà.* There we are. *Vous voilà.* There you are. *Les voilà.* There they are.

D. 1. I'm going to meet Charles. 2. Where could we meet? 3. Are we going to find a free table at that time? 4. I would like to call my friend. 5. I have just arrived at the hotel. 6. She wants to make an appointment. 7. It's necessary to sit indoors. 8. It is necessary to pay the bill. 9. She feels like going to see an exhibition. 10. We are going to celebrate your arrival.

E. 1. *Je sais lire un journal français.* 2. *Nous y allons en métro.* 3. *Je commence à défaire les bagages.* 4. *Est-ce qu'ils vous / t'ont recommandé d'y aller?* 5. *Elle tient à le voir.* 6. *Je refuse tout simplement de rester ici.* 7. *Il leur a demandé s'ils avaient fait bon voyage.* 8. *Je suis telle-ment ravi d'être à Paris.* 9. *C'est l'heure de rencontrer Michel.* 10. *Vous avez le droit de rester à la terrasse toute la journée.*

F. 1. *Je viens d'arriver.* I've just arrived. 2. *Tout de suite, messieurs.* Right away, gentlemen. 3. *Tiens, voici déjà le serveur qui nous apporte les boissons.* Look, here is the waiter bringing us our drinks already. 4. *Et on ne demande jamais aux clients de partir?* And they never ask the customers to leave? 5. *À la terrasse, bien entendu.* On the terrace, naturally (of course). 6. *Il fait chaud aujourd'hui.* It's hot today. 7. *J'ai envie de marcher.* I feel like walking. 8. *Je vais régler l'addition et laisser un pourboire.* I am going to settle the bill and leave a tip.

LESSON 2

L'ACTUALITÉ
THE NEWS

A. DIALOGUE

0. *C'est le soir à Paris chez Michel et Éliane. On sonne
   à la porte. Éliane accueille Jane et Charles et les
   invitent à s'asseoir dans le salon.*
   It's the evening in Paris at Michel and Éliane's
   home. The door rings. Éliane welcomes Jane and
   Charles and invites them to sit in the living room.

1. Éliane: **Je suis très heureuse de vous rencontrer.
   Michel m'a tant parlé de vous.**
   I am very happy to meet you. Michel has spoken to
   me so much about you.

2. Jane: **Le plaisir est partagé. Tenez, voici des
   fleurs.**
   The pleasure is ours. Here are some flowers.

3. Charles: **Michel nous a laissé un message à l'hôtel, à propos d'un rendez-vous de dernière
   minute**.
   Michel left us a message at the hotel about a last
   minute appointment.

4. Éliane: **Ce bouquet est beau, merci. Oui. Il est
   tellement pris par son travail. Cependant, il ne
   devrait pas tarder. En attendant, on pourrait
   prendre un apéritif?**
   This bouquet is beautiful, thanks. Yes, he's so busy
   with his work. But he shouldn't be long. In the
   meantime, we could have a drink?

5. Charles: **Ah! Volontiers.**
Ah! With pleasure.

6. *Quelques minutes plus tard, les trois amis boivent,
discutent et regardent le journal télévisé.*
A few minutes later, the three friends are having a
drink, talking and watching the news on TV.

7. Éliane: **Arte est une très bonne chaîne de télévision publique. Elle présente quotidiennement des
émissions culturelles françaises et allemandes.**
Arte is a very good public TV channel. It shows
French and German cultural programs daily.

8. Jane: **Aux États-Unis, nous avons beaucoup de
chaînes, mais peu sont intéressantes et les actualités sont rarement sérieuses, comme ici. Cette
chaîne-ci semble passionnante.**
In the U.S., we have a lot of channels, but few are
interesting and the news programs are rarely in
depth like here. This channel here looks fascinating.

9. Charles: **Oui, Michel nous a dit que vous étiez
journaliste.**
Yes, Michel told us that you were a journalist.

10. Éliane: **Oui, enfin, je réalise des documentaires. En
fait, mon dernier film sera montré ce soir sur Arte.**
Yes, well, I make documentaries. In fact, my last
film will be shown this evening on Arte.

11. Charles: **Ah, très bien. Et quel est le sujet de ce
documentaire?**
Oh, great. And what is this documentary about?

12. Éliane: **C'est sur l'après-guerre en Angola. J'ai
filmé la population angolaise pendant une quinzaine de semaines, à la fin de la guerre en avril**

2002, à Luanda, la capitale, et dans tout le pays. La situation s'améliore grâce à la paix.

It's about the aftermath of the war in Angola. I filmed the Angolan people for about fifteen weeks at the end of the war in April 2002, in Luanda, the capital, and in the whole country. The situation is getting better thanks to peace.

13. Jane: **Oui, j'ai lu des articles sur la situation dans ce pays. Une guerre de plus de 27 ans!**
    Yes, I've read some articles about the situation in this country. A war that lasted more than 27 years!

14. Charles: **Incroyable**.
    Incredible.

15. *Le téléphone sonne. Éliane s'excuse et va dans une autre pièce.*
    The phone rings. Éliane apologizes and goes into another room.

16. Charles: **Tiens! Regardons la météo pour demain.**
    Here! Let's watch the weather report for tomorrow.

17. Jane: **Ah! Il nous faut absolument du beau temps, si on veut se promener au Jardin du Luxembourg et faire des courses dans le Quartier Latin. Je préfère me promener dans ce quartier-ci.**
    Ah! We absolutely need good weather, if we want to visit the Jardin du Luxembourg and do some shopping in the Latin Quarter. I prefer to walk around in this neighborhood.

18. Charles: **Les dieux t'ont entendue, il semble. Un ciel nuageux mais avec des éclaircies dans l'après-midi.**
    The gods have heard you, it seems. Cloudy sky, but with some sun in the afternoon.

19. *Quand Éliane réapparaît, on sonne à la porte.*
    When Éliane reappears, someone rings at the door.

20. Éliane: **Cela doit être Michel. Il a dû encore oublier ses clés en quittant le bureau!**
    It must be Michel. He's probably forgotten his keys again while leaving the office!

21. Michel: **Bonsoir, Chérie. Charles, Jane, comment allez-vous? Ah, vous avez commencé à prendre l'apéritif. Bien! Moi aussi, j'ai bien besoin d'un verre!**
    Good evening, Dear. Charles, Jane, how are you? Ah, you've started having drinks. Good! I need a drink, too!

22. Tous: **À la vôtre!**
    All: Cheers!

23: Michel: **Encore désolé de ce retard imprévu. Vous aurez fait connaissance sans moi.**
    Sorry again for this unexpected delay. You must have gotten to know one another without me.

24. Charles: **Mais ne t'inquiète pas! Éliane nous parlait de son travail captivant.**
    But don't worry! Éliane was telling us about her captivating work.

25. Michel: **Pouvons-nous continuer à en discuter en mangeant? Je meurs de faim!**
    Can we keep on talking about it while eating? I'm starving!

B. NOTES

0. *On sonne à la porte*: Someone is ringing at the door, but *le téléphone sonne*: the phone is ringing.

Eliane accueille. from the verb *accueillir*: to welcome.

1. *tant* is a synonym of *si* and *tellement*.

2. *Le plaisir est partagé*: The pleasure is ours (literally "shared.")

3. *à propos de*: regarding.
   de dernière minute: last minute.

4. *Il est pris par son travail*: He's very busy at work. *Pris* comes from the verb *prendre*.
   Il ne devrait pas tarder: He should be here soon. Note the use of the conditional in *devrait* (supposition).
   En attendant: in the meantime.
   un apéritif: drinks that are served before a meal with salty snacks such as peanuts, crackers, etc. Again, French will use the verb *prendre*, as in *prendre un apéritif, un repas, un verre* (a drink).

5. *volontiers*: with pleasure.

6. *le journal télévisé*: TV news. *Les actualités, les nouvelles*: news. *Une émission*: a show.

7. *quotidiennement* or *tous les jours*: every day. *un quotidien*: a daily paper. Others are *hebdomadaire*: weekly, *un hebdomadaire*: a weekly paper, *mensuel*: monthly, *un mensuel*: a monthly paper and *annuel*: yearly.

8. *peu sont intéressantes*: few are interesting, also *un peu de*: a little of.
   comme ici: like here.

9. *Il nous a dit que vous étiez . . .* : He said that you were. . . Note the agreement of the tenses.

10. *réaliser*: to direct, to make (films), also *la réalisa-tion*: the making, realization, *le réalisateur*: the director.

   Le film sera montré: The film will be shown.

12. *une quinzaine de semaines*: about fifteen weeks. The suffix *-aine* at the end of a number indicates an approximate amount, such as *une douzaine*: a dozen, *une dizaine*: about ten.

   à la fin de: at the end of.

   s'améliorer: to get better or to be getting better and *améliorer*: to make better.

   grâce à: thanks to and *à cause de*: because of.

16. *la météo*: the weather report

17. *il nous faut*: we need (lit.: "it is necessary for us"). This is the present tense of the verb *falloir,* to be nec-essary to. It is used only in the third person singular. (See Lesson 3.)

   Le Jardin du Luxembourg is located in the *Saint-Michel* neighborhood, also called *Le Quartier Latin* in the *1er arrondissement,* on the Left Bank (of the Seine River), *la Rive Gauche*. It is called the Latin Quarter because during the Middle Ages, all stu-dents spoke Latin.

18. *il semble*: it seems

   Des éclaircies means in the language of *la météo,* the sun will appear and clouds will thin.

20. *Il a dû* + infinitive: He probably had to + infinitive.

23. *(je suis) désolé de*: (I am) sorry for

   ce retard imprévisible: this unforeseeable delay. The adjective *imprévisible* and its opposite, *prévi-*

sible, come from the verb *prévoir,* and the past participle is *prévu.*

faire connaissance: to meet for the first time.

25. *Je meurs de faim*: I'm starving.

C. GRAMMAR AND USAGE

The indefinite relative pronouns, *ce qui* and *ce que* can both be translated by "what."

1. *Ce qui* is subject of the verb that follows.

Ce qui me révolte, c'est l'implication de nos pays dans le trafic d'armes.
   What revolts me is the implication of our countries in arms trafficking.

On ne sait pas ce qui le retarde tant.
   We don't know what's delaying him so much.

Voici ce qui est prévu.
   Here is what is planned.

2. *Ce que* is direct object of the verb that follows.

C'est ce que je te dis.
   That's what I'm telling you.

Ce que vous montrez dans ce documentaire est intéressant.
   What you show in this documentary is interesting.

Je comprends ce qu'Éliane explique.
   I understand what Éliane is explaining.

3. The demonstrative adjectives, just like the articles, agree in gender and numbers with the nouns they precede. They

are used to point to something or someone and are translated by "this" or "that" in the singular form, and "these" or "those" in the plural form.

The masculine singular demonstrative adjectives are *ce* or *cet* (in front of a masculine noun starting with a vowel or a mute *h*).

ce film, ce pays, cet homme, cet hôtel
   this film, this country, this man, this hotel

The feminine singular demonstrative adjective is *cette*.

cette femme, cette histoire
   this woman, this story

Their plural form is *ces* for both genders.

ces films, ces pays, ces hommes, ces hôtels, ces femmes, ces histoires
   these films, these countries, these men, these hotels, these women, these stories

4. To specify the meaning of "this" vs. "that" or "these" vs. "those" while using demonstrative adjectives, attach *-ci* (closer object, as in *ici*) or *-là* (more distant object) to the noun.

Cette chaîne de télévision est intéressante, mais cette chaîne-là ne l' est pas.
   This channel is interesting, but that one is not.

Cet homme-ci est petit, cette femme-là est grande.
   This man is short, that woman is tall.

Je préfère me promener dans ce quartier-ci.
   I prefer to walk around in this neighborhood.

5. Adjectives of nationality are not capitalized in French, and have both a feminine and a masculine form. The plural forms are created by adding a final *-s* to the singu-

lar form. If the singular already ends in -*s*, then nothing is added. Note that adjectives ending in -*ien* in the masculine singular end in -*ienne* in the feminine singular.

Feminine	Masculine	Fem. Plural	Masc. Plural	
belge	*belge*	*belges*	*belges*	Belgian
suisse	*suisse*	*suisses*	*suisses*	Swiss
espagnole	*espagnol*	*espagnoles*	*espagnols*	Spanish
française	*français*	*françaises*	*français*	French
anglaise	*anglais*	*anglaises*	*anglais*	English
chinoise	*chinois*	*chinoises*	*chinois*	Chinese
danoise	*danois*	*danoises*	*danois*	Danish
américaine	*américain*	*américaines*	*américains*	American
sénégalaise	*sénégalais*	*sénégalaises*	*sénégalais*	Senegalese
algérienne	*algérien*	*algériennes*	*algériens*	Algerian
marocaine	*marocain*	*marocaines*	*marocains*	Moroccan
italienne	*italien*	*italiennes*	*italiens*	Italian
canadienne	*canadien*	*canadiennes*	*canadiens*	Canadian
allemande	*allemand*	*allemandes*	*allemands*	German
hollandaise	*hollandais*	*hollandaises*	*hollandais*	Dutch
angolaise	*angolais*	*angolaises*	*angolais*	Angolan

When adjectives of nationality are used as nouns, they are capitalized.

C'est un livre français.
It's a French book.

C'est un Français.
He is a Frenchman.

6. The French expression *en* + present participle can be translated in various ways in English, using "while," "by," "upon," "through," "in," etc.

   En regardant la météo, je pense à demain.
   (While) watching the weather report, I think of tomorrow.

   J'ai mieux compris la situation en lisant des articles.
   I better understood the situation upon/by reading some articles.

   En faisant son documentaire, Éliane s'est exprimée.
   Through/By/In making her documentary, Éliane has expressed her views.

EXERCISES

A. Substitute one of the words or expressions in parentheses for the underlined synonymous word or expression in the pattern sentence. Write the new sentence and say it aloud.

   1. *Je ne comprends pas ce que vous <u>dites</u>.* (*écrivez, faites, expliquez, voulez dire*)

   2. *Je vois ce qui <u>est</u> sur la table.* (*arrive, se passe, il y a, vous inquiète*)

   3. *J'aime ce <u>documentaire</u>-là.* (*livre, compact, film, journal, garçon*)

   4. *Nous regardons le temps prévu pour demain à la météo du <u>journal</u>.* (*du magazine, de la chaîne, du documentaire, des actualités*)

B. Make each of the following masculine. Write complete sentences.

   Example: *C'est une Française: C'est un Français.*

Hollandaise	*Marocaine*
Chinoise	*Espagnole*
Angolaise	*Anglaise*
Italienne	

C. Expand the following sentences by placing *En regardant les actualités* in front of each; then say aloud and translate.

1. _____, *j'ai mieux compris la situation.*

2. _____, *nous apprenons beaucoup.*

3. _____, *on sait ce qui se passe dans le monde.*

4. _____, *nous prenons l'apéritif.*

D. Say the following sentences aloud, and then translate them into English.

1. *Votre documentaire est tellement passionnant!*

2. *Pourriez-vous nous montrer votre film sur l'après-guerre?*

3. *Pourriez-vous nous recommander une bonne chaîne de télévision?*

4. *Est-ce qu'ils présentent les nouvelles quotidiennement?*

5. *J'aimerais regarder la météo.*

6. *Je préfère me promener dans ce quartier-ci.*

7. *Voici une émission captivante.*

8. *Ils vont montrer quelque chose d'important au journal télévisé dans une quinzaine de minutes.*

E. Translate the following sentences into French; then say them aloud.

1. You've already started having aperitifs?

2. Let's choose between this show and that show.

3. He knows what's important.

4. I don't like these newspapers. I prefer those newspapers.

5. Here's what you're looking for.

6. It's what I mean.

7. We read what's necessary.

8. Do you see what's happening?

9. By watching the international news, one can understand better what happens in the world.

10. I understand everything she's saying.

F. From among the three choices given, choose the best translation for the word or phrase at the beginning of each sentence. Write the complete sentence, and translate.

1. (I don't know) _____ *ces journaux.*

   Je ne sais pas / Je ne vois pas / Je ne connais pas

2. (Could you) _____ *nous aider?*

   Pourriez-vous / Auriez-vous / Seriez-vous

3. (a week) *Cette émission est présentée une fois* _____.

   la semaine / par semaine / une semaine

4. (So many) _____ *images!*

   Trop d' / Beaucoup d' / Tant d'

5. (with) *Je commence* _____ *regarder la chaîne Arte.*

   par/sans/comme

6. (fifteen) *Il passe une _____ de jours à Paris.*

   douzaine/dizaine/quinzaine

7. (drink before the meals) *On prend un _____?*

   repas/apéritif/verre

8. (in fact) _____, *je l'ai vu au Jardin du Luxembourg.*

   Enfin / Après tout / En fait

Answer Key

A. 1. *Je ne comprends pas ce que vous <u>expliquez</u>.* 2. *Je vois ce qu'<u>il y a</u> sur la table.* 3. *J'aime ce <u>film-là</u>.* 4. *Nous regardons le temps prévu pour demain à la météo <u>des actualités</u>.*

B. *C'est un Hollandais. C'est un Chinois. C'est un Angolais. C'est un Italien. C'est un Marocain. C'est un Espagnol. C'est un Anglais.*

C. 1. *En regardant les actualités, j'ai mieux compris la situation.* Upon watching the news, I better understood the situation. 2. *En regardant les actualités, nous apprenons beaucoup.* While watching the news, we learn a lot. 3. *En regardant les actualités, on sait ce qui se passe dans le monde.* By watching the news, we know what happens in the world. 4. *En regardant les actualités, nous prenons l'apéritif.* While watching the news, we are having a drink.

D. 1. Your documentary is so fascinating! 2. Could you show us your film about the aftermath of the war? 3. Could you recommend a good TV channel to us? 4. Do they present news daily? 5. I'd like to watch the weather report. 6. I prefer to walk around in this neighborhood. 7. Here is a captivating show. 8. They are going to show something important in the news on TV in about fifteen minutes.

E. 1. *Vous avez déjà commencé à prendre l'apéritif?* 2. *Choisissons entre cette émission-ci et cette émission-là.* 3. *Il sait ce qui est important.* 4. *Je n'aime pas ces journaux-ci. Je préfère ces journaux-là.* 5. *Voici ce que tu cherches.* 6. *C'est ce que je veux dire.* 7. *Nous lisons ce qui est nécessaire.* 8. *Voyez-vous ce qui se passe?* 9. *En regardant les nouvelles internationales, on com-*

prend mieux ce qui se passe dans le monde. 10. *Je comprends tout ce qu'elle dit.*

F. 1. *Je ne connais pas ces journaux.* I don't know those newspapers. 2. *Pourriez-vous nous aider?* Could you help us? 3. *Cette émission est présentée une fois par semaine.* This show appears (or comes out) once a week. 4. *Tant d' images!* So many images! 5. *Je commence par regarder la chaîne Arte.* I start by watching the channel Arte. 6. *Il passe une quinzaine de jours à Paris.* He's spending about fifteen days / two weeks in Paris. 7. *On prend un apéritif?* Shall we have a drink before dinner? 8. *En fait, je l'ai vu au Jardin du Luxembourg.* In fact, I saw him at the Jardin du Luxembourg.

LESSON 3

AU TÉLÉPHONE
ON THE TELEPHONE

A. DIALOGUE

0. *Luc, le fils de Michel, vient de prendre le petit dé-jeuner avec son père dans un café.*
   Michel's son Luc, has just had breakfast with his father in a coffee shop.

1. Michel: **Bon, passe nous voir un de ces soirs ou ce week-end. En plus, Charles et Jane sont de passage à Paris. Cela fera plaisir à tout le monde de te voir!**
   Well, come visit us one of these evenings or this weekend. And Charles and Jane are in Paris. It'll make everyone happy to see you.

2. Luc: **Ok. Je vous téléphonerai en fin de semaine.**
   Okay. I'll call you at the end of the week.

3. Michel: **Allez, prends soin de toi, Luc.**
   All right, take good care of yourself, Luc.

4. Luc: **À la prochaine, papa.**
   See you next time, Dad.

5. *Père et fils s'embrassent à l'extérieur du café avant de se quitter. Luc continue à marcher dans la rue, quand son téléphone portable sonne. Il le sort de son sac à dos, vérifie le numéro et décroche.*
   Father and son hug outside the coffee shop before parting. Luc keeps on walking down the street when his phone rings. He takes it out of his backpack, checks the number and picks it up.

6. Luc: **Allô? Ah, c'est toi, Tony! Quelle coïncidence, j'allais t'appeler. Ouais . . . Comment va?**
Hello? Ah, it's you Tony! What a coincidence, I was going to call you. Yeah . . . How are you doing?

7. Tony: **Ça va. Eh, tu as des plans pour ce soir?**
Good. Hey, do you have any plans for this evening?

8. Luc: **Non, pas vraiment . . . Tu veux aller au ciné?**
No, not really . . . Wanna go to the movies?

9. Tony: **Ouais, pourquoi pas. Quel film veux-tu voir?**
Yeah, why not. Which movie do you want to see?

10. Luc: **Le dernier Téchiné? On m'a dit que c'était pas mal du tout.**
The lastest Téchiné? They said that it's pretty good.

11. Tony: **Ouais, j'en ai entendu parler. Laisse-moi prendre l'Officiel. Aux Halles, je suppose. Ok. À quel cinéma préfères-tu aller, au Quad 3 ou au Cinéplus? Hmm, à 19 heures?**
Yeah, I've heard about it. Let me get the *Officiel*. In Les Halles I guess. Okay. Which theater do you prefer to go to, the Quad 3 or Cineplus? Hmm, at 7:00 p.m.?

12. Luc: **Oui, ça marche.**
Yes, that works.

13. Tony: **Et après, on pourra aller manger un bout au resto vietnamien en face de Beaubourg.**
And after, we could go grab a bite at the Vietnamese restaurant in front of Beaubourg.

14. Luc: **Super! Demande à ta sœur si elle veut venir. Attends un instant, s'il te plaît, j'ai un deuxième appel, c'est mon boulot. Bonjour, Luc Cuvelier à**

l'appareil. Oui, enfin non, il y avait des problèmes dans le métro, mais je serai au bureau dans 15 min. Quel dossier? Allô? Oui, oui, Patrick s'en occupera quand il rentrera. À tout à l'heure. Allô, Tony?

Great! Ask your sister if she wants to come. Hold on a moment please, I have another call, it's my job. Hello, Luc Cuvelier speaking. Yes, well, no, there was a problem in the subway, but I'll be in the office in 15 minutes. Which file? Hello? Sure, Patrick will take care of it when he's back. See you later. Hi Tony?

15. Tony: **T'inquiète! Donc, c'est bon pour ce soir.**
Don't worry. So, everything is set for this evening.

16. Luc: **D'accord, je vais te laisser, car je suis à la bourre. Je viens te chercher à dix-huit heures trente. Et, n'oublie pas de demander à ta sœur. Salut!**
Okay. I have to let you go, because I'm in a rush. I'll come by to pick you up at 6:30 p.m. And don't forget to ask your sister. Bye!

17. *Plus tard dans la journée, Luc est au bureau. Il travaille dans une agence de marketing et comme souvent, il est occupé au téléphone.*
Later in the day, Luc is at the office. He works for a marketing company, and, as is often the case, he's busy on the phone.

18. Luc: **Oui, je lui ferai la commission. Quelle adresse désirez-vous, au bureau ou au studio? Laissez-moi regarder dans mon carnet d'adresses. Ah, je n'ai rien ici. Attendez, je vérifie sur le minitel vite fait. Voilà! 27, rue de la Paix, Paris 8ème. Voulez-vous aussi le numéro de téléphone? Le 01-45-72-06-16. Mais de rien.**
Yes, I'll give him the message. Which address would you like, at the office or the studio? Let me look in

my address book. No, I have nothing here. Wait, let me check quickly on the Minitel. Here it is! 27, rue de la Paix, Paris 8th. Would you like the phone number too? 01-45-72-06-16. You're welcome.

19. *Luc raccroche et va prendre un verre d'eau. En buvant, il regarde la pendule. Presque 17 heures enfin. Il vérifie son portable, mais il n'y a rien. Puis il retourne à son bureau et continue à travailler. Quand il voit sa patronne arriver . . .*
Luc hangs up and goes to get a glass of water. As he's drinking, he looks at the clock. Almost 5 p.m., finally. He checks his cell, but there are no calls. Then, he goes back to his desk and gets back to his work. When he sees his boss arrive . . .

20. Luc: **Pauline. Le Centre Culturel a téléphoné et il leur faut l'heure des réservations.**
Pauline, the Cultural Center called and they need the time of the reservations.

21. Pauline: **Tu leur as demandé de nous envoyer toutes les infos personnelles du groupe?**
Did you ask them to send us all the group's personal information?

22. Luc: **Oui, mais ils ne pourront rien faire avant demain soir car ils attendent un e-mail de New York à ce sujet. Ah, et Aziza Benkimoune a rappelé et laissé un message.**
Yes, but they won't be able to do anything before tomorrow night because they're waiting for an e-mail about this from New York. And Aziza Benkimoune called back and left a message.

23. Pauline: **Comme le proverbe dit: "On n'est jamais si bien servi que par soi-même." Avant de partir, contacte New York s'il te plaît, et demande-leur**

de nous envoyer toutes les informations nécessaires. Merci, Luc.

As the proverb says: "One is never better served than
by oneself." Before leaving, please contact New
York, and ask them to send us all the necessary info.
Thanks, Luc.

24. *Quand Luc quitte le bureau, il est six heures cinq. Il
arrive en retard chez Tony.*

When Luc leaves the office, it's five after six. He
arrives late at Tony's.

25. Luc: **Désolé, Tony. Il y avait des problèmes dans
le métro.**

Sorry, Tony. There were some problems in the subway.

26. Tony: **Oui, c'est ça.**

Yeah, sure.

27. Luc: **Mais non, je ne plaisante pas. Et alors, ta
sœur?**

But, no, I'm not joking. What's up with your sister?

28. Tony: **Eh bien, rien. Elle n'est pas rentrée. Allez,
vite, sinon on va rater la séance de cinéma.**

Well, nothing. She hasn't gotten home. C'mon, let's
hurry up or we're going to miss the movie.

B. NOTES

Title. *Au téléphone*: On the Telephone. Calls can be made
from a café, a post office, and many other public places.
Most public telephones (*les cabines téléphoniques*) now take
a phone card rather than coins.

1. *bon*: well and *allez*: c'mon are common phrases.

3. *Prends soin de toi*: Take care of yourself.

5. *le téléphone portable*: the cellular/portable phone.

6. *Quelle coïncidence!*: What a coincidence!
   Comment va? (colloquial) How you're doing?

7. *Tu as des plans pour ce soir?* (colloquial) You have
   any plans for tonight? The phrase *Qu'est-ce que tu
   fais ce soir?* can also be used.

8. *le ciné*, short for *le cinéma*: the movies.

10. *Téchiné*, that is the famous French director, *André
    Téchiné. Le dernier Téchiné* (colloquial) means the
    last Téchiné's movie.
    On m'a dit que . . .: I was told that . . . , They said
    that . . .
    pas mal du tout: not bad at all.

11. *l'Officiel*, that is *l'Officiel des spectacles,* a pocket-
    size weekly that lists everything that is happening in
    Paris and its environs: films, concerts, exhibitions,
    plays, shows, restaurants.
    Les Halles: a former market and popular neigh-
    borhood in the center of Paris, in the *premier
    arrondissement.*
    J'en ai entendu parler or *on m'en a parlé*: I heard
    about it / I've heard about it.

12. *Ça marche!* (colloquial) is the equivalent of "Sounds
    good!" or "That works!"

13. *Beaubourg* or *le Centre Georges Pompidou,* is *un cen-
    tre culturel multimédia* as well as a huge research cen-
    ter and library which first opened in 1977. Its daring
    architecture by Richard Rogers and Renzo Piano first
    shocked many people, but has since been recognized
    as a unique monument. It is located in *Le Marais.*

14. *J'ai un deuxième appel*: I have a call on the other
    line.
    > *mon boulot*: (colloquial) my job.
    > *Attends un instant, s'il te plaît* (casual) or *Veuillez
    > patienter, s'il vous plaît* (formal): Please hold on.
    > *C'est Luc à l'appareil*: It's Luc on the phone. *Qui
    > est à l'appareil?* Who's on the phone? *L'appareil
    > (de téléphone)* refers to the phone.

15. *T'inquiète!* (colloquial) is the equivalent of "Don't
    worry." Short for *Ne t'inquiète pas*.

16. *Je suis à la bourre*: (colloquial) I'm in a rush or *Je
    suis pressé*.
    > *Et n'oublie pas de* + infinitive: don't forget to +
    > infinitive.

17. *comme souvent*: as often, as is often the case.
    > *Il est occupé au téléphone*: He's busy on the
    > phone. Also, *la ligne est occupée*: the line is busy.

18. *Je lui ferai la commission*: I will give him/her the
    message.
    > *vérifier*: to check.
    > *Le Minitel* is a small computerized device con-
    > nected to the telephone line that allows the user to
    > access many services such as the *annuaire électro-
    > nique*, transportation and theater reservations,
    > e-mail, stock quotes, and computer games, to name
    > a few. It served many of the purposes that people
    > now use the Internet for, but it existed years before
    > the Internet. It is not as widely used as it once was.
    > *Rien* is a negative pronoun used as a part of the
    > negation, as in: *je n'ai rien ici*: I have nothing here.
    > It also can be used in the beginning of the sentence,
    > as in: *Rien ne me surprend*: Nothing surprises me.

Rien is also used in the expression "*de rien*," literally "of nothing," means, "don't mention it."

Vite fait: (colloquial) quickly.

19. *décrocher*: to pick up the phone and, *raccrocher*: to hang up.

en buvant is while drinking. The infinitive form of *buvant* is *boire*.

presque: almost.

22: *à ce sujet*: about this.

Elle a rappelé et laissé un message: She called back and left a message. These common verbs are *appeler* and *laisser un message*.

23. The proverb *on n'est jamais si bien servi que par soi-même* expresses a certain frustration from the speaker, very similar to the expression "If you want a job done right, do it yourself." Note the expression *soi-même*. The rest of the gang is: *moi-même*: myself, *toi-même, vous-même*: yourself, *lui-même*: himself, *elle-même*: herself, *nous-mêmes*: ourselves, *vous-mêmes*: yourselves, *eux-mêmes*: themselves, *elles-mêmes*: themselves.

avant de partir: before leaving. Note the use of the infinitive in French.

toutes les informations nécessaires: all the necessary information. Note the plural form *informations* in French.

24. *Quand il quitte*: When he leaves.

ce dernier: the latter, as opposed to *ce premier* or *celui-ci*: the former.

26. *Oui, c'est ça*, colloquial expression of disbelief or skepticism: Yeah, sure. Yeah, right.

27. *Je ne plaisante pas*: I'm not kidding.

28. *sinon*: otherwise.
     rater la séance de cinéma: to miss the film.

C. GRAMMAR AND USAGE

1. The interrogative adjective *quel* is used in questions and can be translated by "what" or "which." Like other adjectives, it agrees in gender and number with the noun it modifies.

   masculine singular: *quel*

   Quel film veux-tu voir?
      Which movie do you want to see?

   masculine plural: *quels*

   Quels dossiers cherchent-ils?
      What files are they looking for?

   feminine singular: *quelle*

   Quelle adresse désirez-vous?
      Which address would you like?

   feminine plural: *quelles*

   Quelles informations?
      Which information?

   Quel is sometimes used with a preposition corresponding to a verb and its object. *Quel* comes before the verb, parallel to the English "to which . . ." + verb or "for which . . ." + verb.

   À quel cinéma veux-tu aller?
      Which movie theater do you want to go to?

   Par quelle rue es-tu passé?
      Which street did you walk through?

As we saw in the previous lesson, *quel* is also used in exclamations. The forms are like those of the interrogative. Again, the exclamative adjective *quel* agrees in gender and number with the noun it qualifies.

Quel plaisir!
   What a pleasure!

Quelle histoire!
   What a story!

2. In French, direct or indirect object pronouns, such as *me, te, le, la, lui, nous, vous, les, leur,* are placed immediately before the infinitives.

Passe nous voir ce week-end.
   Come and visit us this weekend.

Je vais te laisser.
   I'm going to let you go.

Je viens te chercher à quinze heures cinq.
   I'll come pick you up at 3:05 p.m.

N'oubliez pas de lui demander.
   Don't forget to ask her.

3. In French, the future tense is formed by adding the endings *-ai, -as, -a, -ons, -ez, -ont* either to the infinitive or to an irregular stem. For the regular verbs ending in *-er* (*passer*) or *-ir* (*choisir*), the stem is the same as the full infinitive. For the *-re* verbs (*prendre*), drop the final *-e* before adding the endings.

passer, to stop by

je passerai	*nous passerons*
tu passeras	*vous passerez*
il/elle/on passera	*ils/elles passeront*

choisir, to choose

je choisirai	*nous choisirons*
tu choisiras	*vous choisirez*
il/elle/on choisira	*ils/elles choisiront*

prendre, to take

je prendrai	*nous prendrons*
tu prendras	*vous prendrez*
il/elle/on prendra	*ils/elles prendront*

Je vous téléphonerai en fin de semaine.
   I will call you at the end of the week.

Patrick s'en occupera plus tard.
   Patrick will take care of it later.

Il prendra le métro tous les matins.
   He will take the subway every morning.

Following are some of the most common irregular verbs. It's best to memorize their stems, to which the future endings are added. The same stems are used for the conditional, so it's useful to know them well.

avoir, to have. The stem is *aur-*.

j'aurai	*nous aurons*
tu auras	*vous aurez*
il/elle/on aura	*ils/elles auront*

être, to be. The stem is *ser-*.

je serai	*nous serons*
tu seras	*vous serez*
il/elle/on sera	*ils/elles seront*

aller, to go. The stem is *ir-*.

j'irai	*nous irons*
tu iras	*vous irez*
il/elle/on ira	*ils/elles iront*

venir, to come. The stem is *viendr-*.

je viendrai	*nous viendrons*
tu viendras	*vous viendrez*
il/elle/on viendra	*ils/elles viendront*

faire, to do or to make. The stem is *fer-*.

je ferai	*nous ferons*
tu feras	*vous ferez*
il/elle/on fera	*ils/elles feront*

pouvoir, to be able to. The stem is *pourr-*.

je pourrai	*nous pourrons*
tu pourras	*vous pourrez*
il/elle/on pourra	*ils/elles pourront*

Oui, je lui ferai la commission.
> Yes, I will give him/her the message.

Ils ne pourront rien faire avant demain soir.
> They won't be able to do anything before tomorrow night.

Je serai au bureau dans quinze minutes.
> I'll be at the office in 15 minutes.

The future tense in French is generally used in the same way as the future tense in English. However, there are some important differences.

4. In French, the future is used after *quand* (when), *lorsque* (when), *dès que* (as soon as), *aussitôt que* (as soon as), *tant que* (as long as), where the present is used in English.

Dès que tu arriveras, téléphone-moi.
> As soon as you arrive, give me a call.

Patrick s'en occupera quand il rentrera.
> Patrick will take care of it when he's back.

Aussitôt que vous aurez les réservations, vous viendrez me voir.
> As soon as you arrive, you'll come to see me.

5. As shown in Lesson 2, indirect object pronouns (*me, te, lui, nous, vous, leur*) used with *il faut* (third person singular of *falloir*) are placed between *il* and *faut*. Again, *il me faut* means I need.

Il me faut ces informations.
> I need this information.

Il leur faut les réservations.
> They need the reservations.

Il nous faut du beau temps.
> We need some good weather.

EXERCISES

A. Substitute one of the words or expressions in parentheses for the underlined synonymous word or expression in the pattern sentence. Write the new sentence and say it aloud.

   1. *Au revoir, Tony.* (*bonjour, à plus tard, bonsoir, excusez-moi*)

   2. *J'en ai entendu parler.* (*on m'en a parlé, je lui en ai parlé, je peux en parler, il faut en parler*)

   3. *Il est occupé au téléphone.* (*toujours au téléphone, aime parler au téléphone, est pris au téléphone, entend le téléphone*)

   4. *Ça marche!* (*Que c'est beau, C'est suffisant, C'est bon, C'est à nous*)

B. Transform the following sentences into exclamations by using the proper form of *quel*. Say them aloud and translate them.

Example: *C'est une belle maison.* / *Quelle belle maison!*

1. *C'est un film intéressant.*

2. *C'est un bon café.*

3. *C'est une réalisatrice passionnante.*

4. *C'est une coïncidence.*

5. *C'est un plaisir de te voir.*

6. *C'est un excellent restaurant.*

C. Replace *dès que, lorsque,* and *aussitôt que* by *quand* in each of the following sentences. Say and translate each sentence.

1. *Dès que je pourrai, je passerai vous voir.*

2. *Aussitôt qu'il ira au bureau, on lui fera la commission.*

3. *Lorsqu'il sortira, il ira boire un verre d'eau.*

4. *Dès que tu finiras le boulot, tu passeras me chercher.*

5. *Aussitôt qu'ils auront les informations, ils nous téléphoneront.*

6. *Aussitôt que nous serons au ciné, le film commencera.*

D. Translate the following sentences into English. Then say them aloud.

1. *Il raccroche.*

2. *Faites-lui la commission.*

3. *Quelle coïncidence!*

4. *Avant de partir, contacte-les.*

   5. *Cela fera plaisir à tout le monde.*

   6. *Quel film veux-tu voir?*

   7. *J'en ai entendu parler.*

   8. *Il s'en occupera.*

E. Translate the following sentences into French. Then say them aloud.

   1. They need the reservations. (with *il faut*)

   2. Don't mention it.

   3. There is nothing to say.

   4. I check the Minitel quickly.

   5. As soon as he arrives, I'll tell him.

   6. Take care of yourself. (Familiar.)

F. Match the English phrases in the first column with their correct French equivalents in the second column. Say and write the French sentences.

1. Hold on a moment please.	*Tu pourrais vérifier le Minitel.*
2. Would you like the phone number?	*La ligne est occupée.*
3. Let me look in my address book.	*Tu es occupé au téléphone?*
4. He hangs up.	*Il raccroche.*
5. Give me my cell phone please.	*Je lui ferai la commission.*
6. Are you picking up the phone?	*Laissez-moi regarder mon carnet d'adresses.*

7.	You could check the Minitel.	*Veuillez patienter un instant, s'il vous plaît.*
8.	You are busy on the phone?	*Tu décroches?*
9.	I will give him the message.	*Voudriez-vous le numéro de téléphone?*
10.	The line is busy.	*Donne-moi mon portable, s'il te plaît.*

G. Translate the following dialogue into French.

Mme: Hello, is this 42-81-58-17?

M.: Yes, ma'am.

Mme: I'd like to speak to Mr. Dupont, please.

M.: Who's calling?

Mme: This is Mrs. Lenclos.

M.: Hold on, please. I'm sorry, ma'am, but his line is busy. Do you want to hold on?

Mme: No, thank you. I prefer to leave a message. Please tell him that I'll call back tomorrow.

M.: I'll give him the message.

Mme: Thank you very much. Good-bye, sir.

M.: Good-bye, ma'am.

H. From among the three choices given, choose the best translation for the word or phrase given at the beginning of each sentence, write the complete sentence, and translate.

1. (which) *C'est pour _____ ville?*

   quelle / cette / quoi

2. (Leave a message) _____, *s'il vous plaît.*

   Écrivez un message / Laissez un message / Il n'y a pas de message

3. (on the phone) *Qui est à _____.*

   la télévision / au Minitel / l'appareil

4. (the message) *Dès qu'il arrivera, je lui ferai la _____.*

   communication / message / commission

5. (Would you) _____ *entrer.*

   Pouvez / Veuillez / Voudriez

6. (hold on) *Veuillez _____, s'il vous plaît.*

   patienter / parler / raccrocher

7. (oneself) *On est jamais mieux servi que par _____.*

   soi-même / une autre / moi-même

8. (You will need) _____ *les réservations.*

   tu feras / Vous pourrez / Il vous faudra

9. (late) *Il est toujours _____.*

   en retard / parti / à la bourre

10. (hang up) *Tu _____?*

    décroches / raccroches / vérifies

Answer Key

A. 1. *À plus tard, Tony.* 2. *On m'en a parlé.* 3. *Il est pris au téléphone.* 4. *C'est bon!*

B. 1. *Quel film intéressant!* What an interesting film! 2. *Quel bon café!* What good coffee! 3. *Quelle réalisatrice passionnante!* What a passionate director! 4. *Quelle coïncidence!* What a coincidence! 5. *Quel plaisir de te voir!* What a pleasure to see you! 6. *Quel excellent restaurant!* What an excellent restaurant!

C. 1. *Quand je pourrai, je passerai vous voir.* When I can, I will come and visit you. 2. *Quand il ira au bureau, on lui fera la commission.* When he goes to the office, he will be given the message. 3. *Quand il sortira, il ira boire un verre d'eau.* When he goes out, he'll go drink a glass of water. 4. *Quand tu finiras le boulot, tu passeras me chercher.* When you finish work, you will pick me up. 5. *Quand ils auront les informations, ils nous téléphoneront.* When they have the information, they will call us. 6. *Quand nous serons au ciné, le film commencera.* When we are at the movie theater, the film will start.

D. 1. He is hanging/hangs up. 2. Give him the message, please. 3. What a coincidence! 4. Before leaving, please contact them. 5. It will make everyone happy. 6. What movie do you want to see? 7. I've heard about it. 8. He will take care of it.

E. 1. *Il leur faut les réservations.* 2. *De rien.* 3. *Il n'y a rien à dire.* 4. *Je vérifie le Minitel vite fait.* 5. *Dès qu'il arrivera, je lui dirai.* 6. *Prends soin de toi.*

F. 1. *Veuillez patienter un instant, s'il vous plaît.* 2. *Voudriez-vous le numéro de téléphone?* 3. *Laissez-moi*

regarder dans mon carnet d'adresses. 4. *Il raccroche.*
5. *Donne-moi mon portable, s'il te plaît.* 6. *Tu
décroches?* 7. *Tu pourrais vérifier le Minitel.* 8. *Tu es
occupé au téléphone?* 9. *Je lui ferai la commission.*
10. *La ligne est occupée.*

G. Mme: *Allô, c'est ici le 42-81-58-17?*

M.: *Oui, madame.*

Mme: *Je voudrais parler à Monsieur Dupont, s'il vous
plaît.*

M.: *Qui est à l'appareil?*

Mme: *C'est Madame Lenclos.*

M.: *Ne quittez pas, s'il vous plaît. Je regrette, madame,
mais sa ligne est occupée. Voulez-vous attendre un
instant?*

Mme: *Non, merci. Je préfère laisser un message. Dites-
lui que je le rappellerai demain.*

M.: *Je lui ferai la commission.*

Mme: *Merci beaucoup. Au revoir, Monsieur.*

M.: *Au revoir, madame.*

H. 1. *C'est pour quelle ville?* What city is it for? 2. *Laissez
un message, s'il vous plaît.* Please leave a message.
3. *Qui est à l'appareil?* Who's on the phone? 4. *Dès qu'il
arrivera, je lui ferai la commission.* As soon as he
arrives, I'll give him the message. 5. *Veuillez entrer.*
Please enter. 6. *Veuillez patienter, s'il vous plaît.* Please

hold on. 7. *On n'est jamais si bien servi que par soi-même.* One is never better served than by oneself. 8. *Il vous faudra les réservations.* You will need the reservations. 9. *Il est toujours en retard.* He's always late. 10. *Tu raccroches?* Do you hang up? / Are you hanging up?

LESSON 4

LES TRANSPORTS EN VILLE
CITY TRANSPORTATION

A. DIALOGUE

0. *Jane et Charles se promènent dans Paris. Ils arrivent dans la station de métro Arts et Métiers.*
   Jane and Charles are taking a walk in Paris. They get to the subway station Arts et Métiers.

1. Jane: **Le Marais est même plus beau que je ne le croyais!**
   The Marais is even more beautiful than I thought.

2. Charles: **C'est vrai. Quel dommage que nous ne puissions pas passer plus de temps dans ce quartier.**
   That's right. It's too bad that we can't spend more time in this neighborhood.

3. Jane: **Oui, mais regarde l'heure. On devrait rentrer à l'hôtel avant de rejoindre Nicole. Il faut se changer! Heureusement, le métro est rapide et nous y serons bientôt!**
   Yes, but look at the time. We'd better get back to the hotel before meeting Nicole. We need to change our clothes. Luckily, the metro's fast and we'll be there soon!

4. Charles: **S'il vous plaît, donnez-moi un carnet de dix tickets. Combien vous dois-je?**
   Give me a book of 10 tickets, please. How much do I owe you?

5. Employée de métro: **Voici. Cela fait 15 euros.**
   Subway Employee: Here. It's 15 euros.

6. Charles: **Comment fait-on pour aller à Saint-Sulpice, s'il vous plaît?**
How do we get to Saint-Sulpice?

7. Employée: **Eh bien, prenez d'abord la direction Pont de Levallois. Descendez à la prochaine station, c'est-à-dire, Réaumur Sébastopol. Là, pour la correspondance, prenez la direction Porte d'Orléans, c'est direct pour St-Sulpice. Je crois que vous avez, une, deux . . . neuf stations. Tenez, voici un plan du métro.**
Well, first take the metro towards Pont de Levallois. Get off at the next station, that's Réaumur Sébastopol. There, change to the line toward Porte d'Orléans, it's direct to St-Sulpice. I think you've got one, two . . . nine stops. Here's a map of the metro.

8. Charles: **Merci bien, madame.**
Thank you, Ma'am.

9. *Plus tard, en sortant de l'hôtel.*
Later, coming out of the hotel . . .

10. Jane: **Écoute, chéri, j'ai une bonne idée. Nous avons déjà pris le métro plusieurs fois. Comme Nicole a retardé notre rendez-vous, prenons le bus afin que nous découvrions mieux Paris. Cela prend plus de temps, mais c'est plus intéressant.**
Listen, Dear, I've got a great idea. We've already taken the metro several times. Since Nicole has postponed our meeting, let's take the bus so that we discover Paris better. It takes more time, but it's more interesting.

11. Charles: **Tu as raison. Et en plus, l'arrêt du bus est juste là.** *(Lisant les informations à l'arrêt de bus.)* **Oui, c'est bien ce bus qu'il nous faut. Ah, le voilà.**

You're right. Plus, the bus stop is right there. (Reading the information at the bus stop.) Yes, this is the bus we need. Here it comes.

12. Jane: **Quel monde! Pourvu qu'on puisse monter!**
What a crowd! Let's hope we can get on!

13. Charles: **Malheureusement, c'est l'heure de pointe. Mais, regarde, il y a encore de la place.** *(Au conducteur.)* **Bonjour, nous allons à la Place des Ternes, monsieur. On peut utiliser les mêmes tickets que pour le métro?**
Unfortunately it's rush hour. But look, there's still some space. (To the driver.) Hello, we're going to Place des Ternes, sir. Can we use the same tickets as for the metro?

14. Chauffeur: **Oui, oui. Vous devez juste composter votre ticket. Je vous préviendrai quand vous devez descendre.**
Driver: Sure. You've just got to punch your ticket. I'll let you know when you have to get off.

15. Jane: **Merci! Tiens, deux places à côté de la fenêtre, juste là.**
Thanks! Look, two spaces next to the window, right there.

16. *À la fin de leur soirée avec Nicole, ils s'apprêtent à rentrer à l'hôtel.*
At the end of their evening with Nicole, they get ready to go back to the hotel.

17. Charles: **Merci beaucoup, Nicole, pour cette soirée très agréable.**
Thank you very much, Nicole, for this very pleasant evening.

18. Nicole: **De rien. Cela m'a fait plaisir de vous voir.**
    Don't mention it. I was glad to see you.

19. Jane: **Le restaurant et le spectacle étaient excellents.**
    The restaurant and the show were excellent.

20. Charles: **Y-a-t-il des bus à cette heure-ci?**
    Are there any buses at this time?

21. Nicole: **Il y a juste un bus de nuit, mais je ne crois pas qu'il passe souvent. Je vous conseille de prendre un taxi, vous pourrez toujours voir "Paris by Night"! Il y a une station au coin de la rue. Je vous y accompagne.**
    There's just a night bus, but I don't think it comes often. I suggest that you to take a cab, you'll still be able to see "Paris by Night"! There is a taxi stand at the corner of the street. I'll walk you there.

22. Charles: **Merci, Nicole, bonne nuit.** *(Au chauffeur)* **Bonsoir, Monsieur, nous allons à l'Hôtel de la Paix, rue St-Sulpice.**
    Thank you, Nicole, have a good night. (To the driver.) Good evening sir, we're going to the Hôtel de la Paix on rue St-Sulpice.

23. Chauffeur: **Ça roule.**
    Let's go.

24. Jane: **Je dois avouer que je voyagerais toujours en taxi si c'était possible. C'est de loin le moyen de transport le plus confortable.**
    I have to admit that I would always travel by taxi if it were possible. It's by far the most comfortable means of transportation.

25. *Charles regarde le compteur tourner.*
    Charles looks at the meter running.

26. Charles: *(À voix basse)* **Et le plus cher aussi. Mais à cette heure-ci, comme il n'y a pas de circulation, on sera bientôt à l'hôtel.**
    (Sotto-voce.) And the most expensive as well. But at this hour, since there's no traffic, we'll get to the hotel soon.

B. NOTES

0. *le métro* is short for *le métropolitain*, the subway in Paris, which is a very popular means of transportation.

1. *Le Marais* is a scenic quarter of Paris full of mansions restored as museums. It is especially known for *le Centre Pompidou* and *la Place des Vosges.*
    plus beau que je ne le croyais: After the comparative of an adjective, *ne* generally precedes the verbs *croire* or *penser*. But notice that there's no *pas*.

2. *J'aurais aimé*: past conditional form meaning: I would have liked.
    plus de temps: more time.

3. *on devrait*: we should, we ought to.
    rentrer à (l'hôtel, la maison.): to go back to (the hotel, home.)
    Il est nécessaire que + subjunctive: It is necessary that, the same as *il faut que* + subjunctive.
    avant de + infinitive form: before + verb in-ing.

6. *Comment fait-on pour aller . . . ?* How do you get to . . . ? *pour* + infinitive: in order to.

7. *prenez la direction*: Parisian metro lines are generally identified by the name of the last stations at either end of the line (*le terminus*).

   la correspondance: a transfer to another metro line. Outside of each metro station and on each platform there is a large map of the entire metro system and the possible transfers from one line to another. In larger stations, passengers can press a button on an electronic map indicating the station they'd like to travel to, and the most convenient route will immediately light up on the map.

   c'est direct pour: it goes directly to.

   Tenez!: Here! (see *Tiens!* in Lesson 2)

10. *retarder un rendez-vous*: to postpone a meeting.

    afin que + subjunctive: in order that. Also, *afin de* + infinitive: in order to, as in: *Afin d'arriver à l'heure, on prend le métro*: In order to arrive on time, we take the metro.

11. *C'est ce bus qu'il nous faut*: This is the bus that we need. Note this particular construction.

12. *pourvu que* + subjunctive: let's hope that + present.

13. *l'heure de pointe* or *l'heure d'affluence*: rush hour.

    les mêmes que: the same as.

14. *composter vos tickets*: to punch your tickets.

15. *à côté de la fenêtre*: next to the window. Also, note the use of *côté* in the expression: *côté fenêtre ou côté couloir?* window or aisle?

16. *Ils s'apprêtent à* + infinitive: They are getting ready to. From the adjectives *prêt, prête*: ready.

21. *conseiller de faire*: to advise to do, to suggest or to recommend that one does.

Note the following: *un arrêt de bus, une station de métro, une station de taxi.*

23. *ça roule!* (colloquial) is the equivalent of let's roll! From *rouler*: to roll or to run (car).

24. *C'est de loin le plus (le moins) confortable*: It is by far the most (the least) comfortable.
    si c'était possible: if it were possible.

25. *à voix basse*: in a low voice, sotto voce

C. GRAMMAR AND USAGE

1. The comparatives of adjectives are used to compare two things. In English, just like in French, there are two comparatives. The comparative of superiority is formed in English with more + adjective + than, or adjective + -er. In French it's *plus* + adjective + *que*.

Le taxi est plus confortable que le bus.
    The taxi is more comfortable than the bus.

Ce plan du métro est plus clair que l'autre.
    This map of the metro is clearer than the other.

And the comparative of inferiority is formed in English with less + adjective + than, and in French with *moins* + adjective + *que*.

Les Champs-Élysées sont moins intéressants que le Marais.
    The Champs-Élysées is less interesting than the Marais.

Le bus est moins rapide que le métro.
    The bus is less fast than the metro.

In French, there are also some irregular comparatives of superiority, such as *bon* which becomes *meilleur* (as "good" becomes "better").

Ce restaurant est meilleur que celui-là.
    This restaurant is better than that one.

In English, "bad" always changes to "worse" in a comparative. In French, *mauvais* becomes *pire* only when referring to abstractions. In the other cases, it's *plus mauvais*.

Le trafic est pire à Paris qu'à New York.
    Traffic is worse in Paris than in New York.

Le film est plus mauvais que le livre.
    The movie is worse than the book.

2. The imperative form is used to give directions or orders, or to make requests. The imperative has the same forms as the present tense, but it uses only the *tu*, *vous* and *nous* forms. The only minor difference to remember is that with the verbs ending in *-er*, the *tu* form loses its final *-s*, except when followed by the pronouns *en* or *y*.

Allez, parles-en! or *Vas-y!*
    C'mon, talk about it! or Go on!

Mais parle!
    Speak!

Choisissons un restaurant.
    Let's choose a restaurant.

Descendez à la prochaine station.
    Get off at the next stop.

Prenez la correspondance pour la Porte d'Orléans.
    Change trains to go to Porte d'Orléans.

Note that the imperative forms of *avoir*, *être* are: *aie, ayons,* and *ayez, sois, soyons,* and *soyez*. All irregular forms can be found in the Irregular Verb Charts.

3. The verb *devoir* can usually be translated as "must" or "has/have to." But it can take on different meanings according to its context. *Devoir* can express an obligation.

Nous devons rentrer à l' hôtel.
   We have to go back to the hotel.

Devoir can also express a probability.

Le métro doit passer toutes les deux minutes.
   The metro is supposed to come every two minutes.

Devoir can mean "to owe" when it's used with a noun instead of an infinitive.

Il me doit dix euros.
   He owes me ten euros.

Also, note the different forms of *devoir* in the following sentences.

Je dois partir.
   I must leave.

Je devais partir.
   I was supposed to leave.

Je devrai partir.
   I'll have to leave.

Je devrais partir.
   I should leave.

J' ai dû partir.
   I had to leave.

J' aurais dû partir.
   I should have left.

To study all the forms of *devoir*, please refer to the Irregular Verb Charts.

4. The subjunctive is used to express doubt, emotion, volition, possibility, or necessity. It's generally used in sub-

ordinate clauses after verbs of emotion and wishing, after *il faut que*, and after certain conjunctions, such as: *à moins que* (unless), *de peur que* (for fear that), *pourvu que* (let's hope that), *avant que* (before that). Study the forms of the subjunctive in the Verb Charts.

Il est préférable que j'y aille.
    It is better that I go.

Je doute que le bus passe souvent la nuit.
    I doubt that the bus comes often at night.

Il faut que nous prenions le métro.
    We have to take the metro.

Pourvu que nous puissions monter.
    Let's hope we can get in.

Nous n'irons pas au théâtre demain à moins qu'il ne pleuve.
    We won't go to the theater tomorrow unless it rains.

EXERCISES

A. Substitute one of the words or expressions in parentheses for the underlined synonymous word or expression in the pattern sentence. Write the new sentence and say it aloud.

1. *On <u>rentre</u> à l'hôtel. (quitte, va, retourne, reste)*

2. *<u>On parle</u> français ici. (elle parle, je parle, nous parlons, il parle)*

3. *<u>Je dois</u> partir. (peux, veux, il me faut, il faut)*

4. *Tout ce monde! Cela doit être l'heure <u>de pointe</u>. (de manger, du travail, d'affluence, du trafic)*

B. Transform these familiar singular forms of the imperative to (1) the *vous* form, and (2) the *nous* (Let's) form.

Example: *parle / parlez / parlons*

1. *finis!*

2. *sois!*

3. *apprends!*

4. *mange!*

5. *choisis!*

6. *mets!*

C. Say the following sentences aloud, and then translate them into English.

1. *Quelle est votre adresse?*

2. *Nous devons prendre un bus.*

3. *Elle doit prendre le métro.*

4. *Cela doit être l'arrêt de bus.*

5. *Je devrais prendre un taxi.*

6. *Ils doivent prendre un carnet de tickets.*

7. *Elle devra faire la queue.*

8. *Ils devront payer.*

9. *Il devrait payer, mais il ne veut pas payer.*

10. *Il aurait dû partir.*

11. *Elles auraient dû venir.*

12. *Allons voir la Tour Eiffel.*

13. *Allons passer l'après-midi avec Marie.*

14. *Comment fait-on pour aller à la Place des Vosges?*

D. Translate the following sentences into French. Then say them aloud.

1. How do you ("does one") find a taxi?

2. There is only one station before Concorde.

3. There are only two stops.

4. He said that she would take a taxi.

5. He said that they would have the money.

6. They are richer than the others.

7. The taxis are more expensive than the bus.

8. English is spoken here.

9. The Eiffel Tower can be seen from here.

10. People travel far to see the Eiffel Tower.

11. She wants you to go.

12. I am glad that she is happy.

13. We doubt that he can do that.

14. I will go unless it rains.

E. From among the three choices given, choose the best translation for the English word or phrase given. Write the complete sentence, and translate.

1. (To get back) _____, *prenons un taxi.*

    À rentrer / À la rentrée / Pour rentrer

2. (Let's go) _____ *prendre nos billets.*

    Va / Allons / Allez

3. (at the end) *L'escalier se trouve* _____ *du couloir.*

    à la fin / enfin / au bout

4. (room) *Il y a encore de la* _____.

    chambre / place / pièce

5. (There's a crowd!) _____ *monde!*

   Il y a un / Quel / Il y a beaucoup de

6. (get off) *On doit* _____ *ici.*

   partir / descendre / reprendre

7. (better) *Oui, ça vaudrait* _____ .

   bon / bien / mieux

8. (That one) _____ *doit être occupé.*

   Cela / Il / Celui-là

9. (what) *C'est à* _____ *adresse, s'il vous plaît?*

   quelle / quel / quoi

10. (a train change) *Y a-t-il* _____ *avant Molitor?*

    un changement de train / une correspondance / une station

Answer Key

A. 1. *On retourne à l'hôtel.* 2. *Nous parlons français ici.* 3. *Il me faut partir.* 4. *Tout ce monde! Cela doit être l'heure d'affluence.*

B. 1. *finis / finissez / finissons.* 2. *sois / soyez / soyons.* 3. *apprends / apprenez / apprenons.* 4. *mange / mangez / mangeons.* 5. *choisis / choisissez / choisissons.* 6. *mets / mettez / mettons.*

C. 1. What's your address? 2. We must/have to take a bus. 3. She must/has to take the metro. 4. That must be the bus stop. 5. I should take a taxi. 6. They have to take/get a book of tickets. 7. She'll have to stand in line. 8. They'll have to pay. 9. He should pay, but he doesn't want to pay. 10. He should have left. 11. They (fem.) should have come. 12. Let's go see the Eiffel Tower. 13. Let's go spend the afternoon with Marie. 14. How do you/ does one get to the Place des Vosges?

D. 1. *Comment fait-on pour trouver un taxi?* 2. *Il n'y a qu'une station avant Concorde.* 3. *Il n'y a que deux arrêts.* 4. *Il a dit qu'elle prendrait un taxi.* 5. *Il a dit qu'ils auraient l'argent.* 6. *Ils sont plus riches que les autres.* 7. *Les taxis sont plus chers que le bus.* 8. *On parle anglais ici.* 9. *On peut voir la Tour Eiffel d'ici.* 10. *On voyage loin pour voir la Tour Eiffel.* 11. *Elle veut que vous partiez.* 12. *Je suis content qu'elle soit heureuse.* 13. *Nous doutons qu'il puisse faire cela.* 14. *J'irai à moins qu'il ne pleuve.*

E. 1. *Pour rentrer, prenons un taxi.* To get back, let's take a taxi. 2. *Allons prendre nos billets.* Let's go get our tickets. 3. *L'escalier se trouve au bout du couloir.* The staircase is at the end of the corridor/hallway. 4. *Il y a encore de la place.* There is still room. 5. *Il y a un monde!*

There's a crowd! 6. *On doit descendre ici.* We have to get off here. 7. *Oui, ça vaudrait mieux.* Yes, that would be better. 8. *Celui-là doit être occupé.* That one must be taken / occupied. 9. *C'est à quelle adresse, s'il vous plaît?* What address is it, please? 10. *Y-a-t-il une correspondance avant Molitor?* Is there a train change before Molitor?

LESSON 5

FAISONS UNE PROMENADE À PIED À BRUXELLES
LET'S TAKE A WALK IN BRUSSELS

A. DIALOGUE

0. *Charles et Jane sont dans le train à grande vitesse Thalys qui entre en gare de Bruxelles-Midi. De là, ils prennent un taxi pour se rendre chez leurs amis. Arrivés, ils sonnent. Paule, leur hôtesse, apparaît et les embrasse.*

   Charles and Jane are in the high speed train Thalys, which is pulling into the Brussels-Midi train station. From there, they take a cab to go to their friends'. When they arrive, they ring the bell. Paule, their hostess, appears and hugs them.

1. Paule: **Charles, Jane, quel plaisir de vous voir! Entrez. Vous vous souvenez de Tidjane?**

   Charles, Jane, what a pleasure to see you! Come on in. Do you remember Tidjane?

2. Charles: **Tu sais la dernière fois que nous t'avons vu, tu ne marchais pas encore, et tu as bien grandi depuis!**

   You know the last time we saw you, you weren't walking yet, and since then, you've grown up quite a lot!

3. Jane: **Quel âge as-tu maintenant?**

   How old are you now?

4. Tidjane: **Dix ans. Moi non plus, je ne me souviens pas de vous.**

   Ten years old. I don't remember you, either.

5. *Tout le monde rit alors que Paule guide ses invités dans le salon.*
Eveyone laughs while Paule guides her guests into the living room.

6. Paule: **Asseyez-vous. Si vous désirez vous rafraîchir, la salle de bains est juste là.**
Sit down. If you want to freshen up, the bathroom is right there.

7. Jane: **Oui, je veux bien.**
I wouldn't mind at all.

8. Paule: **Alors, vous avez fait bon voyage?**
So did you have a good trip?

9. Charles: **Parfait! Le train est tellement rapide et confortable. Paris-Bruxelles en 1 heure et 25 minutes! Si on pouvait voyager des États-Unis à l'Europe en train, je viendrais plus souvent!**
Perfect! The train is so fast and comfortable. Paris-Brussels in 1 hour and 25 minutes! If you could travel from the US to Europe by train, I would come more often!

10. Paule: **Je m'excuse de ne pas avoir pu être à la gare. En fait, je viens juste de rentrer.**
I'm sorry not to have been able to be at the station. In fact, I've just gotten home.

11. Jane: **Ne t'inquiète pas. C'était très facile de prendre un taxi et tes indications étaient claires.**
Don't worry. It was very easy to take a taxi, and your directions were clear.

12. *Après dîner, les amis discutent.*
After dinner, the friends have a conversation.

13. Paule: **Malheureusement, je dois travailler demain. C'est une période intense à la Commission Européenne.**
Unfortunately, I have to work tomorrow. It's an intense period at the European Commission.

14. Charles: **Dis-nous, as-tu appris de nouvelles langues? Voyons, tu parles français, anglais, espagnol, allemand et. . .**
Tell us, have you learned any new languages? Let's see, you speak French, English, Spanish, German and . . .

15. Paule: **Je me débrouille plutôt bien en portugais et en suédois.**
I'm doing pretty well in Portuguese and Swedish.

16. Tidjane: **Moi aussi, je parle français et anglais! Et, Maman, pour demain, si j'allais me promener avec eux?**
Me, too, I speak French and English! Mom, about tomorrow, could I walk around with them?

17. Charles: **Oui et comme ça, tu pourrais nous servir de guide. Qu'en pense ta maman?**
Yes, and that way, you could be our guide. What does your mother think?

18. Paule: **C'est une bonne idée, mais juste dans le quartier alors. Comme je sors à 15 heures, on pourra faire une balade en voiture.**
It's a good idea, but just in the neighborhood then. Since I get off at 3 p.m., we'll be able to go for a drive.

19. Tidjane: **Super!**
Great!

20. *Le lendemain matin, Jane et Charles se préparent alors que Tidjane se lave.*
    The next morning, Jane and Charles get ready as Tidjane washes up.

21. Tidjane: **Je me dépêche! Dans cinq minutes, je suis prêt.**
    I'm hurrying up! In five minutes, I'll be ready.

22. *Plus tard, dans la rue.*
    Later, in the street.

23. Charles: **Alors, où est-ce qu'on va, Tidjane?**
    So, where are we going, Tidjane?

24. Tidjane: **Eh bien, si vous voulez faire des achats ou manger, c'est par ici; si vous voulez vous promener dans le Parc du Cinquantenaire, c'est par là. Dis-moi.**
    Well, if you want to do some shopping or eat, it's this way; if you want to walk in the Parc du Cinquantenaire, it's that way. Tell me.

25. Jane: **Pourquoi ne pas faire quelques courses, et puis vers midi, déjeuner. De quoi as-tu envie, Charles?**
    Why not do a few errands and then around noon, have some lunch. What do you feel like, Charles?

26. Charles: **Comme vous voulez.**
    Up to the two of you.

27. Tidjane: **Dans ce cas, on va aller au centre-ville. On va remonter la rue et tourner à droite.**
    In that case, we're going to go downtown. We'll walk up the street and turn right.

28. Charles: **On te suit, mon général!**
We're right behind you, General!

29. *Vingt minutes plus tard.*
Twenty minutes later.

30. Tidjane: **Mais je suis sûr que c'est dans cette direction.**
But I'm sure it's this way.

31. Jane: **Est-ce que nous nous sommes égarés?**
Are we lost?

32. Tidjane: **Non, on ne s'est pas perdu. Mais à cause de tous ces travaux. Si on rebroussait chemin et . . .**
No, we're not lost. But because of all this street work. Why not go back and . . .

33. Charles: **Pourquoi ne pas demander à cette dame?**
Why not ask this lady?

34. Tidjane: **D'accord. Excusez-moi Madame, pouvez-vous nous indiquer le chemin pour aller à la rue des Tongres?**
Okay. Excuse me, Madam, could us show us the way to go to rue Tongres?

35. La femme: **Mais bien sûr, jeune homme. Continuez tout droit dans cette avenue, prenez la première rue à gauche et ensuite prenez la troisième rue à droite. Vous commencerez à voir des boutiques. Vous êtes sur la bonne route!**
Woman: But of course, young man. Keep on going straight on this avenue, take the first street on the left and then the third on the right. You'll start to see some stores. You're on the right track!

B. NOTES

Title *Bruxelles*, or Brussels, capital of Belgium, is also considered the European capital, mainly because it houses *la Commission Européenne*. It is a lively city rich in history and art, where three languages are officially spoken: French, Flemish (Dutch) and English.

0. *de là*: from there, *par là*: that way and *d'ici*: from here, *par ici*: this way.
   se rendre à: to go to. The verbs preceded by the reflexive pronouns *se* (or *me, te, nous, vous*) are called reflexive verbs.

1. *vous vous souvenez de . . .*: you remember . . . is another reflexive verb.

2. *la dernière fois que . . .*: the last time that . . .
   depuis: since.
   grandir (regular verb): to grow up. The tense used in the sentence is the present perfect with past participle, *grandi*.

10. *s'excuser*: to apologize. An other reflexive verb. *Je m'excuse de . . .* I'm sorry to/for . . .
    ne pas avoir pu être: not to have been able to be.

11. *s'inquiéter (de)*: to worry (about) is a reflexive verb.
    les indications: (here) directions.

13. *La Commission Européenne*, or the European Commission, is located in Brussels. It's the main European institution.
    Voyons: Let's see.

15. *je me débrouille* from the reflexive verb *se débrouiller*: to manage, to get by
    plutôt bien: rather well.

16. *Moi aussi, je parle*: I also speak.
    Si j'allais me promener avec eux? The use of the imperfect with *si* corresponds to: how about (doing something)?

17./18. *comme ça*: that way, and *comme* in *comme je sors*: since I'm getting off.

20./21. *se préparer*: to get ready, *se laver*: to wash oneself and *se dépêcher*: to hurry up are all reflexive verbs.
    être prêt (masculine), *être prête* (feminine): to be ready.

25. *Pourquoi ne pas faire quelques courses?*: Why not do some shopping?

27. *au centre-vill*e is the equivalent of "downtown," usually where a lot of shops, banks, post office, etc., are located.
    remonter l'avenue: to walk up the avenue.
    tourner à droite, à gauche: to turn right, left.

30. *dans cette direction*: this way.

31./32. *s'être égaré* or *s'être perdu* is the present perfect of *s'égarer* and *se perdre*.
    rebrousser chemin: to return, to go back, to back track.

33. *cette dame*: this lady. Note the use of *cette dame*. Although this expression is a bit old, it is still used in such circumstances as when one wants to emphasize respect or in front of a child. Similarly, refer to a man as *ce monsieur*, a young woman as *cette demoiselle*.

34. *indiquer le chemin*: to show the way, to point someone in the right direction.

35. *tout droit*: straight ahead. Don't confuse *droit* or its feminine form, *droite* (straight) and *à droite* (on the right).

Vous êtes sur la bonne route: You are on the right track, literally and metaphorically.

C. GRAMMAR AND USAGE

1. The stressed pronouns, also called emphatic pronouns, are:

moi	me	I
toi	you	you
lui	him	he
elle	her	she
nous	us	we
vous	you	you
eux	them (masculine)	they
elles	them (feminine)	they

They are used after a preposition as an object.

Je travaille pour lui.
   I work for him.

Je peux aller avec eux?
   Can I go with them?

They are also used to emphasize a subject or object pronoun.

Moi aussi, je parle français et anglais!
   Me too, I speak French and English!

Toi, tu as faim.
   It looks like you're hungry.

They are used after comparisons as the object of *que*.

Nous sommes moins pressés que vous.
    We are less in a rush than you.

Elle parle plus de langues que nous.
    She speaks more languages than we do.

They are also used after the imperative as an object pronoun.

Dis-moi.
    Tell me.

Indiquez-leur le chemin, s'il vous plaît.
    Show them the way, please.

They can also be used in compound subjects or objects.

Charles et moi, nous aimons voyager en train.
    Charles and I like to travel by train.

But in a compound subject when the two pronouns are of the third person (*lui, elle*), the subject pronoun is omitted and the verb follows directly.

Lui et elle vont se promener avec Tidjane.
    They are going for a walk with Tidjane

Emphatic pronouns are also used after *c'est.*

C'est eux!
    Here they are! / It's them!

C'est à nous.
    It's our turn. It's ours.

Note how they are used in the following phrases.

Moi non plus, je ne me souviens pas de vous.
    I don't remember you, either. / Me neither, I don't
    remember you.

Eux aussi, ils vont venir.
> They're going to come as well.

They can be used alone when given as a response.

Qui veut boire un apéritif?—Nous!
> Who wants a drink?—We do!

Qui a dix ans aujourd'hui?—Moi.
> Who's turning ten today?—I am. / Me.

2. Reflexive verbs are verbs whose action is performed by the subject on itself: *elle se lave, je me prépare*. Note that many verbs that are not reflexive in English are reflexive in French. As you come across new reflexive verbs in French, it's best to memorize them.

Je me débrouille plutôt bien en portugais et en suédois.
> I'm doing pretty well in Portuguese and Swedish.

Nous nous dépêchons.
> We're hurrying up.

Vous vous souvenez de lui?
> Do you remember him?

Ne t'inquiète pas.
> Don't worry.

Study the following forms of a regular reflexive verb in the present tense (and see also the Verb Charts):

se laver	(to wash oneself)
je me lave	I wash myself
tu te laves	you wash yourself
il se lave	he washes himself
elle se lave	she washes herself
nous nous lavons	we wash ourselves
vous vous lavez	you wash yourself (pol.) / yourselves (pl.)

ils se lavent they wash themselves
elles se lavent they wash themselves

Compound tenses of reflexive verbs, such as the present perfect below, are always formed with the auxiliary *être*. Note that the past participle of reflexive verbs agrees with the subject, unless the verb is followed by a direct object, in which case there is no agreement.

Est-ce que nous nous sommes égarés?
  Are we lost? / Have we gotten lost?

Non, on ne s'est pas perdu.
  No, we are not lost. / No, we haven't gotten lost.

Nous nous sommes lavé(e)s.
  We washed ourselves. / We got washed.

Nous nous sommes lavé les mains.
  We washed our hands.

EXERCISES

A. Substitute each of the words in parentheses for the underlined word in the pattern sentence. Write the complete sentence and say it aloud.

1. *Il travaille pour <u>moi</u>. (toi, lui, elle, nous, vous, eux, elles)*

2. *Il est plus riche que <u>moi</u>. (toi, lui, elle, nous, vous, eux, elles)*

3. *Qui sonne à la porte? C'est <u>moi</u>. (toi, lui, elle, nous, vous, eux, elles)*

4. *Elle s'est <u>lavée</u>. (souvenue, dépêchée, levée, égarée, préparée)*

B. Rewrite each sentence by replacing *je* with the other subject pronouns. Make all necessary verb changes, say aloud and translate each sentence.

1. *Je me prépare à neuf heures.*

2. *Je me suis perdue(e).*

C. Change the present to the *passé composé* (the present perfect.) Say aloud and translate each sentence.

> Ex: *Nous nous couchons. / Nous nous sommes couché(e)s.* We went to sleep.

1. *Nous nous lavons.*

2. *Nous nous égarons.*

3. *Nous nous souvenons.*

4. *Nous nous dépêchons.*

5. *Nous nous arrêtons.*

D. Translate the following sentences into French. Then say them aloud.

1. Ask the lady the way.

2. Don't ask this gentleman the way.

3. I wouldn't know how to get there.

4. Where do you want to go? To Paris.

5. They (*elles*) looked at each other.

6. How about going to see the European Commission?

7. How about taking a walk?

8. We've lost our way.

9. We went to the Latin Quarter.

10. Turn to the right.

11. I have to turn to the left.

12. You should have continued straight ahead.

13. She's got to retrace her steps.

14. Is the Parc du Cinquantenaire right there? Yes, it's very near (*tout près d'*) here.

E. From among the three choices, select the best translation for the English word or phrase given. Write the complete sentence, and translate.

1. (How about taking) _____ *une promenade à pied?*

   Comment faire / Si on faisait / Si on prenait

2. (easy) *C' est* _____.

   aisé / facile / agréable

3. (Look at) _____ *ce plan de la ville.*

   Cherchez / Voyez / Regardez

4. (straight ahead) *Il faut continuer* _____.

   droit devant / à droite / tout droit

5. (direction) *Vous allez dans le mauvais* _____.

   sens / côté / coin

6. (left) *Nous avons tourné* _____.

   laissé / à gauche / à droite

7. (now that) *Ah, oui,* _____ *nous avons trouvé le bon chemin.*

   premier/ une fois que / maintenant que

8. (mistaken) *C' est nous qui nous sommes* _____.

   égaré / trompé / trompés

9. (What a pity) _____!

    Quelle pitié! / Quelle sympathie! / Quel dommage!

10. (Don't forget) _____ *que nous avons vu Brux-*
    elles.

    N' oublie pas / Ne revois pas / Ne dis pas

Answer Key

A. 1. *Il travaille pour toi. Il travaille pour lui. Il travaille pour elle. Il travaille pour nous. Il travaille pour vous. Il travaille pour eux. Il travaille pour elles.* 2. *Il est plus riche que toi. Il est plus riche que lui. Il est plus riche qu'elle. Il est plus riche que nous. Il est plus riche que vous. Il est plus riche qu'eux. Il est plus riche qu'elles.* 3. *C'est toi. C'est lui. C'est elle. C'est nous. C'est vous. C'est eux. C'est elles.* 4. *Elle s'est souvenue. Elle s'est dépêchée. Elle s'est levée. Elle s'est égarée. Elle s'est préparée.*

B. 1. *Je me prépare à neuf heures.* I get ready at nine. *Tu te prépares à neuf heures.* You get ready at nine. *Il se prépare à neuf heures.* He gets ready at nine. *Elle se prépare à neuf heures.* She gets ready at nine. *Nous nous préparons à neuf heures.* We get ready at nine. *Vous vous préparez à neuf heures.* You get ready at nine. *Ils se préparent à neuf heures.* They (masc.) get ready at nine. *Elles se préparent à neuf heures.* They (fem.) get ready at nine. 2. *Je me suis perdu(e).* I got lost. *Tu t'es perdu(e).* You got lost. *Il s'est perdu.* He got lost. *Elle s'est perdue.* She got lost. *Nous nous sommes perdu(e)s.* We got lost. *Vous vous êtes perdu(e)(s).* You got lost. *Ils se sont perdus.* They (masc.) got lost. *Elle se sont perdues.* They (fem.) got lost.

C. 1. *Nous nous sommes lavé(e)s.* We washed ourselves. 2. *Nous nous sommes égaré(e)s.* We got lost. 3. *Nous nous sommes souvenu(e)s.* We remembered. 4. *Nous nous sommes dépêché(e)s.* We hurried. 5. *Nous nous sommes arrêté(e)s.* We stopped.

D. 1. *Demandez le chemin à la dame.* 2. *Ne demandez pas le chemin à ce monsieur.* 3. *Je ne saurais pas y aller.* 4. *Où voulez-vous aller? À Paris.* 5. *Elles se sont* *regardées.* 6. *Si on allait voir la Commission européenne?* 7. *Si on allait faire une promenade?* 8. *Nous nous sommes égarés.* 9. *Nous sommes allés au Quartier Latin.* 10. *Tournez à droite.* 11. *Je dois tourner à gauche.* 12. *Vous auriez dû continuer tout droit.* 13. *Elle doit rebrousser chemin.* 14. *Le parc du Cinquantenaire est juste là? Oui, c'est tout près d'ici.*

E. 1. *Si on faisait une promenade à pied?* How about taking a walk? 2. *C'est facile.* It's easy. 3. *Regardez ce plan de la ville.* Look at this map of the city. 4. *Il faut continuer tout droit.* You have to go (to continue) straight ahead. 5. *Vous allez dans le mauvais sens.* You are walking in the wrong direction. 6. *Nous avons tourné à gauche.* We turned left. 7. *Ah oui, maintenant que nous avons trouvé le bon chemin.* Oh, yes, now that we found the right path. 8. *C'est nous qui nous sommes trompés.* It is us/we who made the mistake. 9. *Quel dommage!* What a pity! 10. *N'oublie pas que nous avons vu Bruxelles.* Don't forget that we saw Brussels.

LESSON 6

DANS UN GRAND MAGASIN MULTIMÉDIA
IN A MULTIMEDIA DEPARTMENT STORE

A. DIALOGUE

0. *Charles et Jane, guidés par Luc, arrivent à la FNAC, une grande surface spécialisée dans la vente de livres, de disques compacts, de DVD et de toutes sortes d'appareils électroniques et multimédia.*
Charles and Jane, guided by Luc, arrive at the FNAC, a department store specializing in the sale of books, CD's, DVD's and all types of electronic and multimedia equipment.

1. Luc: **Voilà. Ici, vous devriez trouver tout ce que vous désirez.**
Here we are. Here, you should find everything you need.

2. Charles: **C'est très gentil à toi, Luc, de nous accompagner.**
It's very nice of you to come along, Luc.

3. Jane: **En effet, il semble que nous allons trouver notre bonheur.**
Indeed, it seems that we're going to find everything we'd hoped for.

4. Luc: **En plus, les rayons sont bien indiqués et en général, le personnel s'y connaît.**
And what's more, the departments are well marked and generally the staff knows what it's doing.

5. Charles: **Bon, par quoi commence-t-on? Les disques compacts?**
Well, where should we start? The CD's?

6. Jane: **Oui, puisque c'est au rez-de-chaussée.**
   Yes since that's on the ground floor.

7. Luc: **Quel genre de musique cherchez-vous?**
   What type of music are you looking for?

8. Charles: **De la musique jazz française comme Michel Portal et d'autres. Oui, voilà.**
   French jazz music like Michel Portal and others. Yes, good.

9. Jane: **Regarde, les prix sont à peu près les mêmes qu'à New York. Tiens, tes favoris: Richard Bona et Michel Solal.**
   Look! The prices are about the same as in New York. Here are your favorites: Richard Bona and Michel Solal.

10. Luc: **Bona a beaucoup de succès. Il a gagné les *Victoires du Jazz 2004*, l'équivalent de vos *Grammy Awards*! Sinon, ce CD de Sclavis-Texier-Romano est moins récent, mais il a bien marché aussi. Et Michel Petrucciani, ah c'était vraiment un grand pianiste.**
    Bona is very successful. He won the *Victoires du Jazz 2004*, the equivalent of your *Grammy Awards*! Otherwise, this Sclavis-Texier-Romano CD is less recent but also did very well. And Michel Petrucciani, yes, he was really a great pianist.

11. Charles: **Ah oui, merci. J'en ai entendu parler. Il jouait souvent à New York. On les prend aussi. Et maintenant, pour la variété française?**
    Great, thank you. I've heard of him. He's often performed in New York. We'll take those as well. And now, what about French pop?

12. Jane: **On voudrait trouver Charles Aznavour. J'aime beaucoup ses chansons.**

We would like to find Charles Aznavour. I love his songs.

13. Luc: **En fait, moi, j'écoute surtout de la musique jazz et world. Oui, c'est un classique. Voici une compilation de ses grands succès. Il y en a d'autres: Charle-Elie Couture, Jacques Brel, Bernard Lavilliers, de vrais artistes. Celui-ci de Henri Salvador est très bien, et celui de Jane Birkin a eu un succès bien mérité, aussi.**

In fact, I listen to jazz and world music above all. Yes, this is a classic. Here's a compilation of his big hits. There are others: Charle-Elie Couture, Jacques Brel, Bernard Lavilliers, true artists. This one by Henri Salvador is very good, and that one by Jane Birkin also did very well and really deserved it.

14. Jane: **Bien, on va tous les acheter. En plus, ceux-ci sont bon marché. Et où se trouve la musique internationale, d'Afrique et d'ailleurs?**

Well, we're going to take them all. And these have a good price. And where's the world music from Africa and other places?

15. Luc: **Ici. C'est classé par continent et par pays. Vous avez des artistes en tête?**

Right here. It's sorted by continent and country. Do you have any artists in mind?

16. Charles: **Non, on a décidé de découvrir de nouveaux horizons. Eliane et notre voyage à Bruxelles chez nos amis nous ont inspirés. Alors, dis-nous!**

No, we've decided to discover new horizons. Eliane and our trip to Brussels at our friends' have inspired us. So tell us!

17. Luc: **Bon, là aussi, vous avez l'embarras du choix. Dans mes grands favoris, il y a Bonga, son**

dernier CD, ceux de Oumou Sangaré et Miriam Makeba chez les dames, celui de Corneille.
So here as well, you have a huge selection to choose from. Among my favorites are Bonga, his last CD, the ones by Oumou Sangaré and Miriam Makeba for the ladies, the one by Corneille.

18. Charles: **Corneille, quel nom pour un chanteur!**
Corneille, what a strange name for a singer!

19. Jane: **On pourrait se demander ce que le premier Corneille aurait dit.**
One could wonder what the first Corneille would have said.

20. *Plus tard.*
Later.

21. Jane: **Tu es sûr que tu veux acheter des DVD? Le standard des lecteurs de DVD n'est-il pas différent?**
You're sure you want to buy some DVD's? Isn't the system of DVD players different?

22. Charles: **Oui, mais on devrait ramener des films de comiques français à Carlos, car lui a un lecteur DVD multicanaux. Il serait ravi! Le nôtre, en fait, demande la relève. Peut-être est-ce le moment d'en acheter un nouveau, Jane. Et pourquoi ne pas acheter un enregistreur multicanaux?**
Yes, but we should bring back some movies starring French comedians to Carlos, because he has a multisystem DVD player. He would be so thrilled! Ours, in fact, could be replaced. It may be the moment to buy a new one, Jane. And why not buy a multisystem DVD recorder?

23. Luc: **Vous avez vu la publicité à l'entrée? Il y a des tarifs spéciaux sur les enregistreurs de CD et de DVD. C'est peut-être l'occasion?**
Did you see the advertisement at the entrance? They have special prices on CD and DVD recorders. This may be the right time?

24. Jane: **Bon, je capitule. Allons voir les DVD et ensuite ces enregistreurs multicanaux.**
Alright, I give in. Let's go and see the DVD's and then, these multisystem DVD recorders.

25. *À la caisse.*
At the register.

26. Charles: **Vous acceptez les chèques de voyage?**
Do you accept traveler's checks?

27. La caissière: **Oui, monsieur, si vous avez une pièce d'idendité et si vous les signez devant moi.**
Cashier: Yes, sir, as long as you have an ID card and sign them in front of me.

28. Jane: **En tous cas, Luc, merci beaucoup pour tes conseils. Charles devrait te remercier aussi, car nous n'avions pas prévu de faire un tel achat!**
In any event, Luc, thanks a lot for your insights. Charles should thank you too, because we didn't plan to make such a purchase!

B. NOTES

Title: *un grand magasin* or *une grande surface* has two equivalents: a large store (of any kind) and, more commonly, a department store. The FNAC is a well-known *grand magasin*, which has several locations throughout the country.

0. *de toutes sortes*: of all kinds. *Une sorte de, un genre de, un type de, un espèce de*: a kind of.

1. *tout ce que*: all that.

2. Note the expression *c'est très gentil à toi*: it's very kind of you.

3. *en effet*: indeed.
   Il semble que . . . It seems that . . . The pronoun *il* is impersonal in this expression.
   trouver son bonheur: to find everything that one hopes for.

4. *en plus*: in addition, what's more.
   un rayon: a department or shelf (of a store) or a ray (of the sun.)
   bien indiqués: well marked. Remember that *bien* can be used in front of adjectives.
   le personnel: the staff, the personnel. It is different from the adjective *personnel*: personal.
   un personnel qui s'y connaît: a staff that knows about it, is knowledgeable, knows what it's doing. The irregular verb is *connaître*.

5. Both expressions *disques compacts* or *CD* are used.

6. *Le rez-de-chaussée* is the ground floor. *Le premier étage* is not what is considered to be the first floor in the U.S. but the second floor, *le deuxième étage* is the third floor and so on. *Le sous-sol* is the basement.

9. *à peu près* or *presque*: almost.
   le même (masc.), *la même* (fem.), *les mêmes* (plural) *que*: the same as.

10. *Les Victoires du Jazz, les Victoires du Classique*, and the older *Victoires de la Musique* are the official

music award ceremonies in France, when music and recording professionals are celebrated.

Il a bien marché from *avoir bien marché* is the equivalent here of *avoir du succès*, to be successful. It also means to go well.

11. *La variété*, a typical French expression, corresponds broadly to commercial pop music in the U.S. In this dialogue, you can find some popular singers and musicians, whether *en jazz*, *en musique internationale* or what is also called *la chanson française* or *les variétés*.

13. *un classique*, adjective used as a noun with a different meaning from in *musique classique*, classical music. It is the equivalent of a classic, a standard.

14. *Bon marché*, which is invariable, means inexpensive and *cher* or (*chère, chers, chères*) is expensive. The comparative *meilleur marché* is less expensive.

15. *Vous avez des artistes en tête?* from the expression, *avoir quelque chose en tête*, to have something in mind.

17. *Vous avez l'embarras du choix*, idiomatic expression meaning you have a huge selection to chose from.

21./22. Video equipment in the U.S., Canada and some other countries use the NTSC system, and countries in Europe use the PAL or SECAM system, or *standard* in French. For the DVD's, the differentiation is set by regions, which are numbered. One speaks of *canaux*. Therefore a regular DVD distributed in France would not work on a DVD player, or *lecteur de DVD* in the U.S. However, major brands offer multisystem (*multistandard* or *multicanaux*) VCR's and DVD players and recorders (*enregistreurs*). In the same register, *le magnétoscope* is the VCR, *la cassette vidéo,* the videotape.

le nôtre demande la relève, that is "ours needs to be replaced" (it's too old, or doesn't work well). The expression *prendre la relève* means to take over.

23. *la publicité*: advertisement or commercial.

C'est l'occasion: It is a good opportunity or *c'est l'occasion ou jamais*: It's now or never. Also, *une bonne occasion* means a bargain.

26. *Les chèques de voyage* or traveler's checks are accepted almost everywhere in France.

C. GRAMMAR AND USAGE

1. The present conditional is formed by adding the endings of the imperfect (*-ais, -ais, -ait, -ions, -iez, -aient*) to the future stem of a verb. Remember that the future stem for regular *-er* and *-ir* verbs is the full infinitive, and the infinitive minus the final *-e* for *-re* verbs. Many common verbs have irregular future stems.

Here are the full conjugations of a few verbs in the present conditional.

acheter (to buy)

j' achèterais	I would buy
tu achèterais	you would buy
il, elle, on achèterait	he, she, it, one, we, they would buy
nous achèterions	we would buy
vous achèteriez	you would buy
ils, elles achèteraient	they would buy

finir (to finish)

je finirais	I would finish
tu finirais	you would finish

il, elle, on finirait	he, she, it, one, we, they would finish
nous finirions	we would finish
vous finiriez	you would finish
ils, elles finiraient	they would finish

devoir (have to, must, ought to)

je devrais	I should
tu devrais	you should
il, elle, on devrait	he, she, it, one, we, they should
nous devrions	we should
vous devriez	you would should
ils, elles devraient	they should

pouvoir (be able, can)

je pourrais	I could
tu pourrais	you could
il, elle, on pourrait	he, she, it, one, we, they could
nous pourrions	we could
vous pourriez	you could
ils, elles pourraient	they could

être (to be)

je serais	I would be
tu serais	you would be
il, elle, on serait	he, she, it, one, we, they would be
nous serions	we would be
vous seriez	you would be
ils, elles seraient	they would be

avoir (to have)

j'aurais	I would have
tu aurais	you would have
il, elle, on aurait	he, she, it, one, we, they would have

nous aurions	we would have
vous auriez	you would have
ils, elles auraient	they would have

For other verbs, please consult the verb charts in the grammar summary.

The conditional in French is generally used the same way as it is in English. It expresses a hypothetical statement, a suggestion, an obligation, a duty or a possibility.

En France, nous achèterions des produits spécialisés.
>In France, we would buy specialized products.

On devrait ramener des films de comiques français à Carlos.
>We should bring back movies with French comedians to Carlos.

On pourrait se demander ce que le premier Corneille aurait dit.
>One could wonder what the first Corneille would have said.

The present conditional is also used in polite requests and questions.

Pourriez-vous me montrer celui-là, s'il vous plaît?
>Could you show me that one, please?

Où voudriez-vous aller?
>Where would you like to go?

2. Possessive pronouns replace nouns used with possessive adjectives. In other words, *mon livre* (my book) may be expressed by *le mien* (mine). They agree in gender and number with the noun they replace. Remember that in French, all possessives agree with the thing possessed rather than the possessor. So, *son livre* (his/her book) is masculine because of the gender of *livre*, not because of the gender of the possessor.

	m. sing.	f. sing.	m. plu.	f. plu.
mine	*le mien*	*la mienne*	*les miens*	*les miennes*
yours	*le tien*	*la tienne*	*les tiens*	*les tiennes*
his, hers, its	*le sien*	*la sienne*	*les siens*	*les siennes*
ours	*le nôtre*	*la nôtre*	*les nôtres*	*les nôtres*
yours	*le vôtre*	*la vôtre*	*les vôtres*	*les vôtres*
theirs	*le leur*	*la leur*	*les leurs*	*les leurs*

> *C'est mon disque compact, pas le tien.*
>> It's my CD, not yours.

> *Votre lecteur de DVD est nouveau, mais le nôtre demande la relève.*
>> Your DVD player is new but ours needs to be replaced.

When the possessive pronoun is preceded by *à* or *de*, the article is contracted in the ususal way.

> *La caissière a besoin de ta carte d'identité, mais pas des nôtres.*
>> The cashier needs your ID card, but not ours.

3. Likewise demonstrative pronouns replace nouns used with demonstrative adjectives. For example, *ce livre* (this book) may be expressed by *celui* (this one). Like any other pronoun, the demonstrative pronouns agree in gender and number with the nouns they replace.

m. sing.	f. sing.	m. plu.	f. plu.
celui	*celle*	*ceux*	*celles*

Demonstrative pronouns can be used on their own or can be followed by *-ci or -là* to specify a meaning of "this one here" vs. "that one there." They can also be used with the relative pronouns *qui, que, dont, où* or a preposition.

> *Celui de Carlos est intéressant.*
>> This one belonging to Carlos is interesting.

Nous allons acheter ceux qui sont multicanaux.
> We are going to buy these multi-standard ones.

En plus, ceux-ci sont bon marché.
> And these (here) are cheap.

4. When a verb has two objects, they can be replaced by two object pronouns, but there are rules regarding the order of pronouns. In the affirmative or negative forms the order is:

me, te, se, nous, vous are used first

le, la, l', les are used in second

lui, y, leur are used third

en is used last

Il nous le montre.
> He shows it to us.

Il le lui a prêté.
> He lent it to him/her.

Il les leur a achetés.
> He bought them for them.

Il y en a d' autres.
> There are others.

In a negative command, the order is the same. But in an affirmative command, all direct object pronouns come before all indirect object pronouns, which come before *y* and *en*.

Donnez-m' en.
> Give me some.

Ne m' en donnez pas.
> Don't give me any.

Ne le lui dis pas!
> Don't say it to him/her!

Finally, *me* and *te* become *moi* and *toi* after *le, la, les*.

Donnez-le moi!
   Give it to me!

EXERCISES

A. Substitute one synonymous word or expression in parentheses for the underlined word or expression in the model sentence. Write the complete sentence and say it aloud. Change the main verb if necessary.

   1. *En effet, vous pourriez le faire.* (*bien sûr, en fait, maintenant, avant*)

   2. *J' aime le mien.* (*son CD, mon CD, ton CD, leur CD*)

   3. *Nous allons trouver notre bonheur.* (*le bonheur, ce que nous désirons, la vérité, quelque chose*)

   4. *Le personnel s' y connaît.* (*mes amis, les clients, les employés, la dame*)

B. Replace the underlined adjective-noun combination with the corresponding demonstrative pronoun.

   Example: *Je ne veux pas cette robe-ci./Je ne veux pas celle-ci.*

   1. *Donnez-moi ce lecteur-ci.*

   2. *Je préfère ces livres-là.*

   3. *Prenez ces disques compacts-ci.*

   4. *Regardez ces cassettes-ci.*

C. Expand the following by placing *Celui dont je vous ai parlé* in front of each of the following. Write the entire sentence, say it, and give the English translation.

   1. _____ *a été vendu.*

2. _____ *coûte trop cher.*

3. _____ *ne me plaît pas.*

4. _____ *est excellent.*

5. _____ *est le frère de Michel.*

6. _____ *est venu me voir.*

D. Replace the object nouns with object pronouns, and translate them.

Example: *Il me donne les livres./Il me les donne*: He gives them to me.

1. *Il lui donne le chèque de voyage.*

2. *Il nous montre les enregistreurs de DVD.*

3. *Ne me donnez pas ce magnétoscope.*

4. *Il me montre des disques compacts.*

5. *Il y a des vidéos.*

6. *Je leur parle de musique de jazz.*

E. Make the following commands negative. Translate these negative sentences.

Example: *Donnez-le-moi./Ne me le donnez pas.* Don't give it to me.

1. *Montrez-la leur.*

2. *Vendez-les lui.*

3. *Donnez-m'en.*

4. *Prête-le moi.*

F. Translate the following into French. Then say them aloud.

1. I prefer this one.

2. This is a DVD player, and those are recorders.

3. What type of music would you like?

4. Here is something (*quelque chose de*) beautiful.

5. There is nothing else (*rien d'autre*) here.

6. He's going to send it to you with ours.

7. You could pay with a traveler's check.

8. The staff is knowledgeable and the departments are well marked.

9. Do you have anyone in mind?

10. You have a huge selection.

11. These CD's are cheap.

12. The video department is in the basement.

G. From among the three choices, select the best translation for the English word or phrase given at the beginning of each sentence. Write the complete sentence, and translate.

1. (bargain) *C'est une _____.*

   bonne occasion / bonne opportunité / bon marché

2. (What) _____ *vous désirez, madame?*

   Que / Qu'est-ce que / Quoi

3. (All that) _____ *vous voulez est ici.*

   Tout / Tous ceux qui / Tout ce que

4. (Indeed) _____, *c'est un excellent artiste!*

   En fait / En effet / En tout

5. (almost) *Les prix sont* _____ *les mêmes qu'à New York.*

   tous / enfin / à peu près

6. (cheap) *Ceux-là sont* _____.

   bonne qualité / bien indiqués / bon marché

Answer Key

A. 1. *Bien sûr, vous pourriez le faire.* 2. *J'aime mon CD.*
3. *Nous allons trouver ce que nous désirons.* 4. *Les
employés s'y connaissent.*

B. 1. *Donnez-moi celui-ci.* 2. *Je préfère ceux-là.* 3. *Prenez
ceux-ci.* 4. *Regardez celles-ci.*

C. 1. *Celui dont je vous ai parlé a été vendu.* The one I
spoke to you about has been sold. 2. *Celui dont je vous
ai parlé coûte trop cher.* The one that I spoke to you
about costs too much. 3. *Celui dont je vous ai parlé ne
me plaît pas.* I don't like the one (the person) I spoke to
you about. 4. *Celui dont je vous ai parlé est excellent.*
The one I spoke to you about is excellent. 5. *Celui dont
je vous ai parlé est le frère de Michel.* The person (the
one) whom I spoke to you about is Michel's brother.
6. *Celui dont je vous ai parlé est venu me voir.* The one
(the person) whom I spoke to you about came to see me.

D. 1. *Il le lui donne.* He is giving it to him. 2. *Il nous les
montre.* He is showing them to us. 3. *Ne me le donnez
pas.* Don't give it to me. 4. *Il m'en montre.* He shows
some to me. 5. *Il y en a.* There are some. 6. *Je leur en
parle.* I am speaking to them about it.

E. 1. *Ne la leur montrez pas.* Don't show it to them. 2. *Ne
les lui vendez pas.* Don't sell them to him/her. 3. *Ne m'en
donnez pas.* Don't give any to me. / Don't give me any.
4. *Ne me le prête pas.* Don't lend it to me.

F. 1. *Je préfère celui-ci.* 2. *C'est un lecteur de DVD, et
ceux-là sont des enregistreurs.* 3. *Quel genre de musique
aimeriez-vous?* 4. *Voici quelque chose de beau.* 5. *Il n'y
a rien d'autre ici.* 6. *Il va vous l'envoyer avec les nôtres.*
7. *Vous pourriez payer avec un chèque de voyage.* 8. *Le*

personnel s'y connaît et les rayons sont bien indiqués.
9. *Est-ce que vous avez quelqu'un en tête?* 10. *Vous avez l'embarras du choix.* 11. *Ces disques compacts sont bon marché.* 12. *Le rayon vidéo est au sous-sol.*

G. 1. *C'est une bonne occasion.* It is a bargain. 2. *Qu'est-ce que vous désirez, madame?* What would you like, Ma'am? 3. *Tout ce que vous voulez est ici.* All that you want is here. 4. *En effet, c'est un excellent artiste!* Indeed, he's an excellent artist! 5. *Les prix sont à peu près les mêmes qu'à New York.* Prices are almost the same as in New York. 6. *Ceux-là sont bon marché.* Those (ones there) are cheap.

LESSON 7

RENCONTRE DE NOUVEAUX AMIS
MEETING NEW FRIENDS

A. DIALOGUE

0. *Ce soir, Jane et Charles se promènent aux alentours de la rue Mouffetard à la recherche d'un restaurant. C'est leur anniversaire de mariage!*
   Tonight, Jane and Charles are walking around the rue Mouffetard searching for a restaurant. It's their anniversary!

1. Charles: **Regarde! Ce restaurant-ci a l'air très bien et . . .**
   Look! This restaurant looks very nice and . . .

2. Jane: **Oui, mais il y a beaucoup trop de monde, tu ne trouves pas?**
   Yes, but there are too many people, don't you think?

3. Charles: **Tu as raison, il y a même des gens qui attendent sur le trottoir.**
   You're right, there are even people waiting on the sidewalk.

4. Jane: **Et celui-là de l'autre côté de la Place de la Contrescarpe? Quel en est le nom?**
   And that one on the other side of the Place de la Contrescarpe? What's its name?

5. Charles: **Chez Zila. Quel joli nom! Allons voir!**
   Chez Zila. What a pretty name! Let's go and see!

6. *Au restaurant "Chez Zila", Jane et Charles s'installent à une table ronde en bois, quand un serveur*

*ne tarde pas à venir les accueillir en leur apportant
une carafe d'eau et une corbeille de pain.*

In the restaurant "Chez Zila", Jane and Charles sit
down at a round wooden table, when a waiter
appears right away to welcome them by bringing
them a pitcher of water and a basket of bread.

7. Le serveur: **En vacances à Paris? Bien. Je reviens
   aussitôt avec les menus.**
   Waiter: On vacation in Paris? Good. I'll be right
   back with the menus.

8. Charles: **Chérie, je crois que nous avons fait un
   bon choix! L'endroit est joli, la lumière tamisée et
   les gens ont l'air de bien s'amuser!**
   Sweetheart, I think we made a good choice! The
   place is lovely, the light is soft and the people seem
   to be enjoying themselves!

9. Jane: **Oui, il y a une bonne ambiance! Regarde,
   les gens au bar sont sur leur 31, et au fond de la
   salle, il y en a qui dansent.**
   Yes, there's a great atmosphere! Look, people at the
   bar are all dressed-up and in the back of the room,
   some are dancing.

10. *Le serveur est de retour avec les menus.*
    The waiter is back with the menus.

11. Le serveur: **Madame, c'est une soirée bien parti-
    culière, car la patronne célèbre son mariage.
    D'ailleurs, elle offre à tous ses clients un apéritif.
    Alors, que pourrions-nous vous servir?**
    Madam, it's a very special evening because the
    owner is celebrating her wedding. And, she's offer-
    ing an aperitif to all her customers. So, what could
    we bring you?

12. Charles: **C'est merveilleux! D'abord, nos félicitations aux mariés. Puis . . .**
That's wonderful! First our congratulations to the bride and groom. Then . . .

13. Jane: **Et transmettez-leur, s'il vous plaît, nos meilleurs vœux de bonheur!**
And please give them our best wishes of happiness!

14. Le serveur: **Je n'y manquerai pas, mais je crois que vous aurez l'occasion de le faire en personne lorsque Madame Zila viendra dans la salle.**
Certainly, but I think you'll have the opportunity to do so in person when Mrs. Zila comes into the room.

15. Charles: **Bien. C'est une coïncidence heureuse car aujourd'hui, c'est notre anniversaire de mariage! 25 ans!**
Great. It is a happy coincidence because today is our wedding anniversary! 25 years!

16. Le serveur: **Ah ça, ça va lui faire plaisir.**
Ah, that's going to make her happy!

17. *Peu après, une femme élégante avec le bras dans le plâtre s'approche de leur table.*
Shortly after, an elegant woman with her arm in a cast approaches their table.

18. Madame Zila: **Excusez-moi, mais est-ce vous qui célébrez votre anniversaire de mariage?**
Madame Zila: I beg your pardon but are you the couple celebrating their wedding anniversary?

19. Jane: **Oui, c'est bien nous! Et nous vous souhaitons beaucoup de bonheur!**
Yes, we are indeed. And we wish you much happiness!

20. Madame Zila: **Merci! À vous aussi, je vous adresse mes meilleurs vœux! Ah, je n'en reviens pas. Vous permettez que je m'asseoie un instant?**
Thank you! My best wishes to you as well! Ah, I can't believe it. Would you allow me to sit for a moment?

21. Jane: **Mais naturellement!**
Of course!

22. Madame Zila: **Je vais vous faire une confession. Depuis une semaine, tout s'annonçait assez mal: mes deux enfants ne pouvaient venir assister à mon mariage, je me suis cassé le bras et j'ai dû me le faire plâtrer, le gérant et le chef de mon restaurant sont tous les deux tombés malades et . . .**
I'm going to make a confession. For a week, everything was looking pretty bad: my two children couldn't attend my wedding, I broke my arm and had to have it put in a cast, the manager and the chef of my restaurant both got sick and . . .

23. Le serveur: **. . . la salle que vous aviez louée pour le mariage n'était plus libre!**
. . . the room you'd rented for the wedding was no longer available!

24. Madame Zila: **C'est pour ça que nous faisons la fête ici. Enfin, plus que jamais, je commençais à me poser des questions. Mais hier soir, enfin, j'ai eu un coup de téléphone de ma fille. Elle s'apprêtait à prendre l'avion pour Paris. Elle vit à New York.**
That's why we are celebrating here. Well, more than ever, I was starting to wonder. But yesterday evening, finally, I got a phone call from my daughter. She was about to take the plane to Paris. She lives in New York.

25. Jane: **Tout comme nous!**
So do we!

26. Madame Zila: **Vraiment? Vous voyez? C'est incroyable! Donc, ma fille arrive, mon autre fille et son mari me font la surprise d'arriver à minuit et en plus, mon gendre a gentiment offert de s'occuper du restaurant ce soir et il a amené son meilleur ami qui est un chef réputé!**
Really? You see? It's incredible! So my daughter is here, my other daughter and her husband surprised me last night when they came at midnight, and what's more, my son-in-law kindly offered to take care of the restaurant this evening and brought along his best friend who is a renowned chef!

27. Jane: **Quelle histoire!**
What a story!

28. Charles: **Oui, de temps en temps la vie est surprenante! Est-ce votre beau-fils?**
Yes, at times, life is surprising! Is this your son-in-law?

29. Madame Zila: **Oui, il est charmant, n'est-ce pas? Et, en plus de tout ça, c'est votre anniversaire de mariage et vous êtes de New York City! J'y ai rencontré mon mari lors de ma dernière visite. Alors, comme je ne crois pas aux coïncidences, je considère ça plutôt comme un bon présage, je voudrais vous inviter à nous joindre ...**
Yes, he's charming, isn't he? And in addition to all this, it's your anniversary and you're from New York City! I met my husband there during my last visit. So, since I don't believe in coincidences, I rather consider this as an omen, I'd like you to join us ...

30. Charles: **Mais vous êtes trop aimable . . .**
But you're too kind . . .

31. Jane: **On ne voudrait pas s'imposer . . .**
We wouldn't want to impose . . .

32. Madame Zila: **Absolument pas . . . Si, bien sûr, vous ne préférez pas dîner en amoureux, cela me ferait un grand plaisir de partager ce moment avec vous!**
Not at all . . . If, of course, you don't prefer having an intimate dinner, it'd be a great pleasure for me to share this moment with you!

33. Charles: **Dans ce cas-là, nous acceptons votre invitation!**
In that case, we accept your invitation!

B. NOTES

0. *aux alentours de, vers*: around, about, in the vicinity of. *La rue Mouffetard* is a picturesque street near the *Quartier Latin*. It's lined with a great variety of *restaurants*, *cafés* and passes through la *Place de la Contrescarpe*, whose *bars* and *cafés* are popular after dark.

2. *Tu ne trouves pas?* is a common colloquial expression equivalent to: Don't you think?

5. *Chez Zila*: At Zila's. The expression *chez* + noun means: at the home of, at the place of, at the place of work of: *chez le docteur, chez l'avocat, chez mes parents, chez moi*.

8. *Ils ont l'air de s'amuser*: They seem to be having fun. *Avoir l'air de* corresponds to: to look like, to seem.

9. *être sur son 31*: to be all dressed-up, to be dressed to kill.

   Note the phrase: *il y en a qui* + verb: there are some who + verb.

10. *être de retour*: to be back

14. *lorsque Madame Zila viendra*: when Ms. Zila comes. Note the use of the future tense in this phrase. In many instances where the future is only implied in English, it is used in French.

15. *une coïncidence* is one of the few words using the dieresis or *tréma*, which is the two little dots used above a vowel to indicate that the vowel has to be pronounced separately.

    Another common word with a *tréma* is *Noël* (Christmas)

16. *Cela va lui faire plaisir*: It's going to make her happy. Note the construction of this expression, *faire plaisir à quelqu'un*: to make someone happy.

20. *Vous permettez que je* + verb: Would you allow me to + verb

    je n'en reviens pas: I can't believe it

22. *Les choses s'annoncent bien* or *mal* means things look good or bad.

24. *c'est pour ça que*: this is why. The pronoun *ça* is the contracted form of *cela*.

    Plus que jamais, that is, more than ever, can be used as is, or with an adjective or an adverb as in *plus vite que jamais*: faster than ever, *moins sympathique que jamais*: less kind than ever.

    un coup de téléphone: a phone call. Literally, the expression *un coup de* means a blow or stroke of or with something, as *un coup de pied* (a kick), *un coup de coude* (a nudge).

s'apprêter à faire: to be ready to. From *prêt*, ready.

26. *mon gendre*: my son-in-law

faire la surprise de + infinitive: to surprise by + verb in -ing. *Mon gendre m'a fait la surprise d'amener son ami.*

29. *plutôt*: rather

C. GRAMMAR AND USAGE

1. The verbs *vouloir* (to want, to desire) and *pouvoir* (can, may), whose conjugation is similar, can be followed by the infinitive form of a second verb.

Je veux célébrer mon mariage à ce restaurant.
   I want to celebrate my wedding in this restaurant.

Nous ne pouvons pas venir.
   We can't come.

Puis-je vous appeler?
   Could I call you?

When used with an object pronoun, the pronoun comes after *pouvoir / vouloir* and immediately before the infinitive of the second verb.

Pourriez-vous nous donner le menu?
   Could you give us the menu?

Nous ne voudrions pas vous déranger.
   We wouldn't want to bother you.

Je voudrais vous inviter à mon mariage.
   I would like to invite you to my wedding.

Note the use of *pouvoir* and *vouloir* in the conditional to express a request or a desire.

2. The causative form, using *se faire*, is followed by the infinitive.

   Je me suis fait plâtrer le bras.
   > I got my arm put in a cast.

   Il se fait couper les cheveux.
   > He's getting / having his hair cut.

   Il se les fera couper plus tard.
   > He'll get / have it cut later.

   Elle s'est fait renvoyer de son travail.
   > She got fired from her job.

   Note that the auxiliary *être* must be used when *se faire* is used in the *passé composé* and that the past participle of *faire* does not agree-is invariable-when followed by the infinitive. Finally, note the position of the object pronoun of the infinitive before *faire*, after the reflexive pronoun *se*.

3. In French, when describing an action involving parts of the body, the definite article is used—and not the possessive adjective as in English.

   Tu t'es fait couper les cheveux.
   > You got / had your hair cut

   Je me suis cassé le bras.
   > I broke my arm.

   Il baisse la tête.
   > He lowers his head.

4. The prepositions *à* and *de*, when used with the masculine or plural definite article, are contracted, such as:

   à le (masculine singular) becomes *au*

à les (masculine plural) becomes *aux*

de le (masculine singular) becomes *du*

de les (masculine plural) becomes *des*

With *à la*, *de la* and *à l'* and *de l'*, there's no contraction.

Le gérant et le chef du restaurant sont tombés malades.
　　The manager and the chef of the restaurant got sick.

*Nous sommes allés au restaurant Chez Zila pour célébrer
notre anniversaire de mariage.*
　　We went to the restaurant Chez Zila to celebrate our
　　wedding anniversary.

À l'hôtel, tout se passe bien.
　　At the hotel, all goes well.

La fille de la mariée est arrivée.
　　The bride's daughter has arrived.

EXERCISES

A. Write out each of the following sentences after the following phrase, and say aloud.

　　Elle parle . . .

　　1. *à son beau fils qui lui rend visite.*

　　2. *des jours précédant son mariage.*

　　3. *au couple américain qui célèbre leur anniversaire
　　　de mariage.*

　　4. *de tous ses problèmes à ses clients.*

B. Substitute each word in parentheses for the underlined
word in the model sentence. Say and write the entire new
sentence.

　　1. *Vous pouvez la <u>voir</u> plus tard.* (*faire, chercher,
　　　manger, boire*)

2. *Nous voudrions vous y inviter.* (*le donner, le deman-der, l'expliquer, le recommander*)

C. Change each sentence below to indicate that the subject is having somebody else perform the action, using *se faire.*

Example: *Je me coupe les cheveux. Je me fais couper les cheveux.*

1. *On se lave les cheveux.*

2. *Elle s'est coupé les cheveux.*

3. *On me renvoie.*

4. *On plâtre son* (her) *bras.*

D. Change each sentence below from present to *passé composé.* Say and translate each.

1. *Nous nous faisons renvoyer.*

2. *Elle se fait aider par sa famille.*

E. Translate the following sentences into French. Then say them aloud.

1. What luxury to go to Paris!

2. I'd like a haircut for my wedding.

3. Do it as you wish. (familiar)

4. Do you (polite) want to go to her wedding?

5. Besides, there's a lot of food for everyone.

6. Allow me to sit for a moment.

7. There are a lot of people who are waiting on the sidewalk.

8. Since it's her wedding, she'd like to offer a drink to all her clients.

F. Say the following sentences aloud, and then translate them into English.

1. *Des gens sont sur leur 31, d'autres dansent.*

2. *Il y a une bonne ambiance.*

3. *Félicitations et meilleurs vœux à vous et votre mari!*

4. *Est-ce vous qui célébrez votre anniversaire de mariage?*

5. *Je n'en reviens toujours pas.*

6. *Elle s'apprêtait à prendre l'avion.*

G. From among the three choices given, select the best translation for the English word or phrase given at the beginning of each sentence. Write the complete sentence and translate.

1. (Besides) _____ *on voudrait vous offrir un verre.*

   Toujours / À nouveau / D'ailleurs

2. (dressed to kill) *Ils sont* _____.

   sur leur 31 / élégants / bien habillés

3. (Around) _____ *de la rue Mouffetard.*

   À / Vers / Aux alentours

4. (at . . . 's) *Nous allons manger* _____ *nos parents.*

   à / avec / chez

5. (look like) *Elle* _____ *heureuse.*

   a l'air / est / a envie de

6. (look promising) *La soirée* _____.

   est / s'annonce bien / se prépare

Answer Key

A. 1. *Elle parle à son beau fils qui lui rend visite.* 2. *Elle parle des jours précédant son mariage.* 3. *Elle parle au couple américain qui célèbre leur anniversaire de mariage.* 4. *Elle parle de tous ses problèmes à ses clients.*

B. 1. *Vous pouvez la <u>voir</u> plus tard. Vous pouvez la <u>faire</u> plus tard. Vous pouvez la <u>chercher</u> plus tard. Vous pouvez la <u>manger</u> plus tard. Vous pouvez la <u>boire</u> plus tard* 2. *Nous voudrions vous <u>y inviter</u>. Nous voudrions vous <u>le donner</u>. Nous voudrions vous <u>le demander</u>. Nous voudrions vous <u>l'expliquer</u>. Nous voudrions vous <u>le recommander</u>.*

C. 1. *On se fait laver les cheveux.* 2. *Elle s'est fait couper les cheveux.* 3. *Je me fais renvoyer.* 4. *Elle se fait plâtrer le bras.*

D. 1. *Nous nous sommes fait renvoyer.* We got/were fired. 2. *Elle s'est fait aider par sa famille.* She got/was helped by her family.

E. 1. *Quel luxe d'aller à Paris!* 2. *J'aimerais me faire couper les cheveux pour mon mariage.* 3. *Fais comme tu désires / veux.* 4. *Voudriez-vous aller à son mariage?* 5. *D'ailleurs, il y a beaucoup de nourriture pour tout le monde.* 6. *Vous permettez que je m'asseoie un instant?* 7. *Il y a beaucoup de gens qui attendent sur le trottoir.* 8. *Puisque c'est son mariage, elle aimerait offrir un verre à tous ses clients.*

F. 1. Some people are dressed to kill, others are dancing. 2. There's a good atmosphere. 3. Congratulations and best wishes to you and your husband! 4. Are you the couple who's celebrating their wedding anniversary? 5. I still can't believe it. 6. She was getting ready to take a plane.

G. 1. *D'ailleurs on voudrait vous offrir un verre.* Besides we would like to offer you a drink. 2. *Ils sont sur leur 31.* They are dressed to kill. 3. *Aux alentours de la rue Mouffetard.* Around the rue Mouffetard. 4. *Nous allons manger chez nos parents.* We are going to eat at our parents'. 5. *Elle a l'air heureuse.* She looks happy. 6. *La soirée s'annonce bien.* The evening looks promising.

LESSON 8

AU CINÉMA
AT THE MOVIES

A. DIALOGUE

0. *Luc et Tony arrivent essoufflés au cinéma Quad dans le quartier des Halles. Il s'agit d'un cinéma d'art et d'essai.*
   Luc and Tony arrive breathless at the Quad Cinema in the Halles neighborhood. It's a movie theater for art and experimental films.

1. Luc: **Tiens, il ne semble pas qu'il y ait le film de Téchiné.**
   Look, there doesn't seem to be the Téchiné film.

2. Tony: **J'ai dû regarder le programme de la semaine dernière . . . Bon, qu'est-ce qu'on fait, on va voir un autre film?**
   I must have looked at last week's program. Well, what do we do? Go see another movie?

3. Luc: **Oui, puisqu'on est là. Voyons, qu'est-ce qui se joue? Une rétrospective des films de Pierre Richard. Bien! Aujourd'hui, c'est . . .**
   Yes since we're here. Let's see what's playing. A retrospective of Pierre Richard films. Good. Today is . . .

4. Tony: **C'est *Le Jouet*. C'est un très bon film, mais . . . ça a déjà commencé. Quoi d'autre?**
   It's *The Toy*. It's a very good movie but . . . it's already started. What else?

5. Luc: **Carnets de Voyage?**
   The Motorcycle Diaries?

6. Tony: **Ah oui, c'est le film du réalisateur brésilien Walter Salles qui retrace le premier voyage en Amérique du sud d'Ernesto Guevara et d'un ami. Ce film était au festival de Cannes. Je ne l'ai pas vu quand il est sorti. Il paraît que c'est super.**
Ah yes, it's the movie by Brazilian director Walter Salles about the first trip to South America by Ernesto Guevara and a friend of his. This movie was at the Cannes Festival. I didn't see it when it came out. It's supposed to be great.

7. Luc: **Je voulais justement le voir. Allons-y! Mais à quelle heure commence la séance? Je ne vois personne attendre.**
Well, I wanted to see it. Let's go! But what time does the movie start? I don't see anyone waiting.

8. Tony: **À 19h30, et il est . . .**
At 7:30 p.m., and it's . . .

9. Sonja: **Exactement 18 heures 41 minutes!**
Exactly 6:41 p.m.!

10. Tony: **Mais . . . Qu'est-ce que tu fais là, toi?**
But . . . What are you doing here?

11. Sonja: **Et vous, alors?**
Well, what about you two?

12. Luc: **Sonja, tu tombes à pic! Ton frère te cherchait.**
Sonja, you came at the right time! Your brother was looking for you.

13. Sonja: **Qu'est-ce qu'il y a?**
What's the matter?

14. Tony: **Dis-moi, je croyais que tu avais cours ce soir?**
Tell me, I thought you had a class this evening?

15. Sonja: **Eh bien, mon cours a été annulé. D'ailleurs, je suis là avec deux potes de la fac. On prend un pot au café d'en face en attendant la séance.**
Well, my class was cancelled. And I'm here with two classmates from the university. We're having a drink in the café across the street waiting for the movie to start.

16. Luc: **Et vous allez voir quel film?**
And what movie are you going to see?

17. Sonja: *Diarios de Motocicleta.* **C'est basé sur le journal que Che Guevara écrivait à l'époque . . . Enfin, à l'époque, il ne s'appelait pas Che, et c'était un étudiant tout comme nous. Notre prof d'histoire cubaine nous l'a recommandé, en version originale, naturellement.**
The Motorcycle Diaries . . . It's based on the diary Che Guevara was writing then . . . Well, at the time, his name wasn't Che and he was a student just like us. Our teacher in Cuban History recommended it to us, in original version, naturally.

18. Tony: **T'as appelé maman pour lui dire que tu rentreras plus tard?**
Did you call Mom to tell her that you'll be back later?

19. Sonja: **Mais oui. Bon, vous voulez nous accompagner? Le film ne commence pas avant 19h30.**
Yes. So, do you want to go with us? The movie doesn't start until 7:30 p.m.

20. *Vers 19h15, les amis font la queue au guichet pour prendre leur place.*
Around 7:15 p.m., the friends are waiting in line to get their tickets.

21. Luc: **Bonjour, une place s'il vous plaît, et voici ma carte de fidélité.**
Hello, one ticket, please, and here's my frequent customer card.

22. L'ouvreuse: **Cela fait 7 euros, s'il vous plaît. Merci. Et voici votre carte.**
The ticket seller: That's 7 euros please. Thanks. And here's your card.

23. *À l'intérieur de la salle qui se remplit vite, les amis s'apprêtent à s'asseoir.*
Inside the room, which is filling up quickly, the friends get ready to sit down.

24. Tony: **C'est bien, là, non?**
It's nice here, isn't it?

25. Sonja: **Il n'y a pas assez de places. Asseyez-vous là, nous on se met derrière.**
There aren't enough seats. You sit here and we'll sit behind you.

26. *Peu de temps après, les lumières s'éteignent et le projecteur commence à tourner.*
Shortly after, the lights fade and the projector starts to roll.

27. *Plus tard, au resto vietnamien où Sonja, Tony et Luc dînent.*
Later, in the Vietnamese restaurant where Sonja, Tony and Luc are having dinner.

28. Sonja: **J'ai adoré. Je crois que j'irais même le revoir . . .**
I loved it. I even think that I'd go to see it again . . .

29. Tony: **Et les acteurs étaient bons et j'aime beaucoup la façon dont c'est tourné.**
And the actors were good, and I really like the way
it is shot.

30. Luc: **Rien de mieux que les voyages pour former
la jeunesse! Vous avez raison, c'est un bon film,
vraiment. C'était sympa de vous voir les gars,
mais je dois y aller car j'ai un rendez-vous à 9
heures demain matin et si je suis en retard une
fois de plus, je vais avoir tout le temps de voyager!**
There's nothing like traveling to shape youth!
You're right, it's a great movie, really. It was nice
to see you guys, but I have to go because I have
an appointment at 9 tomorrow morning, and if
I'm late one more time, I'll have all the time to
travel!

B. NOTES

0. *Un cinéma d'art et d'essai* is an independant movie
theater that shows less commercial films, such as art
and experimental films, as well as older movies.
Tributes to film directors or actors and retrospectives
of their work are often given.

1. *Il ne semble pas que* (it does not seems that) is followed by the subjunctive. *Il semble que* can be followed by the indicative or the subjunctive according
to meaning.

3. Pierre Richard is a comedian, *un comique*, who was
very popular until the 1980's. His screen character
as a dreamer and unwilling trouble maker seduced
the audiences for more than a decade.

4. *Quoi d'autre?* What else?

5. *Carnets de voyage* means "travel notebooks." The actual English title is given in the translation.

6. *le réalisateur*: director, *les acteurs, les actrices* (feminine): actors, *le producteur*: producer. In the same topic: *la réalisation*: direction, *la production*: production, *réaliser*: to direct, *produire*: to produce, *jouer*: to act.

    Le Festival de Cannes is one of the most renowned film festival in the world. It takes place every year in spring in Cannes on the Riviera.

9. Official time is given on the 24-hour clock when announcing starting, ending, departure, and arrival times for activities related to public entertainment, transportation, private invitations, and many formal events. But the 12-hour clock is also heard in everyday conversation.

13. *Qu'est-ce qu'il y a?* What's the matter?

15. *deux potes*: two buddies and *un pot*: a drink are two colloquial expressions.

    La fac is short for: *la faculté* or *l'université*.

21. *la carte de fidélité*: Most independent film theaters give discount prices or have a card system, stamping the card each time a customer buys a ticket. After a certain number of stamps, the customer gets a free movie ticket.

C. GRAMMAR AND USAGE

1. The adverb *ne . . . que*, which means "only", indicates a restriction. It is not a negation and should not be con-

fused with *ne . . . pas*. The *ne* goes between the subject and the verb, and the *que* is placed just before the restricted element in the sentence.

Ce n' est qu' un étudiant.
    He's just a student.

Je n' en veux qu' un.
    I just want one of them.

Il ne reste que trois places.
    There are only three seats left.

Nous n' allons au cinéma que le dimanche.
    We only go to the movies on Sunday.

Tu ne vas voir que des films commerciaux.
    You only go to see commercial films.

2. The partitive article designates a part of a whole, and is the equivalent of the English "some" or "any." This concept is expressed in French by the use of *de* and the definite article (*le, la, les*). Note that "some" or "any" may be implied in English, but it's always expressed in French. The partitive articles are:

masculine singular : *de l'* or *du*

du pain, de l' ananas
    some/any bread, some pineapple

feminine singular: *de l'* or *de la*

de la chance, de l' imagination
    some/any luck, some imagination

plural: *des*

des places, des amis
    some seats, some friends

Je voudrais des nems.
    I would like some spring rolls.

Ce réalisateur a du talent.
This director has talent.

Note that the negative form is *pas de* + noun.

Je n'ai pas assez d'argent liquide sur moi.
I don't have enough cash on me.

Je n'ai pas de programme.
I don't have any/a program.

When an adjective is placed before a plural noun, the preceding plural partitive article *des* changes into *de*.

J'ai des places de ciné. / J'ai de bonnes places de ciné.
I have seats for the movie. / I have good seats for the movie.

Ce sont des films. / Ce sont de longs films.
These are films. / These are long films.

Finally, the partitive article is not used with verbs of liking and disliking. The regular definite article is used instead.

J'adore les films sud-américains.
I love South American movies.

Est-ce que tu aimes la nourriture vietnamienne?
Do you like Vietnamese food?

3. Imperatives that take indirect object use disjunctive pronouns, which are *moi, toi, lui, soi, nous, vous, leur.*

Permettez-moi de vous offrir la place.
Allow me to pay for your ticket.

Donnons-leur le programme de cinéma.
Let's give them the movie program.

Dites-nous comment est ce film.
Tell us how this movie is.

However, in the negative form, these disjunctive pronouns are replaced by object pronouns and are positioned just after the negation *ne*.

Ne lui permettez pas de vous offrir la place.
Don't allow him / her to offer you the ticket.

Ne leur donnons pas le programme de cinéma.
Let's not give them the movie program.

Ne nous dites pas comment est ce film.
Don't tell us how this movie is.

4. In the *passé composé*, although most verbs are conjugated with the auxiliary *avoir* (to have), many verbs use the auxiliary *être* (to be). They are usually verbs expressing movement or a change of state. And don't forget that all reflexive verbs take *être* as well.

Note that with the auxiliary *être*, the past participle agrees with the subject in number (singular and plural) and gender (masculine or feminine).

Ils se sont assis devant.
They sat in the front.

Ma sœur est née avant moi.
My sister was born before me.

Nous ne nous sommes pas rappelés de l'heure de la séance.
We didn't remember the time the film started.

Some verbs can be used with *être* ou *avoir* according to the situation. For instance:

Elle est montée dans la salle.
She went up in the room.

Elle a monté les bagages.
She took up the luggage.

Elle est sortie.
   She went out.

Elle a sorti le chien.
   She took the dog out.

EXERCISES

A. Replace *seulement* by *ne . . . que* in each of the following sentences. Write the complete sentence, say it aloud, and translate.

Example: *J'ai seulement des places séparées.* / *Je n'ai que des places séparées.*

1. *Elle a seulement deux sœurs.*

2. *Le film dure seulement une heure dix.*

3. *J'ai seulement cours le lundi.*

4. *Nous avons seulement trois places.*

B. Expand the following sentences by placing *bons* or *bonnes* before the noun. Make any necessary changes. Say aloud and translate.

Example: *J'ai des amis.* / *J'ai de bons amis.*

1. *Vous avez des idées.*

2. *J'ai lu des livres.*

3. *Nous avons vu des films.*

4. *J'ai mangé des nems.*

C. Write the following phrases in the negative.

Example: *Parlez-moi.* / *Ne me parlez pas.*

1. *Pardonne-lui.*

2. *Regardons-les.*

3. *Écoutez-nous.*

4. *Excusez-la.*

5. *Lève-toi.*

6. *Asseyons-nous.*

D. Substitute each of the words or expressions in parentheses for the underlined word in the model sentence. Write and say each new sentence.

1. *Nous sommes entrés.* (*partis, arrivés, venus, restés, tombés*)

2. *Elle est sortie.* (*partie, devenue riche, restée, née, montée*)

E. Write the following sentences in the *passé composé.* (Make sure the past participle agrees with the subject.) Say and translate the new sentences.

Example: *Nous arrivons.* / *Nous sommes arrivés.*

1. *Elle descend de taxi.*

2. *Ils viennent au ciné avec nous.*

3. *Vous* (plural masculine) *arrivez en retard.*

4. *Nous restons pour la prochaine séance.*

F. Say the following sentences aloud, and then translate them into English.

1. *On ne veut que deux places.*

2. *Il y a des places au café.*

3. *On a de bonnes salles de cinéma à Paris.*

4. *Je suis avec des potes de la fac.*

5. *Ne me montre pas le programme.*

6. *Hier, il est aussi parti à neuf heures.*

7. *Donne-nous l'argent. Ne lui donne pas l'argent.*

8. *Aujourd'hui, je ne suis pas en retard.*

G. Translate the following sentences into French, and then say them aloud.

1. She stayed at the office until eight o'clock.

2. She is pleased to see the actors.

3. I'll have the time to do it.

4. Will they have the chance (*l'occasion*) to do it?

5. What interests me is the directing.

6. What interests him is the action.

7. Give me my ticket please. (familiar)

8. It's a good movie.

H. From among the three choices, select the best translation for the English word or phrase given at the beginning of each sentence. Write the complete sentence, and translate.

1. (good seats) *J'ai encore _____.*

   bonnes places / des bonnes places / de bonnes places

2. (to) *Quel plaisir _____ vous revoir!*

   de / à / pour

3. (Permit me) *_____, Sonja, de t'offrir la place.*

   Me permet / Permettez-me / Permets-moi

4. (Let's hurry) *_____, alors!*

   Laissons vite / Passons rapide / Dépêchons-nous

5. (drink) *Venez boire _____ avec nous.*

   un pote / un repas / un pot

6. (tickets) *Bonjour, il me faut deux _____ pour ce film.*

   billets / tickets / places

Answer Key

A. 1. *Elle n'a que deux sœurs.* She only has two sisters.
2. *Le film ne dure qu'une heure dix.* The film lasts only one hour and ten minutes. 3. *Je n'ai cours que le lundi.* I have classes only on Monday. 4. *Nous n'avons que trois places.* We have only three seats/tickets.

B. 1. *Vous avez de bonnes idées.* You have (some) good ideas. 2. *J'ai lu de bons livres.* I've read some good books. 3. *Nous avons vu de bons films.* We've seen some good films. 4. *J'ai mangé de bons nems.* I ate some good spring rolls.

C. 1. *Ne lui pardonne pas.* 2. *Ne les regardons pas.* 3. *Ne nous écoutez pas.* 4. *Ne l'excusez pas.* 5. *Ne te lève pas.* 6. *Ne nous asseyons pas.*

D. 1. *Nous sommes entrés. Nous sommes partis. Nous sommes arrivés. Nous sommes venus. Nous sommes restés. Nous sommes tombés.* 2. *Elle est sortie. Elle est partie. Elle est devenue riche. Elle est restée. Elle est née. Elle est montée.*

E. 1. *Elle est descendue de taxi.* She got off a cab. 2. *Ils sont venus au ciné avec nous.* They came to the movies with us. 3. *Vous êtes arrivés en retard.* You arrived late. 4. *Nous sommes restés pour la prochaine séance.* We stayed for the next film.

F. 1. We only want two tickets. 2. There are some seats at the café. 3. We have good movie theaters in Paris. 4. I am with some buddies from the university. 5. Don't show me the program. 6. Yesterday he also left at nine o'clock. 7. Give us the money. Don't give him the money. 8. Today I am not late.

G. 1. *Elle est restée au bureau jusqu'à huit heures.* 2. *Elle est contente de voir les acteurs.* 3. *J'aurai le temps de le faire.* 4. *Auront-ils l'occasion de le faire?* 5. *Ce qui m'intéresse, c'est la réalisation.* 6. *Ce qui l'intéresse, c'est l'action.* 7. *Donne-moi ma place, s'il te plaît.* 8. *C'est un bon film.*

H. 1. *J'ai encore de bonnes places.* I still have some good seats. 2. *Quel plaisir de vous revoir!* What a pleasure to see you again! 3. *Permets-moi, Sonja, de t'offrir la place.* Allow me, Sonja, to offer you the ticket. 4. *Dépêchons-nous, alors!* Let's hurry up, then! 5. *Venez boire un pot avec nous.* Come and have a drink with us. 6. *Bonjour, il me faut deux places pour ce film.* Hello, I need two tickets for this movie.

LESSON 9

AU LOUVRE
AT THE LOUVRE

A. DIALOGUE

0. *Jane et Charles profitent d'une journée pluvieuse pour visiter le Louvre, d'autant plus que Charles est un grand amateur d'art. À l'entrée, un employé du musée s'approche d'eux.*
Jane and Charles are taking advantage of a rainy day to visit the Louvre, since Charles is a real art lover. At the entrance, a museum employee approaches them.

1. L'employé: **Bonjour Madame, Monsieur. Est-ce votre première visite au Louvre?**
The employee: Good afternoon Madam, Sir. Is this your first visit to the Louvre?

2. Jane: **Oui, en effet.**
Actually, yes.

3. L'employé: **Puis-je vous proposer une visite guidée?**
May I suggest a guided tour?

4. Jane: **Qu'en penses-tu Charles? J'aimerais bien une visite guidée. Mon mari s'y connaît en peinture, mais pas moi.**
What do you think, Charles? I'd like a guided tour. My husband knows about paintings, but not me.

5. Charles: **En fait, je ne suis qu'un humble amateur et je n'ai jamais visité le Louvre, ce dont j'ai un peu honte. Aussi, c'est une excellente idée.**

In fact I'm only a humble amateur and I've never visited the Louvre, which I'm a bit ashamed of. So, it's an excellent idea.

6. L'employé: **Dans ce cas, je vous suggère la visite découverte. Vous pouvez acheter les billets pour cette visite avec le billet d'entrée. Les caisses sont juste en face. Un conférencier du musée sera là dans un instant.**
In that case, I suggest the discovery visit. You can buy the tickets for this visit with the admission. The registers are right across from us. A museum lecturer will be here in a moment.

7. La caissière: **Donc deux entrées à 8,50 euros et deux visites découverte à 5 euros . . . Cela fait 27 euros, s'il vous plaît.**
The cashier: So two at 8.50 euros and two discovery visits at 5 euros . . . That's 27 euros, please.

8. Charles: **Voici, madame. Est-ce qu'il y a des vestiaires?**
Here you are, madam. Is there a coat check?

9. La caissière: **Merci. Oui, les vestiaires sont de ce côté au bout du couloir.**
Thanks. Yes, the coat check is on this side at the end of the hall.

10. *Au début de la visite.*
At the beginning of the visit.

11. Le guide: **Vous trouverez ici bien de l'inspiration. Le Louvre est probablement le musée d'art le plus riche du monde. Allons-y.**
The guide: You'll find plenty of inspiration here. The Louvre is probably the richest art museum in the world. Let's go.

12. Jane: **Où commence-t-on?**
Where're we starting?

13. Le guide: **Puisque nous sommes au rez-de-chaussée, je vais d'abord vous faire voir les anti-quités orientales, grecques, égyptiennes, étrusques et romaines, ensuite, des sculptures européennes, et finalement, la collection d'arts d'Afrique, d'Asie, d'Océanie et d'Amérique.**
Since we're on the ground floor, I'll first show you the Oriental, Greek, Egyptian, Etruscan and Roman antiquities, some European sculptures and finally, the collection of art pieces from Africa, Asia, the Pacific and America.

14. Jane: **Enfin, je vois de près cette statue: la Vénus de Milo! Elle est d'une beauté!**
At last I'm seeing this statue up close: the Venus de Milo! She's so beautiful!

15. Le guide: **Ah, vous n'êtes pas la seule à l'admirer. Regardez à droite, voici la Victoire de Samo-thrace, qui est également bien connue.**
Ah, you're not the only one to admire it. Look on the right, here's the Winged Victory, which is equally well known.

16. *Au premier étage.*
On the second floor.

17. Le guide: **Vous allez découvrir des sculptures de toutes les grandes époques: du Moyen Âge, de la Renaissance, du dix-septième siècle.**
You're about to discover sculptures of all the great periods: from the Middle Ages, the Renaissance, the seventeenth century.

18. Jane: **Cette exposition de meubles anciens est magnifique.**
This exhibition of antique furniture is magnificent.

19. Le guide: **Absolument! Ici sont rassemblés les plus grandes merveilles du mobilier, de l'orfèvrerie, de la tapisserie. Admirez aussi les bronzes, les ivoires et les bijoux de la couronne de France.**
Absolutely! Gathered here are the greatest wonders of furniture, goldsmiths' work, tapestry. Admire as well the bronzes, the ivories, and the French crown jewels.

20. Charles: **Que de richesses! Il faudra revenir. Mais n'y a-t-il pas de peintures?**
What riches! We'll have to come back. But aren't there any paintings?

21. Le guide: **Par ici et au deuxième étage. Comme vous allez le voir, il y a des peintures classiques et modernes, des gouaches, des aquarelles, des huiles, ainsi que des gravures, des eaux-fortes lesquelles représentent la plus grande collection du monde.**
This way and on the third floor. As you'll see, there are classical and modern paintings, gouaches, watercolors, oils, as well as engravings, etchings, which represent the largest collection in the world.

22. Charles: **Les genres et les époques sont différents— paysages, natures—mortes, nus-mais tous sont de véritables chefs-d'œuvre.**
The genres and the periods are varied—landscapes, still lifes, nudes—but all are real masterpieces.

23. Le guide: **Veuillez me suivre, s'il vous plaît, dans la Grande Galerie. Je vous ferai voir une toile**

que vous reconnaîtrez et devant laquelle des gens restent émerveillés pendant des heures entières.
Please follow me into the Great Gallery. I'll show you a canvas that you'll recognize, and in front of which people stay filled with wonder for entire hours.

24. Charles: **Ah! Madame La Joconde, Mona Lisa!**
Ah! Madam the Joconde, Mona Lisa!

25. Jane: **Encore plus belle que sa légende . . . Mais où sont les tableaux de l'école impressionniste? Je n'en vois nulle part.**
Even more beautiful than her legend. . . But where are the pictures of the Impressionist School? I don't see any anywhere.

26. Le guide: **Pour les impressionnistes, il faudra aller au musée d'Orsay.**
For the Impressionists, you'll have to go to the Musée d'Orsay.

27. Charles: **Ce sera pour un autre jour. En attendant, voyons ces superbes tableaux pointillistes.**
That'll be for another day. In the meantime, let's see these superb pointillist paintings.

28. Le guide: **En fait, j'aimerais vous suggérer de faire une pause d'une demi-heure durant laquelle vous pourrez vous rafraîchir et, si le temps le permet, jeter un coup d'œil à la pyramide en verre. Ah, et voici de la documentation en anglais sur l'association:** *The American Friends of the Louvre.*
Actually, I'd like to suggest that we take a half an hour break during which you'll be able to refresh, and weather permitting, take a look at the glass Pyramide. Ah, and here's some information about the organization: *The American Friends of the Louvre.*

B. NOTES

0. *Le musée du Louvre*, 800 years old, was originally a medieval castle, then became the palace of the kings of France before becoming a museum in 1793 under the first French Republic. One can say *Le Louvre* or *le musée du Louvre*.

3. The verb *proposer* means to suggest.

4. *Mon mari s'y connaît en peinture*: My husband is knowledgeable about paintings.

5. *avoir honte de*: to be ashamed of

8. *le vestiaire* or *les vestiaires*: the coat check

14. *Elle est d'une grande beauté*: She's of a great beauty. Note the similar emphatic construction in French and in English.

22. Note the plural form of *chef-d'œuvre*: *des chefs-d'œuvre*. Only the first noun takes *-s*.

23. *montrer* or *faire voir quelque chose à quelqu'un*: to show something to someone

26. *Le musée d'Orsay*, formerly a train station, houses the city's Impressionist art.

28. *faire une pause*: to take a break
    jeter un coup d'œil: to take a quick look, to glance at
    La pyramide du Louvre is the work of the Chinese-American architect Ieoh Ming Pei. This projet, inaugurated in 1989, represents a large glass pyramid surrounded by water fountains and is located in the center of *la cour Napoléon*. The pyra-

mid shelters the *Hall Napoléon*, where all the con-
veniencies of the Museum are found, an exhibition
hall, the *Auditorium*, a projection hall, as well as,
since 1999, le *CyberLouvre*.

C. GRAMMAR AND USAGE

1. You've already seen *se faire* used as a causative. The verb
faire (to make, to do) followed by the infinitive expresses
the notion of causing something to be done by someone
else.

Je vous ferai visiter le musée.
   I will show you the Museum.

Il nous a fait voir la Joconde.
   He showed us the Joconde.

Ils feront inviter tous les membres du musée.
   They will get all the museum members invited.

Elle m'a fait tomber.
   She made me fall.

Note that the indirect object pronoun is used when the
subject is not having something done to itself, as in the
last example. Also when replacing the object with an
object pronoun, the latter precedes the verb *faire*.

Finally, unlike *se faire*, *faire* uses the auxiliary *avoir* in
compound tenses. The past participle *fait* remains invariable.

*Elle lui a fait découvrir la pyramide du Louvre. / Elle la
lui a fait découvrir.*
   She made him discover the Pyramide of the Louvre. /
   She made him discover it.

2. When using the verb *aller* with *y* in the imperative form, note that the pronoun *y* is attached to the end of the verb with a hyphen.

Allons-y.
   Let's go. / Let's go there.

Allez-y.
   Go ahead. / Go there.

Vas-y.
   Go ahead. / Go there.

In the negative form, the construction changes. The pronoun *y* comes directly after *n'*.

N'y allons pas.
   Let's not go there.

N'y allez pas. / N'y va pas.
   Don't go there.

3. The invariable relative pronoun, *dont* (about whom, of whom, of which, about which) is used to connect two ideas or clauses. It's placed before the subject of the subordinate clause.

L'exposition dont je vous ai parlé a débuté hier.
   The exhibition which I told you about began yesterday.

Les autres peintres dont on entend parler ont une exposition au musée.
   The other painters we hear about are having a show in the museum.

The relative pronoun *dont* can also have a possessive meaning and is translated as "whose."

Le sculpteur dont je connais le travail est là.
   The sculptor whose work I know is here.

4. The relative pronoun *lequel* can be translated in different cases as "which," "who" or "that." It has the following four forms: *lequel* (m. sing.), *laquelle* (f. sing.), *lesquels* (m. pl.) and *lesquelles* (f. pl.). These forms are mostly used with prepositions (*sur lequel* / on which) or to refer back to a noun which was specifically mentioned earlier, especially in legal language, such as a mortgage contract, etc.

Mélangez les œufs dans lesquels vous avez ajouté le sucre.
  Mix the eggs into which you've added the sugar.

On lui donnera un délai de trois jours, lequel sera annulé si le montant n'est pas accordé.
  We will give him a grace period of three days, which will be cancelled if the amount is not granted.

The forms of *lequel* can be used with prepositions, giving the equivalents of the English "to which," "for which," with whom," etc. Notice that *lequel*, *lesquels* and *lesquelles* contract with the prepositions *de* and *à*: *duquel*, *desquels*, *desquelles* (but *de laquelle*), and *auquel*, *auxquels* and *auxquelles* (but *à laquelle*). There is no contraction with other prepositions.

Le musée duquel nous nous approchons date du Moyen Âge.
  The museum we're coming up to dates from the Middle Ages.

Ce sont les guides auxquels on m'a présenté(e).
  These are the guides to whom I was introduced.

C'est l'amie avec laquelle je suis allé(e) au Louvre.
  This is the friend with whom I went to the Louvre.

Note it's much more common to use *qui* instead of *lequel* as the subject of the clause. The pronoun *qui* can be used with any of the prepositions as well.

Admirez ces peintures qui représentent la plus grande collection du monde.
> Admire these paintings, which represent the largest collection in the world.

C'est le guide qui nous a fait voir la Grande Galerie.
> This is the guide who showed us the Grand Gallery.

Ce sont les guides à qui on m'a présenté(e).
> These are the guides to whom I was introduced.

C'est l'amie avec qui je suis allé(e) au Louvre.
> This is the friend who I went to the Louvre with.

Finally, in some cases *dont* may be replaced by *de qui* for people or *duquel, de laquelle, desquels*, or *desquelles* for things.

Le musée dont nous nous approchons date du Moyen Âge. / *Le musée duquel nous nous approchons date du Moyen Âge.*
> The museum we're coming up to dates from the Middle Ages.

Le guide dont je vous ai parlé travaille au Musée d'Orsay. / *Le guide de qui je vous ai parlé travaille au Musée d'Orsay.*
> The guide I talked to you about works at the Musée d'Orsay.

EXERCISES

A. Substitute each of the words or expressions in parentheses for the underlined word or expression in the model sentence. Write the complete sentence and say it aloud.

1. *Il __me__ fera visiter le Louvre.* (*lui, nous, leur*)

2. *Nous vous avons fait __voir__ le musée.* (*visiter, connaître, découvrir*)

B. Expand the phrases below by placing *il y a* in front of each. Say the entire sentence, then write it.

Example: *une femme à la porte / Il y a une femme à la porte.*

1. *quatre peintures au mur*

2. *vingt personnes dans la salle*

3. *des touristes devant le musée*

4. *de magnifiques sculptures*

C. Transform the following sentences from affirmative to negative, say out loud, and write out their translations.

1. *Vas-y.*

2. *Allez-y.*

3. *Il y va.*

4. *Il y est allé.*

5. *Nous y sommes allés.*

6. *Elles y sont allées.*

D. Replace *de* and the relative pronoun by *dont* in the following sentences and translate.

1. *L'homme de qui je t'avais parlé est arrivé.*

2. *La femme de qui j'avais fait la connaissance hier s'appelle Mme Dupont.*

3. *Les peintres desquels j'avais entendu parler sont partis pour Paris.*

4. *La sculptrice de qui vous discutez sera présente.*

E. Say the following sentences aloud, and then translate them into English.

1. *Elle vous fera visiter le Louvre.*

2. *Nous lui ferons voir les peintures.*

3. *Je leur ferai regarder les statues.*

4. *Voilà l'Opéra! Il y a aussi un bel Opéra à Milan.*

5. *Voilà la Place de la Concorde. Il y a aussi une belle place à Rome.*

6. *Voilà le Louvre! Il y a aussi un beau musée à New-York.*

7. *Voici les objets d'art dont il vous a parlé.*

8. *Voici les sculptures dont ils lui ont parlé.*

F. Translate the following sentences into French. Then say them aloud.

1. Here are the paintings which she spoke to them about.

2. Here are the masterpieces which we spoke to you about.

3. There are the painters who we always hear about.

4. There are the Impressionists who I always hear about.

5. My wife knows (is knowledgeable about) music.

6. I know painting.

G. Translate the following dialogue.

I'd like to go to the Louvre.

Let's go there right away.

Where are the paintings?

They're at the end of the exhibition hall.

I'd also like to see the statues.

Look! There are the masterpieces!

H. From among the three choices, select the best translation for the English word or phrase given at the beginning of each sentence. Write the complete sentence, and translate.

1. (each) *Vingt francs* _____, *s'il vous plaît.*

   l'un / chacun / chaque

2. (We should have) _____ *venir dimanche.*

   Nous devons / Nous avons dû / Nous aurions dû

3. (knows about) *Mon mari* _____ *peinture.*

   s'y connaît en / se connaît autour / sait de

4. (One can admire) _____ *les chefs-d'œuvre.*

   On doit admirer / On sait admirer / On peut admirer

5. (Follow me) _____, *s'il vous plaît.*

   Conduisez-moi / Venez-moi / Suivez-moi

6. (How well displayed it is!) _____ *(la peinture)*

   Comment bien exposée elle est! / Qu'elle est bien exposée! / Qu'il est bien exposé!

Answer Key

A. 1. *Il me fera visiter le Louvre. Il lui fera visiter le Louvre. Il nous fera visiter le Louvre. Il leur fera visiter le Louvre.* 2. *Nous vous avons fait voir le musée. Nous vous avons fait visiter le musée. Nous vous avons fait connaître le musée. Nous vous avons fait découvrir le musée.*

B. 1. *Il y a quatre peintures au mur.* 2. *Il y a vingt personnes dans la salle.* 3. *Il y a des touristes devant le musée.* 4. *Il y a de magnifiques sculptures.*

C. 1. *N'y va pas.* Don't go there. 2. *N'y allez pas.* Don't go there. 3. *Il n'y va pas.* He isn't going there. 4. *Il n'y est pas allé.* He didn't go (hasn't gone) there. 5. *Nous n'y sommes pas allés.* We didn't go there. 6. *Elles n'y sont pas allées.* They didn't go there.

D. 1. *L'homme dont je t'avais parlé est arrivé.* The man about whom I had spoken to you has come. 2. *La femme dont j'avais fait la connaissance hier s'appelle Mme Dupont.* The name of the woman (whom) I had met yesterday is Mme Dupont. 3. *Les peintres dont j'avais entendu parler sont partis pour Paris.* The painters (whom) I had heard about have left for Paris. 4. *La sculptrice de qui/dont vous discutez sera présente.* The (woman) sculptor whom you are discussing will be here.

E. 1. She'll have you visit the Louvre. / She'll take you to visit the Louvre. 2. We'll have him see the paintings. / We'll take him to see the paintings. 3. I'll have them look at the statues. 4. There's the Opera! There's also a beautiful opera in Milan. 5. There's the Place de la Concorde! There's also a beautiful square in Rome. 6. There's the Louvre! There's also a beautiful museum in New York.

7. Here are the pieces of art which he spoke to you about.

8. Here are the sculptures which they spoke to him about.

F. 1. *Voici les peintures dont elle leur a parlé.* 2. *Voici les chefs-d'œuvre dont nous vous avons parlé.* 3. *Voilà les peintres dont nous entendons toujours parler.* 4. *Voilà les impressionnistes dont j'entends toujours parler.* 5. *Ma femme s'y connaît en musique.* 6. *Je m'y connais en peinture.*

G. *Je voudrais aller au Louvre.*

Allons-y tout de suite (or: *Allons-y immédiatement*).

Où se trouvent les peintures (or: *Où sont les peintures*)?

Elles se trouvent au bout de la salle d'exposition.

Je voudrais voir aussi les statues (or: *Je voudrais voir également les statues*).

Regardez! Voilà les chefs-d'œuvre.

H. 1. *Vingt francs chacun, s'il vous plaît.* Twenty francs each, please. 2. *Nous aurions dû venir dimanche.* We should have come Sunday. 3. *Mon mari s'y connaît en peinture.* My husband knows about painting. 4. *On peut admirer les chefs-d'œuvre.* One can admire the masterpieces. 5. *Suivez-moi, s'il vous plaît.* Follow me, please. 6. *Qu'elle est bien exposée!* How well displayed it is!

LESSON 10

AU MARCHÉ AUX PUCES
AT THE FLEA MARKET

A. DIALOGUE

0. *Un dimanche beau et frais, Michel invite Jane et Charles à aller au marché aux puces. Il vient les chercher en compagnie de sa belle-sœur, Danièle.*
   One beautiful and cool Sunday, Michel invites Jane and Charles to go to the flea market. He comes to pick them up along with his sister-in-law Danièle.

1. Michel: **Bonjour Charles, Jane, comment allez-vous? J'aimerais vous présenter Danièle Dagmi, la sœur d'Éliane. Danièle, voici Jane et Charles McGrath.**
   Hello Charles, Jane, how are you? I'd like to introduce you to Danièle Dagmi, Eliane's sister. Danièle, this is Jane and Charles McGrath.

2. Jane: **Nous sommes enchantés de faire votre connaissance, Danièle!**
   We're delighted to make your acquaintance, Danièle.

3. Danièle: **Pareillement.**
   Likewise.

4. Michel: **Danièle, qui adore les brocantes, est la spécialiste des marchés aux puces.**
   Danièle, who loves antique markets, is the flea market specialist.

5. Danièle: **Oui, c'est vrai. J'y vais pratiquement tous les dimanches. Tenez, ma voiture est garée ici.**

Yes, it's true. I go there almost every Sunday. Look, my car is parked here.

6. *Ils montent tous dans la voiture de Danièle qui ne tarde pas à démarrer.*
They all get into Danièle's car which is soon off and running.

7. Jane: **Nous avons souvent entendu parler des marchés aux puces, mais nous n'y sommes encore jamais allés. Y en-a-t-il plusieurs à Paris?**
We've often heard about the flea market, but we haven't gone there yet. Are there many of them in Paris?

8. Danièle: **Oui, en fait, il y en a trois principaux: les puces de Saint-Ouen au Nord de Paris, qui est en fait le marché le plus vieux—je crois qu'il date du XIX ème siècle—et le plus grand: on dit qu'il s'étend sur 15 kilomètres!**
Yes, in fact, there are three main ones: the Saint-Ouen Flea Market in the north of Paris, which is actually the oldest—I think it started in the 19th century—and the largest: they say it spreads over 15 kilometers!

9. Charles: **Cela doit être un vrai spectacle!**
That must really be something to see!

10. Michel: **Oui, mais c'est aussi trop fréquenté. Si vous êtes d'accord, nous allons aux puces de Vanves**.
Yes, but it's also too crowded. If it's okay with you, we're going to the Vanves Flea Market.

11. Charles: **Volontiers! On vous suit.**
Gladly! We're in your hands.

12. Danièle: **C'est mon préféré et on peut y trouver de tout, des meubles, des bibelots ou des antiquités, des fripes . . . Vous verrez. Et donc, il y a les puces de Montreuil qui sont bien aussi.**
It's my favorite one, and you can find everything there: furniture, knicknacks or antiques, second hand clothes . . . You'll see. And then there's the Montreuil flea market which is quite good too.

13. Jane: **Il semble qu'il y aura beaucoup de choses qui pourront nous intéresser!**
It seems that there'll be a lot of things that could interest us!

14. *Ils arrivent au marché aux puces et Danièle, après dix minutes, trouve enfin une place et peut garer sa voiture. Ils se promènent au milieu de la foule et du brouhaha.*
They arrive at the flea market and, after ten minutes, Danièle finally finds a space and can park her car. They walk among the crowd and the hubbub.

15. Michel: (*en aparté*) **N'oubliez pas qu'il ne faut pas tout croire et qu'il faut marchander.**
(Aside) Don't forget that you mustn't believe everything and that you have to bargain.

16. Danièle: **Il y a l'air d'avoir des choses bien ici. Ah oui, cette dame est là tous les dimanches. Bonjour, ça va?**
There seem to be good things here. Ah yes, this lady is here every Sunday. Hello, how are you?

17. La dame: **Bonjour! Eh bien, on fait aller!**
The lady: Hello! Well, getting by!

18. Jane: **Charles, regarde cette cafetière en porcelaine jaune clair, elle est jolie et en bon état. Quel en est le prix, madame?**

Look, Charles at this light yellow china coffeepot, it's pretty and in good shape. How much is it, Ma'am?

19. La dame: **Quarante-cinq euros, ma bonne dame. Ah! C'est du Limoges . . .**
Forty-five euros, my dear lady. Ah! It's Limoges porcelain.

20. Jane: **Oui, en effet, c'est de la porcelaine de Limoges. Je vous en offre trente euros.**
Yes, as a matter of fact, it is Limoges porcelain. I'll give you thirty euros for it.

21. La dame: **Madame, c'est une de nos plus belles cafetières, pratiquement une pièce de collection! Remarquez cette fine bordure d'or, et peinte à la main aussi.**
Madam, it's one of our most beautiful coffeepots. Almost a collection piece. Notice this thin golden border, and handpainted as well.

22. *Danièle, qui a l'habitude de marchander, vient à la rescousse de Jane . . .*
Danièle, who is used to bargaining, comes to Jane's rescue . . .

23. Danièle: **Bien sûr, c'est une jolie pièce, mais bon, un petit effort! Vous nous la laissez à trente-cinq euros?**
Of course, it's a nice piece, but still, a little effort! Will you give it to us for thirty-five euros?

24. La dame: **Va pour quarante euros! Allez!**
Sold for forty euros. Go on!

25. Michel: **Regardez en face! Quels beaux meubles de style!**

Look across the way! What beautiful antique furniture!

26. Charles: **Oui, en effet. En particulier cette magnifique bergère Louis XV. Celle qui est recouverte de tapisserie d'Aubusson. Tu la vois Jane?**
Yes, indeed. Particularly that magnificent Louis XV easy chair. The one that's upholstered in Aubusson tapestry. Do you see it Jane?

27. Jane: **C'est de loin la plus belle de toutes. Ces couleurs fauves et roses sont superbes. Qu'en pensez-vous, Danièle, Michel?**
It's by far the most beautiful of all. Its fawn and pinkish colors are superb. What do you think, Danièle, Michel?

28. Charles: **On l'achète?**
How about buying it?

29. Jane: **Ne sois pas trop impulsif, Charles. Voyons d'abord quel en est le prix**.
Don't be too impulsive, Charles. Let's first see how much it is.

30. Charles: **Je vous avertis que je ne sais absolument pas marchander.**
I'm warning you that I don't know at all how to bargain.

31. Michel: **Ah, à toi, Danièle! Danièle? Ah, elle est là-bas. Restez-là, je vais la chercher.**
Ah, your turn, Danièle! Danièle? Ah, she's over there. Stay here, I'm going to get her.

B. NOTES

0. Another way to say *inviter* is *convier*, but this is used specifically for a dinner or celebration involving food.

3. *pareillement*: likewise

4. *La brocante* is a type of flea market, where old objects, art pieces, knicks-knacks and furniture are sold. *Le brocanteur* leads the *brocante*. There are also various *foires à la brocante* in most big cities.

5. *pratiquement*: practically, virtually

   garée: parked, the verb *se garer*: to park and the noun is *un garage*: a parking garage

10. *trop fréquenté* or *avec trop de monde*: crowded. The verb *fréquenter* means to hang out with, to spend time with / at.

12. *c'est mon préféré, c'est ma préférée*: it's my favorite, from the verb *préférer*

    Montreuil-sous-Bois is a town southeast of Paris next to the *Château de Vincennes*. It was founded in the 8th century and was an agricultural site with vineyards and fruit trees for centuries. After the French Revolution in 1789, it became politically active, and in the 19th century, a great deal of industries moved into the vicinity. Director George Méliès built the first film studio there in 1896, followed a few years later by Pathé. During the Second World War, a lot of *Montreuillois*—people who live in Montreuil—belonged to the Resistance, and in fact, Montreuil was the first town around Paris to be liberated from the occupation. Among the famous of Montreuil are Jacques Brel, Lino Ventura, Serge Reggiani, and Kenny Clark.

14. Note this funny word, *le brouhaha,* the hubbub. This is also used in English sometimes.

15. *marchander*: to bargain, to haggle, to negotiate prices

17. *Eh bien, on fait aller*: is a colloquial expression that doesn't have a translation in English but corresponds more or less to: "Well, one must keep going."

19. *la porcelaine de Limoges*: the name of a famous expensive porcelain made in the city of *Limoges*, about 200 miles southwest of Paris. The city of *Sèvres*, near *Versailles*, is also well known for porcelain.

22. *Venir à la rescousse de quelqu'un* is a colloquial expression, synonymous with *aider, secourir*.

24. *Va (pour)* is an old colloquial expression to indicate that something (usually a selling price) has been agreed upon.

26. *Aubusson*: the name of the town renowned for the manufacture of tapestries. Other fine tapestries are made in *Beauvais* and at the *Manufacture des Gobelins* in Paris.

27. *elle est / il est / c'est / de loin* . . . she / he / it is by far . . .

C. GRAMMAR AND USAGE

1. In French, the relative pronoun *qui* (who, which, that) is used for persons, things and places. It replaces the subject of the relative clause. Its use and construction are similar to English, except that unlike in English, *qui* cannot be omitted.

   Danièle, qui adore les brocantes, est la spécialiste des marchés aux puces.
   Danièle, who loves antique markets, is very familiar with flea markets.

La bergère qui est en soie rose est jolie.
The easy chair (which is) covered in silk is pretty.

Celle qui est recouverte de tapisserie d'Aubusson?
The one that's upholstered in Aubussson tapestry?

2. The relative pronoun *que* (whom, which, that) is used for persons, things and places. It replaces the object of the relative clause. Its use and construction are similar to English, except that just like *qui*, the relative pronoun *que* cannot be omitted.

Le marché que je préfère est celui-ci.
The market (that) I prefer is this one.

La personne que j'ai rencontrée n'est pas là.
The person (whom) I met is not there.

Les films que nous avons vus sont très longs.
The films that we saw are very long.

Note that the past participle of the relative clause agrees with the antecedent of *que* in number and gender. In other words, in the second example above, *rencontrée* is feminine and singular, because *que* refers back to *la personne*, which is also feminine and singular. The same is true in the third example, where *vus* refers ultimately back to *films*. Also notice that *que* can be used to introduce entire clauses, just like the English "that." But in French, *que* cannot be omitted.

Je crois qu'il date du XIXème siècle et on dit qu'il s'étend sur 15 kilomètres!
I think it started in the nineteenth century, and one says that it spreads over 15 kilometers!

Je vous avertis que je ne sais absolument pas marchander.
I'm warning you that I don't know at all how to bargain.

3. The circumstancial relative pronoun *où* can be used to introduce a clause specifying location. It can be translated as "where," "which," "in which," "at which" or "to which."

Le stand où on vend la porcelaine est plus loin.
   The stand at which (where) they sell porcelain is further away.

Voici le marché où vous pouvez la trouver tous les weekends.
   Here's the market where you can find her every weekend.

Il faut passer par la rue où sont tous les brocanteurs.
   We have to go down the street where all the antique merchants are.

4. In English, superlative adjectives are formed by adding -est or with the adverb "most." In French, the superlative is formed by placing the appropriate definite article (*le, la, les*) or possessive (*mon, ma, mes, notre*, etc.) before *plus* or *moins*.

Ce marché est le plus ancien et le plus vaste.
   This market is the oldest and the largest.

C'est de loin la plus belle de toutes.
   It's by far the most beautiful of all.

Note that *de* is placed after the superlatives and in front of a noun or pronoun to express "in, of, among."

Note these irregular comparatives and superlatives.

Adjective	Comparative	Superlative
bon (good)	*meilleur*	*le meilleur*
mauvais (bad)	*pire*	*le pire*
mauvais (bad)	*mauvais*	*le plus mauvais*

Note that *pire* is used primarily in a moral, judgemental sense.

C'est le pire accident que j'aie vu.
　　It's the worst accident I've seen.

Aujourd'hui, nous avons le plus mauvais temps du mois.
　　Today, we're having the worst weather of the month.

Tu es la meilleure!
　　You're the best!

5. Usually the names of colors are placed after nouns and, as with all other adjectives, they agree in gender and number with those nouns. Certain adjectives that can also be used as nouns are invariable: *marron, orange, ivoire*, etc.

Le tapis rouge, la voiture bleue, les meubles bruns.
　　The red carpet, the blue car, the brown pieces of furniture.

But when modified by a second adjective or noun, the names of colors are invariable.

La voiture bleu clair de Danièle.
　　Danièle's light blue car.

EXERCISES

A. Substitute each word in parentheses for the underlined word in the model sentence. Write the complete sentence and say it aloud.

1. *La porcelaine que j'ai achetée est <u>belle</u>*. (*chère, rose pâle, de collection*)

2. *Le marchand qui arrive est son <u>père</u>*. (*ami, oncle, grand-père*)

B. In the sentence *L'armoire que j'ai vendue est belle*, replace *je* by the other subject pronouns (*tu, il, elle, nous, vous, ils, elles*). Make all necessary verb changes.

C. Say the following sentences aloud, then translate them into English.

    1. *Le marchand qui vend la cafetière est sympathique.*

    2. *La dame qui achète les meubles est ma femme.*

    3. *Le marchand que vous voyez est sympathique.*

    4. *C'est l'allée la plus longue du marché.*

    5. *C'est le peintre le plus reconnu de Paris.*

    6. *C'est le meilleur dessin de la collection.*

    7. *C'est le plus vieux tableau de la collection.*

    8. *Il y aura des meubles au marché.*

D. Translate the following sentences into French; then say them aloud.

    1. It will be necessary to bargain.

    2. It will be necessary to wear old clothes.

    3. She looks (*a l'air*) elegant.

    4. I wonder if he has a sofa.

    5. We wonder if you have any art objects.

    6. I'd like to see it up close.

    7. Show me a sky-blue easy chair.

    8. Do you prefer the tapestry on the right?

E. From among the three choices, select the best translation for the English word or phrase given at the beginning of each sentence. Write the complete sentence, and translate.

1. (heard) *Nous avons si souvent* _____ *du marché aux puces.*

   entendu / écouté parler / entendu parler

2. (that we could buy) *Il y aura quelque chose* _____ .

   que nous pourrons acheter / que nous pouvions acheter / que nous avons pu acheter

3. (bargain) *Il faut* _____ .

   marchander / marcher / acheter

4. (across the way) *Regardez* _____ .

   à travers le chemin / en face / en traversant la route

5. (Don't be [formal]) _____ *trop impulsif.*

   N'êtes pas / Ne soyez pas / Ne faites pas être

6. (the one [m.] who) _____ *a une exposition à Beaubourg est excellent.*

   Où / Que / Celui qui

Answer Key

A. 1. *La porcelaine que j'ai achetée est belle. La porcelaine que j'ai achetée est chère. La porcelaine que j'ai achetée est rose pâle. La porcelaine que j'ai achetée est de collection.* 2. *Le marchand qui arrive est son père. Le marchand qui arrive est son ami. Le marchand qui arrive est son oncle. Le marchand qui arrive est son grand-père.*

B. *L'armoire que tu as vendue est belle. L'armoire qu'il a vendue est belle. L'armoire qu'elle a vendue est belle. L'armoire que nous avons vendue est belle. L'armoire que vous avez vendue est belle. L'armoire qu'ils ont vendue est belle. L'armoire qu'elles ont vendue est belle.*

C. 1. The merchant who sells the coffeepot is nice. 2. The lady who is buying the furniture is my wife. 3. The merchant (whom) you see is nice. 4. It's the longest row (aisle) in the market. 5. He's the most recognized painter in Paris. 6. It's the best design in the collection. 7. It's the oldest picture in the collection. 8. There will be (some) furniture at the market.

D. 1. *Il faudra marchander.* 2. *Il faudra porter de vieux vêtements.* 3. *Elle a l'air élégant.* 4. *Je me demande s'il a un canapé.* 5. *Nous nous demandons si vous avez des objets d'art.* 6. *Je voudrais le voir de près.* 7. *Montrez-moi un fauteuil bleu ciel.* 8. *Préférez-vous la tapisserie de droite?*

E. 1. *Nous avons si souvent entendu parler du marché aux puces.* We've heard so much about the flea market. 2. *Il y aura quelque chose que nous pourrons acheter.* There will be something we'll be able to buy. 3. *Il faut marchander.* One has/You have to haggle. 4. *Regardez en face.* Look across the way. 5. *Ne soyez pas trop impulsif.* Don't be too impulsive. 6. *Celui qui a une exposition à Beaubourg est excellent.* The one who has an exhibition in Beaubourg is excellent.

LESSON 11

PRENONS DES PHOTOS
LET'S TAKE SOME PICTURES

A. DIALOGUE

0. *Dans leur chambre d'hôtel, Jane et Charles s'apprêtent à faire une randonnée photographique dans la capitale quand le téléphone sonne.*
   In their hotel room, Jane and Charles are getting ready for a day of taking photos in the capital when the phone rings.

1. Charles: **Allô? Oui, bien sûr. Dites-lui, s'il vous plaît, que nous descendons dans quelques minutes.**
   Hello? Yes, of course. Please tell him we'll be down in a few minutes.

2. Jane: **Qui est-ce qui a appelé?**
   Who called?

3. Charles: **C'est Luc, il est déjà en bas. Bon, on va descendre. N'oublie pas de mettre des chaussures confortables car on va beaucoup marcher.**
   It's Luc, he's already downstairs. So then, let's go down. Don't forget to wear comfortable shoes because we're going to walk a lot.

4. Jane: **Bien sûr! Dis-moi, est-ce que nous avons assez de pellicules pour l'appareil?**
   Of course! By the way, do we have enough film for the camera?

5. Charles: **Oui, je crois, mais je voudrais quand même passer chez le photographe pour en acheter d'autres et pour demander quelques conseils.**

Yes, I think so, but I'd like to stop by the camera store anyway to buy more rolls and to ask for some advice.

6. Jane: **N'oublions pas d'acheter également des pellicules diapo et quelques cassettes mini DV pour le caméscope.**
    Let's not forget to buy some film for slides and some mini DV tapes for the camcorder, too.

7. *Dans l'ascenseur.*
    In the elevator.

8. Charles: **Absolument. La qualité de la couleur est meilleure avec les diapos et j'aimerais vraiment reproduire la beauté des couleurs vives des cafés du Marais.**
    Absolutely. The quality of color is better with slides, and I'd really like to reproduce the beauty of the bright colors of the cafés in the Marais.

9. Jane: **Bonjour Luc, qu'est-ce que c'est gentil de ta part de nous accompagner.**
    Hello Luc, how nice it is for you to come along with us.

10. Luc: **C'est avec plaisir. Alors, comment allez-vous?**
    It's my pleasure. So, how are you?

11. Charles: **Nous allons bien. Cela me rappelle lorsque, adolescent, tu venais te promenener avec nous, alors que maintenant, c'est toi qui nous guides...**
    We're doing well. This reminds me when, as a teenager, you used to come along with us, and now you're the one leading us.

12. *Chez le photographe.*
    At the camera store.

13. Charles: **Je voudrais deux pellicules 200 ASA 24 poses pour cet appareil 35 mm.**
I'd like two rolls of 200 ASA 24 exposure film for this 35 mm camera.

14. L'employé: **Voici. C'est un très bon appareil que vous avez là. On en voit de moins en moins. De nos jours, les gens ont surtout des appareils digitaux.**
The employee: Here they are. That's a very good camera you have there. We see less and less of them. Nowadays, more and more people have digital cameras.

15. Charles: **Oui. J'en suis très satisfait. Donnez-moi aussi deux pellicules-diapo, s'il vous plaît.**
Yes. I'm very happy with it. Give me two rolls of slide film too, please.

16. L'employé: **Vingt-quatre poses et 200 ASA aussi?**
Twenty-four exposures and 200 ASA too?

17. Charles: **Oui, c'est cela. Aussi, est-ce que vous pourriez jeter un coup d'œil à l'appareil?**
Yes, that's it. Also, could you take a look at the camera?

18. L'employé: **Euh oui, qu'est-ce qui ne va pas?**
Uh yes, what's the trouble?

19. Charles: **Parfois quand j'appuie sur le déclencheur, l'appareil reste coincé.**
Sometimes when I press on the release, the camera gets stuck.

20. L'employé: **Voyons ça . . . Il n'y a pas de pellicule n'est-ce pas? Oui . . . Il y a une petite résistance. En fait, regardez, il faut appuyer sur le bouton ni trop fort, ni trop longtemps. Appuyez et retirez**

aussitôt votre doigt. **Ce sont de bons appareils, mais en vieillissant, ils prennent des habitudes!**
Let's see. . . . There's no film, is there? Yes . . . There's a little resistance. In fact, look, you can't press the button too hard or too long. Press and take your finger off right away. They're very good cameras but as they get old, they develop habits!

21. Charles: **Ah! Merci beaucoup, monsieur. Nous prendrons aussi des cassettes mini DV. Donnez-nous en trois, s'il vous plaît.**
Ah! Thank you very much, sir. Also, we'll take some mini DV tapes. Give us three of them, please.

22. L'employé: **Voilà . . . Vous désirez autre chose?**
Here we go . . . Is there anything else?

23. *Après quelques heures de balades et de photos, Jane, Charles et Luc s'arrêtent pour manger un plat de saucisses-frites.*
After a few hours of walking around and taking pictures, Jane, Charles and Luc stop to eat a dish of sausages and fries.

24. Luc: **Tenez, je vais vous prendre en photo en train de déguster de la grande cuisine française! En fait, je vais utiliser mon portable, comme ça, je pourrai l'envoyer à votre fIlle Natalie quand je rentrerai chez moi.**
Hey, I'm going to take a photo of you while you're eating high French cuisine! In fact I'm going to use my cell phone, so that I can send it to your daughter Natalie when I go home.

25. *En fin d'après-midi, à Montmartre, quand la lumière devient plus orangée.*
At the end of the afternoon, in Montmartre, when the light becomes more orange.

26. Charles: **C'est magnifique. Je vois parfaitement tous les cafés, les kiosques et les couleurs sont si belles dans cette lumière. Jane et Luc, reculez juste un peu . . . Parfait! Il me tarde déjà de les faire développer.**
    This is wonderful. I see all the cafés, the newspaper stands perfectly, and the colors are so beautiful in this light. Jane and Luc, step back just a little . . . Perfect! I already can't wait to have them developed.

27. Jane: **Charles, laisse-moi en prendre quelques-unes ou tu ne seras pas beaucoup sur ces photos! J'aimerais prendre le Sacré-Cœur et ces deux restaurants. Ah, c'était la dernière photo.**
    Charles, let me take a few or you won't be in many of these pictures! I'd like to get Sacré-Cœur and these two restaurants. Ah, it was the last picture.

28. Charles: **Bon, attends, je vais vite changer la pellicule. La lumière commence à tomber. Je ferais mieux d'augmenter l'ouverture. Voilà.**
    Well, wait, I'll reload the camera quickly. The light is beginning to fade. I'd better enlarge the aperture. Here.

29. Jane: **Merci. J'espère qu'il est bien réglé. J'aimerais faire agrandir cette série.**
    Thank you. I hope it's set up well. I'd like to enlarge this series.

30. Charles: **Ne t'en fais pas. Il y a quinze ans que je prends des photos avec cet appareil, et elles sont toujours réussies.**
    Don't worry. I've been taking pictures with this camera for fifteen years, and they always turn out great.

B. NOTES

Title: *La photo* is the customary short form of *la photographie*: photograph, photography. Beware *le photographe* is the photographer, and to take a photo is *prendre une photo*.

3. The following indicate location: *en bas* (at the bottom), *en haut* (at the top), *à droite* (on the right), *à gauche* (on the left), *au-dessous* (below, beneath), *au-dessus* (on top, above). Here, *en bas* means downstairs.

4. Note that *une pellicule* is a (roll of) film used in a still camera, and *un film* is what is seen on TV or at the movies. *L'appareil photo* is short for *appareil photographique*, any still camera or digital camera (*appareil digital* or *numérique*). *La caméra* is used only for a video or film camera. A camcorder is *le caméscope*.

5. *quand même*: however, nevertheless, still
    Note that *le conseil* or *les conseils* (advice), which is always used in the singular in English, can be plural in French.

6. *une diapo, une diapositive*: slide

11. *se souvenir de* and *se rappeler* both mean: to remember. With *se souvenir* you must use *de* before the object. Example: *je me souviens de votre nom, je me rappelle votre nom.*: I remember your name. Use *se souvenir de* when remembering people.

12. *chez le photographe*: at the camera store

14. *de moins en moins*: less and less, and *de plus en plus*: more and more

15. *être satisfait de quelque chose*: to be satisfied about something

18. *Qu'est-ce qui ne va pas?*: What's wrong with it? or literally: what is not going (well)?

19. *Il reste engagé* or *il reste bloqué*: It gets stuck

20. *ni . . . ni*: neither . . . nor

23. *un plat de saucisses-frites*: a real French specialty from the very North of France. The sausages are supposedly from Strasbourg or Frankfurt in Germany.

25. *en fin de, en début de*: at the end of, at the beginning of

   Montmartre: a renowned neighborhood on the hill in the North of Paris, with a lot of museums, galeries, little shops and cafés. The hill is called *la Butte Montmartre*. Montmartre, which was the center of the greatest painting movements of the 19th and 20th centuries (Impressionism, Cubism, Fauvism, Futurism, Surrealism) has preserved its cultural and artistic identity in spite of being a major tourist attraction. Visitors can take a small bus, or *le funiculaire*—a type of air tramway—to go on the top of the hill, or walk up the numerous stairs in the park.

26. *Il me tarde de* + infinitive: I can't wait to + infinitive

27. *La Basilique du Sacré-Cœur* or *Le Sacré-Cœur* is the basilica with a spectacular example of Byzantine style architecture. It dominates Montmartre so that it can be seen from almost anywhere in Paris.

28. *changer la pellicule*: to change the film or to reload the camera
   je ferais mieux de: I'd better

30. *Ne t'en fais pas* or *ne t'inquiète pas*: Don't worry.

C. GRAMMAR AND USAGE

1. The pronoun *en* (some of it; some of them; of it; of them) is invariable, and it is used to replace the partitive article *de* and its noun. The pronoun *en* precedes the verb, and is never omitted, unlike the English equivalents.

J'ai beaucoup de photos.	*J'en ai beaucoup.*
I have a lot of pictures.	I have a lot (of them)
Ne me donnez pas de cartes postales.	*Ne m'en donnez pas.*
Don't give me any postcards.	Don't give me any (of them).
J'ai besoin du flash.	*J'en ai besoin.*
I need the flash.	I need it.

But in requests, *en* comes after the verb and any other pronouns.

Montrez-moi des kiosques à journaux.	*Montrez-m'en.*
Show me some newspapers stands.	Show me some.

When *en* replaces a noun with a quantity (*un / une, deux . . .*), the quantity expression remains.

J'ai acheté un appareil photo.	*J'en ai acheté un.*
I bought a camera.	I bought one.
Il m'a donné trois pellicules.	*Il m'en a donné trois.*
He gave me three rolls of film.	He gave me three.
Ont-ils mangé beaucoup de frites?	*En ont-ils mangé beaucoup?*
Did they eat a lot of fries?	Did they eat a lot (of them)?

2. The adverb *assez* means "enough", and it is placed after the verb. The form *assez de* means "enough of (some-

thing)", and it is used with a partitive noun. Note that *de*, which comes after *assez*, is invariable.

On ne marche pas assez vite.
    We don't walk fast enough.

| *Tu as assez de pellicules?* | *J'en ai assez.* |
| Do you have enough rolls of film? | I have enough. |

| *Nous avons pris assez de photos.* | *Nous en avons pris assez.* |
| We took enough pictures. | We took enough. |

The expression *en avoir assez* means "to have enough of it" or "to be fed up."

J'en ai assez de marcher.
    I have had enough of walking.

On en a assez!
    We're fed up! / We've had enough!

3. The interrogative form *qu'est-ce qui* (lit.: "what is it that") is used as a subject, always referring to things.

Qu'est-ce qui ne va pas?
    What's wrong?

Qu'est-ce qui se passe?
    What's happening?

Qu'est-ce qu'il y a?
    What's the matter?

4. The preposition *pour* is always followed by the infinitive. It means "to" or "in order to."

On va s'arrêter pour manger.
    We're going to stop to eat.

Ils sont ici pour prendre des photos.
    They are here in order to take some pictures.

Allons au magasin pour acheter des pellicules.
   Let's go to the store to buy rolls of film.

EXERCISES

A. Substitute each of the words in parentheses for the underlined word in the model sentence. Write the complete sentence and say it aloud, and then translate it.

   1. *J'en ai acheté. (des pellicules, des cassettes mini DV, des frites, des chaussures confortables)*

   2. *Allez au magasin pour en acheter. (voir, trouver, admirer, essayer)*

B. Expand the expressions below by placing *Qu'est-ce qui* in front of each. Write the complete sentence and say it aloud.

   1. _____ *se passe?*

   2. _____ *ne marche pas?*

   3. _____ *vous ennuie?*

   4. _____ *est arrivé?*

   5. _____ *l'inquiète?*

   6. _____ *ne va pas?*

C. Replace the underlined expression by *en*. Say and write the entire new sentence, and translate. Example: *Il faut faire des photos. / Il faut en faire*: We have to take some.

   1. *J'ai acheté des cassettes mini DV*.

   2. *Je voudrais un appareil photo*.

   3. *Nous avons assez de lumière*.

   4. *Il m'a donné quatre pellicules*.

    5. *Montrez-moi des chaussures confortables*.

    6. *Prenez des photos de Montmartre*.

D. Translate the following sentences into French. Then say them aloud.

    1. Photos? He took several of them.

    2. I'd like four of them.

    3. Don't give me any film; I have enough.

    4. Do you have enough film for the camera?

    5. Yes, but there's not enough light.

    6. What's on the table?

    7. What's going to happen?

    8. What's bothering you? (*ennuyer*)

    9. In order to learn, one must understand.

    10. I don't have enough money to buy this camcorder.

E. From among the three choices, select the best translation for the English word or phrase given at the beginning of each sentence. Write the complete sentence, and translate.

    1. (enough) *As-tu _____ pellicules-diapo?*

      assez / assez de / assez des

    2. (at least) *Il nous en faudra _____ deux.*

      à moins / moins / au moins

    3. (remember) *Je voudrais _____ des couleurs.*

      se souvenir / me souvenir / me rappeler

    4. (Here they are) _____.

      Voici / Les voici / Ici ils sont

5. (a glance) *Veuillez aussi jeter* _____ *à cet appareil.*

   un coup / un regard / un coup d'œil

6. (anything else) *Y a-t-il* _____?

   autre chose / quoi d'autre / rien d'autre

7. (as far as) *Je vois* _____ *l'Arc de Triomphe.*

   haut à / jusqu'à / assez de

8. (I'd better) _____ *de changer l'ouverture.*

   Je pourrais / Je ferais mieux de / Je devrais

Answer Key

A. 1. *J'en ai acheté. J'ai acheté des pellicules. J'ai acheté des cassettes mini DV. J'ai acheté des frites. J'ai acheté des chaussures confortables.* 2. *Allez au magasin pour en acheter. Allez au magasin pour en voir. Allez au magasin pour en trouver. Allez au magasin pour en admirer. Allez au magasin pour en essayer.*

B. 1. *Qu'est-ce qui se passe?* 2. *Qu'est-ce qui ne marche pas?* 3. *Qu'est-ce qui vous ennuie?* 4. *Qu'est-ce qui est arrivé?* 5. *Qu'est-ce qui l'inquiète?* 6. *Qu'est-ce qui ne va pas?*

C. 1. *J'en ai acheté.* I bought some. 2. *J'en voudrais un.* I'd like one. 3. *Nous en avons assez.* We have enough. 4. *Il m'en a donné quatre.* He gave me four (of them). 5. *Montrez-m'en.* Show me some. 6. *Prenez-en.* Take some.

D. 1. *Des photos? Il en a pris plusieurs.* 2. *J'en voudrais quatre.* 3. *Ne me donnez pas de pellicules, j'en ai assez.* 4. *Avez-vous assez de pellicules pour l'appareil?* 5. *Oui, mais il n'y a pas assez de lumière.* 6. *Qu'est-ce qui est sur la table?* 7. *Qu'est-ce qui va arriver?* 8. *Qu'est-ce qui vous ennuie?* 9. *Pour apprendre, il faut comprendre.* 10. *Je n'ai pas assez d'argent pour acheter ce caméscope.*

E. 1. *As-tu assez de pellicules-diapo?* Do you have enough slide film? 2. *Il nous en faudra au moins deux.* We'll need at least two. 3. *Je voudrais me souvenir des couleurs.* I'd like to remember the colors. 4. *Les voici.* Here they are. 5. *Veuillez aussi jeter un coup d'œil à cet appareil.* Would you please also take a look at this camera. 6. *Y a-t-il autre chose?* Is there anything else? 7. *Je vois jusqu'à l'Arc de Triomphe.* I see as far as the Arch of Triumph. 10. *Je ferais mieux de changer l'ouverture.* I'd better change the aperture.

LESSON 12

À L'AGENCE DE VOYAGE
AT THE TRAVEL AGENCY

A. DIALOGUE

0. *Un matin, Jane et Charles entrent dans une agence de voyage de la SNCF pour demander des renseignements.*
   One morning, Jane and Charles enter an SNCF travel agency to get some information.

1. L'agent de voyage: **Bonjour, messieurs dames. En quoi puis-je vous être utile?**
   The travel agent: Good day, sir, madam. How can I help you?

2. Charles: **Nous voudrions explorer la région parisienne. Pourriez-vous nous suggérer quelques itinéraires?**
   We'd like to explore the area around Paris. Could you suggest some itineraries?

3. L'agent de voyage: **Avec plaisir. Où voudriez-vous aller plus précisément?**
   With pleasure. Where would you like to go more precisely?

4. Charles: **Nous pensions aller à Fontainebleau et à Versailles pour visiter les châteaux. Mais comment s'y rendre?**
   We were thinking of going to Fontainebleau and to Versailles to visit the châteaux. But how do you get there?

5. L'agent de voyage: **Pour Fontainebleau, je vous conseille de prendre le train. En fait, nous offrons un forfait train, bus et visites au château.**
For Fontainebleau, I advise you to take the train. In fact, we offer a package that covers train, bus and visits to the château.

6. Jane: **Merci. Et pour le château de Versailles?**
Thanks. And for the Château of Versailles?

7. L'agent de voyage: **Vous pouvez y aller en RER ou en train.**
You can go there by RER or train.

8. Charles: **Ensuite, nous voudrions voir d'autres régions en France. Par exemple, la Côte d'Azur.**
Then we'd like to see other regions in France. For instance, the French Riviera.

9. L'agent de voyage: **Où que vous alliez, vous pouvez prendre le train, et souvent, le T.G.V. qui est rapide, pratique et plutôt agréable.**
Wherever you go you can take the train, and often, the T.G.V. which is fast, practical and quite pleasant.

10. Jane: **Nous voudrions aussi aller en Italie et en Suisse. Mais mon mari préférerait aller d'abord en Espagne et au Portugal. Mais bon, ce sera pour plus tard . . .**
We'd also like to go to Italy and to Switzerland. But my husband would prefer to go to Spain and Portugal first. Well, that'll be for later . . .

11. L'agent de voyage: **Vous pouvez faire tous ces voyages en train, bien sûr. La SNCF offre des tarifs avantageux sur les grandes distances, mais l'avion, bien entendu, est plus rapide. Tout dépend du temps que vous avez.**

You can take all these trips by train, of course. The
SNCF offers good deals on long distances, but the
plane of course is faster. It all depends on the time
you have.

12. Charles: **Merci bien, Monsieur. Nous devons
réfléchir sérieusement à toutes ces possibilités.**
Thank you so much, sir. We need to think about all
these possibilities seriously.

13. L'agent de voyage: **Voulez-vous réserver vos
places aujourd'hui? Nous pourrions nous occuper de tout maintenant.**
Do you want to reserve your tickets today? We could
take care of everything now.

14. Jane: **Si vous permettez, nous allons y réfléchir, et
nous reviendrons demain.**
If you don't mind, we're going to think about it, and
we'll come back tomorrow.

15. *Le lendemain.*
The next day.

16. L'agent de voyage: **Ah, bonjour. Alors, qu'est-ce
que vous avez décidé?**
Oh, hello. So, what have you decided?

17. Charles: **Voyons. Nous voudrions deux billets
de train aller et retour pour Fontainebleau
pour demain matin. Après neuf heures trente, si
possible . . .**
Let's see. We'd like two round-trip train tickets for
Fontainebleau for tomorrow morning. After nine
thirty, if possible . . .

18. L'agent de voyage: **Tout est possible! Voilà. Vous
partirez de la gare de Lyon et vous arriverez à la**

gare de Fontainebleau-Avon. De là, un service de bus vous conduira au château.

Everything's possible! Here. You'll leave from the Gare de Lyon and you'll arrive at the Fontainebleau-Avon Station. From there, a bus service will drive you to the château.

19. *Plus tard* . . .
    Later . . .

20. Jane: **Et deux billets de train aller et retour pour Versailles pour dimanche matin. On nous a dit qu'on ne peut voir les Grandes Eaux que le dimanche.**

    And two train tickets, round-trip, for Versailles for Sunday morning. We were told that we can only see the fountain display on Sundays.

21. L'agent de voyage: **Oui, c'est juste, le dimanche ainsi que les jours de fête**.

    Yes, that's correct, on Sundays and during the holidays as well.

22. *Enfin* . . .
    Finally . . .

23. Charles: **Et dans un premier temps, nous avons décidé d'aller sur la Côte d'Azur, à Nice. Nous voudrions donc deux aller et retour Paris-Nice en train pour mardi prochain, le matin de préférence.**

    And to start with, we've decided to go to the Riviera, to Nice. So we'd like two round trips Paris-Nice by train for this coming Tuesday, in the morning preferably.

24. L'agent de voyage: **D'accord. Voyons ce que nous avons de disponible. De la gare de Lyon, vous**

avez un train direct partant à 9h34 et qui arrive à 15h12.
Okay. Let's see what we have available. From the Gare de Lyon, you have one direct train leaving at 9:34 a.m. and arriving at 3:12 p.m.

25. Jane: **Super. Pensez-vous que vous puissiez réserver des chambres d'hôtel? Bien, je crois que nous aimerions un hôtel qui donne sur la mer.**
Great. Do you think you could book us hotel rooms? Well, I think we'd like a hotel facing the sea.

26. L'agent de voyage: **Oui, mais si cela ne vous dérange pas, je vais m'occuper de tout cela cet après-midi. Il est midi trente, et, malheureusement, on doit fermer. Vous avez un numéro de téléphone où je peux vous joindre ou désirez-vous repasser en fin d'après-midi?**
Yes, but if you don't mind, I'll take care of all that this afternoon. It's 12:30, and, unfortunately, we have to close. Do you have a phone number where I can reach you, or do you want to come back in the late afternoon?

B. NOTES

0. *La SNCF* (*Société nationale des chemins de fer français*) is the national railroad company of France. It now makes plane reservations and offers both domestic (*nationaux*) and international (*internationaux*) packages.

1. Note the idiomatic expression of courtesy: *en quoi puis-je vous être utile?* Literally, how can I be useful to you? That is, how can I help you?

4. *Fontainebleau* is a small town near Paris noted for its beautiful *château*, built by François I as a hunting lodge, and its surrounding large forest. On another note, the art school in Fontainebleau is highly regarded.

6. *Versailles*, a town west of Paris, is renowned for its château, built in the XVIIth century by architect Louis Le Vau for Louis XIV, known as the Sun King, *le Roi Soleil*. The château is also noted for its gardens, its fountains and its Hall of Mirrors. The treaty ending World War I was signed there.

7. *Le RER* is the name for the express commuter rail system linking Paris to its suburbs. There are currently five lines (A, B, C, D, E) with various directions and which criss-cross Paris and its suburbs from East to West or South to North.

9. The *T.G.V.*, or *train à grande vitesse*, is France's high-speed train. It covers a great deal of territory and conveniently connects with other trains.

11. *dépendre de*: to depend on
    avoir du temps: to have time

17. *un aller et retour*: a round trip

18. There are several train stations in Paris: *la gare de Lyon, la gare du Nord, la gare de l'Est, la gare Saint-Lazare, la gare d'Austerlitz, la gare Montparnasse.*

26. Although the practice has started to change, at least in Paris and other big cities, many businesses still close at lunch time.

C. GRAMMAR AND USAGE

1. In French, geographic names—names of countries, continents, states, provinces—have a gender just like every other noun. Most of the time the gender can be determined as follows:

All names ending in *-e* are usually feminine, except *le Mexique, le Cambodge.*

> *L'Algérie, l'Europe, la Californie, la France, L'Amérique, l'Espagne, la Suède, la Catalogne, la Provence, l'Asie, l'Allemagne, l'Italie,* etc.

Note also that most geographic names that end in -a in English (except: Angola, Canada, Cuba, Guatemala, Venezuela, Panama, etc. which are the same in French), end in *-e* in French, and thus are feminine.

> *l'Afrique, la Chine, l'Australie, la Lituanie, la Russie, la Floride,* etc.

All other geographic names, ending with any other vowel or a consonant, tend to be masculine.

> *le Portugal, l'Angola, le Vietnam, le Japon, le Canada, le Sénégal, le Maroc, l'Irak, le Massachusetts, le Languedoc,* etc.

There are a few geographic names that are not used with articles: *Cuba, Tahiti, Hong Kong, Haïti, Trinidad, Sainte Lucie, Porto Rico, Fidji.* Notice that they're all islands.

2. The prepositions which precede geographic names vary. Before a feminine continent, country, state or region, use *en*, to mean either "to" or "in / at."

J'ai voyagé en Asie.
> I traveled in Asia.

Je vais en France tous les ans.
  I go to France every year.

Pauline habite en Floride.
  Pauline lives in Florida.

Nous passons tous nos étés en Provence.
  We spend all our summers in Provence.

Before a masculine continent, country, state or region, use *au* (or *aux* in front of a plural noun).

Nous sommes aux États-Unis depuis 1990.
  We've been in the United States since 1990.

Êtes-vous allés au Venezuela?
  Did you go to Venezuela?

Non, nous sommes allés seulement au Brésil.
  No, we just went to Brazil.

If the masculine geographic name starts with a vowel, use *en*.

Ils ont habité en Irak.
  They lived in Iraq.

Use the preposition *à* ("in", "to", or "at") before the names of cities that don't begin with an article.

J'ai habité à Paris pendant trois ans.
  I've lived in Paris for three years.

Maintenant, je suis à New York.
  Now I'm in New York.

Ma mère adore aller à Londres.
  My mother loves to go to London.

But some cities have an article in their name (think of The Hague in English): *La Nouvelle-Orléans, Le Havre, Le Mans, La Havane,* etc. Use *à* and the article, contracted if possible.

Nous ne sommes jamais allés à La Nouvelle-Orléans.
  We've never been to New Orleans.

Ma sœur est étudiante au Mans.
  My sister is a student in Le Mans.

Finally, to express "from" or "of", use the preposition *de*. As usual, *de* may be contracted to *du* when used with the masculine article *le*, and to *des* with a plural noun. In the same way, *de* becomes *d'*, in front of a noun starting with a vowel.

Je suis du sud de la France.
  I'm from the South of France.

Le Festival de Jazz de La Havane est génial.
  The Havana Jazz Festival is great.

La musique d'Angola est belle et dansante.
  Music from Angola is beautiful and good to dance to.

Elle rentre des Açores.
  She is coming back from the Azores.

Mes amis sont tous de Paris.
  My friends are all from Paris.

Ma famille est du Maroc.
  My family is from Morocco.

3. There are two prepositions that can be used with means of transportation. The preposition *à* is used essentially with *pied, cheval* and *bicyclette* and its synonym, *vélo*.

On est allé à pied à l'agence de voyage.
  We went to the travel agency on foot.

J'adore rouler à bicyclette.
  I love to ride (on) the bicycle.

Autrefois, les gens se déplaçaient à cheval.
  In the past, people got around on horseback.

The preposition *en* is used with all other means of transportation.

en bateau, en avion, en voiture, en moto, en train . . .
    by boat, by plane, by car, by motorbike, by train . . .

4. The subjunctive is used in French after the interrogative and negative forms of the verbs *croire, trouver* and *penser,* because there is a sense of doubt. For the forms of the subjunctive, check the Verb Charts.

Croyez-vous qu'il soit préférable d'aller à Nice en voiture ou en train?
    Do you think it's better to go to Nice by car or by train?

Je ne pense pas qu'il y ait de la place dans le train de demain.
    I don't think there will be any seats in tomorrow's train.

Trouves-tu que ce soit un bon hôtel?
    Do you think it's a good hotel?

EXERCISES

A. Substitute each of the words or expressions in parentheses for the underlined word or phrase in the model sentence. Write the complete sentence and say it aloud.

1. *Il voudrait aller en <u>France</u>. (Afrique, Provence, Asie, Europe)*

2. *Il doit aller à <u>Paris</u>. (Londres, Madrid, Buenos Aires, Genève)*

3. *Il est revenu hier de <u>La Nouvelle-Orléans</u>. (Angola, Brésil, Les Antilles, Cuba)*

4. *Elle aime voyager en <u>avion</u>. (autobus, voiture, train, bateau)*

B. Replace *je* with the other subject pronouns (*tu, elle, il, nous, vous, ils, elles*). Make the necessary changes in the verb forms. Say and write the new sentences.

1. *Croit-il que je puisse voyager?*

2. *Je ne pense pas que j'aie vos billets.*

C. Translate the following sentences into French; then say them aloud.

1. They went to Italy last year.

2. There is a beautiful cathedral in Perpignan.

3. In West Africa, people (*on*) speak French.

4. We received a letter from our aunt from Québec.

5. She came back from Paris yesterday.

6. This wine comes from Portugal.

7. They always travel by car.

8. I returned home on foot.

9. I don't think they're very expensive.

10. Do you believe that he came yesterday?

D. From among the three choices, select the best translation for the English word or phrase given at the beginning of each sentence. Write the complete sentence, and translate.

1. (outside of) *Je voudrais voyager _____ Paris.*
   hors / en dehors de / loin de

2. (anywhere) *Vous pouvez aller _____.*
   n'importe où / de tout / toujours

3. (by) *Vous pouvez y aller _____ train.*
   à / au / en

4. (road map) *J'ai besoin d' _____.*
   un plan / une carte postale / une carte routière

5. (What) _____ *vous avez décidé?*

   Qu'est-ce que / Que / Quoi

6. (on Sundays) *On peut voir les Grandes Eaux seulement* _____.

   dimanche / sur dimanche / le dimanche

7. (hotel rooms) *Voudriez-vous bien nous réserver des* _____?

   hôtels / chambres d'hôtel / pièces d'hôtel

8. (round trips) *Nous prendrons deux* _____.

   allers et retours / voyage autour / aller et venir

Answer Key

A. 1. *Il voudrait aller en France. Il voudrait aller en Afrique. Il voudrait aller en Provence. Il voudrait aller en Asie. Il voudrait aller en Europe.* 2. *Il doit aller à Paris. Il doit aller à Londres. Il doit aller à Madrid. Il doit aller à Buenos Aires. Il doit aller à Genève.* 3. *Il est revenu hier de La Nouvelle-Orléans. Il est revenu hier d'Angola. Il est revenu hier du Brésil. Il est revenu hier des Antilles. Il est revenu hier de Cuba.* 4. *Elle aime voyager en avion. Elle aime voyager en autobus. Elle aime voyager en voiture. Elle aime voyager en train. Elle aime voyager en bateau.*

B. 1. *Croit-il que je puisse voyager? Croit-il que tu puisses voyager? Croit-il qu'elle puisse voyager? Croit-il qu'il puisse voyager? Croit-il que nous puissions voyager? Croit-il que vous puissiez voyager? Croit-il qu'ils puissent voyager? Croit-il qu'elles puissent voyager?* 2. *Je ne pense pas que j'aie vos billets. Je ne pense pas que tu aies vos billets. Je ne pense pas qu'elle ait vos billets. Je ne pense pas qu'il ait vos billets. Je ne pense pas que nous ayons vos billets. Je ne pense pas que vous ayez vos billets. Je ne pense pas qu'ils aient vos billets. Je ne pense pas qu'elles aient vos billets.*

C. 1. *Ils sont allés en Italie l'année dernière.* 2. *Il y a une belle cathédrale à Perpignan.* 3. *En Afrique de l'Ouest, on parle français.* 4. *Nous avons reçu une lettre de notre tante du Québec.* 5. *Elle est revenue de Paris hier.* 6. *Ce vin vient du Portugal.* 7. *Ils voyagent toujours en voiture.* 8. *Je suis rentré à pied.* 9. *Je ne pense pas qu'ils soient très chers.* 10. *Croyez-vous qu'il soit venu hier?*

D. 1. *Je voudrais voyager en dehors de Paris.* I would like to travel outside of Paris. 2. *Vous pouvez aller n'importe où*. You can go anywhere. 3. *Vous pouvez y aller en train.*You can go there by train. 4. *J'ai besoin d'une carte routière.* I need a road map. 5. *Qu'est-ce que vous avez décidé?* What have you decided? 6. *On peut voir les Grandes Eaux seulement le dimanche.* You can see the fountains only on Sundays. 7. *Voudriez-vous bien nous réserver des chambres d'hôtel?* Would you please reserve hotel rooms for us? 8. *Nous prendrons deux allers et retours.* We'll take two round trips.

LESSON 13

ON LOUE UNE VOITURE
WE'RE RENTING A CAR

A. DIALOGUE

0. *Jane et Charles sont à Nice où ils profitent du doux soleil d'automne. Ils veulent louer une voiture pour visiter la région et se rendre à Monaco.*
   Jane and Charles are in Nice, where they're enjoying the warm autumn sun. They want to rent a car to visit the region and go to Monaco.

1. L'agent de location: **Hmm . . . Pour lundi, il ne nous reste plus qu'une seule automatique, c'est une Mercedes E Clim . . . Non? Bien, il n'y a plus grand chose. Voyons. Une Renault Twingo, c'est un petit modèle deux portes.**
   The rental agent: Hmm . . . For Monday, we only have one automatic left, it's a Mercedes E Clim . . . No? Well, there's not much left. Let's see. A Renault Twingo, it's a small model with two doors.

2. Jane: **Y-a-t-il la climatisation?**
   Does it have air conditioning?

3. L'agent de location: **Non, pas vraiment; sinon, nous avons, ah bien . . . une Renault Vel Satis, cinq portes et air climatisé. Voulez-voir celle-ci?**
   No, not really; otherwise, we have, ah good . . . a Renault Vel Satis, five doors and air conditioning. Would you like to see this one?

4. Charles: **Oui, cela semble bien . . .**
   Yes, that seems good . . .

5. L'agent de location: **Pour quelles dates vous la faudrait-il?**
Which dates will you need it for?

6. Jane: **Du 25 octobre au matin au 29 octobre.**
From October 25 in the morning until October 29.

7. L'agent de location: **Oui, c'est bon. Le tarif est de 516 euros TTC, c'est-à-dire, toutes taxes comprises, pour quatre jours.**
Yes, that's no problem. The price is 516 euros TTC, that is, all taxes included, for four days.

8. Charles: **Mais c'est assez cher pour quatre jours. Quel serait le prix pour la Mercedes automatique?**
But that's pretty expensive for four days. What would the price be for the Mercedes automatic?

9. L'agent de location: **La Mercedes est un modèle G, tandis que celle-ci est un modèle E. La location en serait beaucoup plus chère. Je peux vérifier, mais la Vel Satis est une très bonne voiture stable, endurante et confortable. Si vous désirez, il nous reste encore quelques petites voitures.**
The Mercedes is a G model, while this one is an E model. To rent it would be much more expensive. I can check, but the Vel Satis is a very good car, stable, sturdy and comfortable. If you want, we still have a few small cars.

10. Jane: **Et qu'est-ce qui est inclus dans le prix?**
And what's included in the price?

11. L'agent de location: **Ce forfait comprend toutes les taxes ainsi que l'assurance avec franchise en cas d'accident, l'assurance avec franchise en cas de vol du véhicule et en plus, vous avez 1 000 kilo-**

mètres inclus. Au-delà, ce n'est seulement que 0,38 euro TTC par kilomètre.

This package includes all the taxes, as well as insurance with damage waiver and insurance with theft waiver, and in addition, you get 1,000 kilometers included. Beyond that, it's only 0.38 euros all taxes included per kilometer.

12. Charles: (*en aparté*) **Qu'en penses-tu Jane?**
(aside) What do you think Jane?

13. Jane: **Puisque cela semble être une bonne voiture, prenons-la. (*À l'agent*) C'est d'accord, nous la prenons.**
Since it looks like a good car, let's take it. (To the agent) Okay, we'll take it.

14. L'agent de location: **Très bien. Je vais avoir besoin du permis de conduire de . . . Monsieur? D'accord. Vous seul pensez conduire?**
Very well. I'm going to need the driver's licence of . . . you, Sir? Okay. Only you intend to drive?

15. Jane: **Oui, car je n'ai l'habitude que des voitures automatiques.**
Yes, because I'm only used to driving automatics.

16. L'agent de location: **Vous devriez essayer un jour, ce n'est pas si compliqué . . . Enfin, pas . . . , pas avec celle-ci! J'aurai aussi besoin de votre carte de crédit, ainsi que de votre passeport.**
You should try one day, it's not so complicated . . . Well not . . . , not with this one! I'll also need your credit card, and your passport as well.

17. Charles: **Voici mon permis, mon passeport et ma carte de crédit.**
Here are my licence, my passport and my credit card.

18. L'agent de location: **Donnez-moi quelques minutes, je vais enregistrer la location. Le montant est payable maintenant et une caution remboursable de 150 euros sera déduite de votre carte de crédit lorsque vous viendrez prendre la voiture. Veuillez vous asseoir en attendant.**
Give me a few minutes, I'm going to put the rental through. The amount is payable now and a refundable deposit of 150 euros will be deducted from your card when you come to pick up the car. Please have a seat in the meantime.

19. Jane: **Allez, Charles, on ne part même pas en vacances deux fois par an! Quelle chance nous avons d'être dans cette si jolie région!**
C'mon Charles, we don't even go on vacation twice a year! What luck we have to be in such a pretty region!

20. Charles: **Tu as totalement raison. J'étais juste un peu surpris. Les prix sont plus élévés qu'à New York. Mais comme tu dis, profitons du temps présent!**
You are entirely right. I was just a bit surprised. Prices are much higher than in New York. But, as you say, let's enjoy the present!

21. L'agent de location: **Ça y est, tout est prêt. J'aurai juste besoin que vous vérifiiez et signiez les copies du contrat.**
That's it, everything is ready. I'll just need you to review and sign the copies of the contract.

22. Charles: **Très bien . . . Ici?**
Very well . . . Here?

23. L'agent de location: **Oui, c'est ça . . . Donc, vous viendrez chercher la voiture à cette même**

adresse, lundi à 9 heures. Nous ouvrons à huit heures. Et vous la ramènerez ici vendredi matin au plus tard à 10 heures.

Yes, that's it . . . So you'll get the car at this same address, on Monday at 9 a.m. We open at 8 a.m. And you'll bring it back Friday morning at the latest 10 a.m.

24. Charles: **Merci bien. On vous verra donc lundi?**

Thank you very much. So we'll see you on Monday?

25. L'agent de location: **Non, je ne serai pas là, mais un de mes collègues s'occupera de vous. Voici votre copie du contrat et notre carte. Merci. Alors, où pensez-vous aller?**

No, I won't be here, but a colleague of mine will take care of you. Here's your copy of the contract and our card. Thank you. So where do you think you'll go?

26. Jane: **Très probablement, à Cannes, à Monte-Carlo, peut-être ailleurs, enfin, jusqu'à la frontière italienne et nous reviendrons par l'arrière-pays.**

Most probably to Cannes, Monte-Carlo, maybe somewhere else and then, up to the Italian border, and we'll come back through the inland.

27. L'agent de location: **C'est une très belle région et c'est une bonne chose que vous ayez choisi la semaine pour faire ce petit voyage. Car il y a bien plus de monde sur les routes le week-end. Dans tous les cas, profitez-en bien!**

It's a very beautiful region, and it's a good thing you've chosen the week to take this little trip. Because there are many more people on the road during the weekend. In any case, enjoy!

B. NOTES

0. *louer une voiture, un appartement, de l'équipement*: to rent a car, an apartment, equipment. *une location*: a rental

1. *Il ne reste plus que* . . . is the equivalent of *il n'y a plus que* . . . : There is only . . . left

2. *l'air climatisé* or *la climatisation*: air conditioning

3. *Renault* is a brand of French car. Others are *Citroën* and *Peugeot*.

7. *c'est-à-dire*: that is, that's to say

10. *Qu'est-ce qui est inclus dans le prix?* What is incuded in the price? The past participle *inclus,* from the verb *inclure,* is synonymous with *compris* from the verb *comprendre.*

11. *Un forfait* is a special all-included price or rate.

    In most of Europe, distances are measured in kilometers. *Un kilomètre* is five-eighths of a mile. Parallel to mileage is *le kilométrage*.

    Note the way one thousand is written, again, in most of Europe . . . 1.000 instead of 1,000. Where English uses a comma, a period is used, and vice versa (0,38 euros in French would be noted in English 0.38 euros). It's also possible to see a number with a space in place of a period/comma.

    en cas d'accident, en cas de vol du véhicule: in case of accident, in case of vehicule theft

16. *J'aurai besoin de votre passeport et* . . . *de votre carte de crédit*. Note that in French, you need to repeat the preposition *de* in each phrase connected by *et*.

25. *s'occuper de*: to take care of

26. *ailleurs*: somewhere else, elsewhere

27. *Profitez-en bien*: Enjoy. The verb *profiter (de quelque-
    chose)* is to enjoy (something).

C. GRAMMAR AND USAGE

1. The question word *quel* and its various forms *quels,
   quelle, quelles* can be pronouns or adjectives. As an interrogative pronoun, *quel* agrees with the gender and number of the noun it refers to.

   Quel serait le prix?
     What would the price be?

   Quelle est votre nationalité?
     What nationality are you?

   Quelles sont vos suggestions?
     What are your suggestions?

   The interrogative adjective *quel* is followed by a noun,
   and it agrees with that noun in gender and number. It can
   be translated as "what" or "which."

   Quel type de voiture préférez-vous?
     What type of car do you prefer?

   Quelle heure est-il?
     What time is it?

   Quels modèles cherchez-vous?
     Which models are you looking for?

   In some instances, *quel* can be preceded by a preposition,
   just like English "what" or "which."

   Pour quelles dates vous la faudrait-il?
     For which dates do you need it?

   À quelle heure devons-nous ramener la voiture?
     At what time do we need to bring back the car?

De quel pays êtes-vous?
From which country are you? / Which country are you from?

2. The preposition *par* is used to express a frequency or a ratio.

Ce n'est que 0,38 euro par kilomètre.
It's only 0.38 euro a kilometer.

Nous partons en voyage une fois par mois.
We go on vacation once a month.

En France, beaucoup de gens travaillent trente-cinq heures par semaine.
In France, a lot of people work thirty-five hours a week.

3. The regular verb *penser* can be followed by the infinitive when it means to think of, to consider, or to intend to.

Où pensez-vous aller?
Where do you think you'll go? / Where are you thinking of going?

Il pense apprendre à conduire.
He intends to learn how to drive.

Nous ne pensons pas y aller cette année.
We aren't considering going there this year.

EXERCISES

A. Substitute each of the words in parentheses for the underlined word in the model sentence. Make the necessary changes. Write each new sentence and say it aloud.

1. *Quel est votre <u>but</u>? (profession, hôtel, préférences)*

2. *J'y vais trois fois par <u>semaine</u>. (mois, an, heure)*

3. *Ils pensent <u>partir</u> demain matin. (venir, téléphoner, commencer)*

B. Complete the sentences below by placing *par an* at the end of each one, and translate.

1. *Il part en vacances trois fois*

2. *Ils se voient deux fois*

3. *Ils louent une voiture une fois*

4. *Elle me téléphone plusieurs fois*

C. Transform each of the following sentences according to the model.

J'ai besoin de cent euros. / Il me faut cent euros.

1. *Nous avons besoin d'une voiture automatique.*

2. *Il avait besoin de son permis.*

3. *Vous en avez besoin lundi?*

4. *On aura besoin d'une assurance.*

D. Say each of the following sentences aloud, and then translate them into English.

1. *Quelle est sa question?*

2. *Quelle voiture a-t-il louée?*

3. *Quel voyage feront-ils?*

4. *Je ne la vois qu'une fois par an.*

5. *Combien de fois par jour conduisez-vous?*

6. *J'ai besoin de louer une voiture pour mon travail.*

E. Translate the following sentences into French. Then say them aloud.

1. You need your driver's licence, your passport and your credit card.

2. Which model do you prefer, automatic or not?

3. At what time do we need to be here?

4. Is the mileage unlimited?

5. We intend to drive along the French Riviera.

6. That is to say, you have to bring the car back to the same location.

F. From among the three choices, select the one that correctly renders the English word or phrase given at the beginning of each sentence, write the complete sentence, and translate.

1. (were thinking about) *Nous _____ aller en Espagne.*

   allons croire de / avons pensé de / pensions

2. (depends on) *Cela _____ dates.*

   vaut les / dépend sur les / dépend des

3. (What) _____ *est inclus dans le forfait?*

   Quel / Quoi / Qu'est-ce qui

4. (return) *Nous paierons quand nous _____ la voiture.*

   rendrons / rendons / retournons

5. (elsewhere) *Mais si on la laisse _____?*

   autre place / d'ailleurs / ailleurs

6. (The insurance) *est comprise dans le prix.*

   L'assurance / le confort / la climatisation

Answer Key

A. 1. *Quel est votre but? Quelle est votre profession? Quel est votre hôtel? Quelles sont vos préférences?* 2. *J'y vais trois fois par semaine. J'y vais trois fois par mois . J'y vais trois fois par an. J'y vais trois fois par heure.* 3. *Ils pensent partir demain matin. Ils pensent venir demain matin. Ils pensent téléphoner demain matin. Ils pensent commencer demain matin.*

B. 1. *Il part en vacances trois fois par an.* He goes on vacation three times a year. 2. *Ils se voient deux fois par an.* They see each other twice a year. 3. *Ils louent une voiture une fois par an.* They rent a car once a year. 4. *Elle me téléphone plusieurs fois par an.* She telephones me several times a year.

C. 1. *Il nous faut une voiture automatique.* 2. *Il lui fallait son permis.* 3. *Il vous le / la / en faut lundi?* 4. *Il nous faudra une assurance.*

D. 1. What's her/his question? 2. Which car did he rent? 3. What trip will they take? 4. I see her only once a year. 5. How many times a day do you drive? 6. I need to rent a car for my work.

E. 1. *Vous avez besoin de votre permis de conduire, de votre passeport et de votre carte de crédit.* 2. *Quel modèle préférez-vous, automatique ou non?* 3. *À quelle heure devons-nous être là?* 4. *Est-ce que le kilométrage est illimité?* 5. *Nous pensons rouler le long de la Côte d'Azur.* 6. *C'est-à-dire, vous devez ramener la voiture au même endroit.*

F. 1. *Nous pensions aller en Espagne.* We were thinking about going to Spain. 2. *Cela dépend des dates.* That depends on the dates. 3. *Qu'est-ce qui est inclus dans le forfait?* What's included in the package? 4. *Nous paierons quand nous rendrons la voiture.* We will pay when we return the car. 5. *Mais si on la laisse ailleurs?* But if we leave it somewhere else? 6. *L'assurance est comprise dans le prix.* Insurance is included in the price.

LESSON 14

SUR LA ROUTE
ON THE ROAD

A. DIALOGUE

0. *Charles et Jane sont sur la route de leur découverte de la Côte d'Azur. C'est Charles qui conduit.*
   Charles and Jane are on their way to discovering the French Rivera. Charles is driving.

1. Jane: **Quel beau temps nous avons! En cette saison, on a de la chance.**
   What beautiful weather we're having! In this season, that's called luck.

2. Charles: **Oui, cela rend tout plus agréable. Même la conduite! D'autant plus qu'il n'y a pas beaucoup de circulation.**
   Yes, it makes everything all the more pleasant. Even driving! And there isn't even much traffic.

3. Jane: **Alors, elle n'est pas si mal, cette voiture . . .**
   So, this car isn't that bad . . .

4. Charles: **Non, elle est même très confortable. La seule chose, c'est que j'ai l'impression qu'un des pneus est un peu dégonflé. On va s'arrêter à la prochaine station service, car de toutes façons, on va bientôt devoir faire de l'essence.**
   No, it's even very comfortable. The only thing is that I have the feeling that one of the tires is a bit flat. We're going to stop at the next gas station, since we'll have to get gas soon anyway.

5. Jane: **Tiens, il y a une pancarte indiquant une station d'essence à droite. Allons-y.**

Here, there's a sign pointing to a gas station on the right. Let's go there.

6. *À la station d'essence, le garagiste se dirige vers la voiture qui s'arrête près de l'une des pompes à essence.*
At the gas station, an attendant comes out and makes his way to the car, which stops near one of the gas pumps.

7. Le garagiste: **Bonjour! Le plein?**
Station Attendant: Hello. Fill it up?

8. Charles: **Oui, le plein de super, s'il vous plaît. Regarde Jane, il y a un garage aussi, je vais parler au garagiste.**
Yes, fill it up, please. Look Jane, they have a garage as well, I'm going to speak to the attendant.

9. Jane: **Vas-y, moi, je vais en profiter pour me rafraîchir un peu. Excusez-moi, les toilettes, s'il vous plaît?**
Go ahead. I'm going to take the opportunity to freshen up a bit. Excuse me, the restrooms please?

10. Le garagiste: **Du côté droit, là, face au grand arbre.**
On the right side, there, opposite the big tree.

11. Charles: **Monsieur, pouvez-vous vérifier les pneus, s'il vous plaît?**
Sir, could you check the tires please?

12. Le garagiste: **Bien sûr, qu'est-ce qui se passe? Ils sont un peu dégonflés? Je finis avec ça et je vais y jeter un coup d'œil.**
Of course, what's the trouble? They're a little deflated? I'll finish with this and I'll take a look at it.

13. Charles: **Merci bien. On est loin de Monte-Carlo?**
    Thanks very much. Are we far from Monte-Carlo?

14. Le garagiste: **Non, vous y arrivez là, à quatre
    kilomètres environ. Bon, voyons ces pneus . . . Ah
    ben oui. Y en a un qui est vraiment dégonflé. Il a
    même l'air crevé. Les autres sont bons, neufs
    apparemment . . . Vous avez une roue de secours?**
    No, you're almost there, in about four kilometers.
    Well, let's take a look at these tires . . . Ah yes.
    There's one that's really deflated. It even looks flat.
    The others are good, brand new, obviously. Do you
    have a spare tire?

15. Charles: **Vraiment? Oui, il y en a une dans le cof-
    fre, je crois.**
    Really? Yes, there's one in the trunk, I think.

16. Le garagiste: **C'est une voiture de location?**
    Is it a rental car?

17. Charles: **Oui. Cela nous est probablement arrivé
    à la sortie de Nice. Il avait dû y avoir un accident,
    car sur la route, il y avait beaucoup de débris de
    verre et . . .**
    Yes. It probably happened to us coming out of Nice.
    There must have been an accident because on the
    road, there was a lot of glass debris and . . .

18. Le garagiste: **Et des petits morceaux de métal.
    Tenez, regardez . . . Vous avez eu de la chance.
    Vous auriez pu avoir un accident à cause de ça . . .**
    And little pieces of metal. Here, look . . . You were
    lucky. You could have gotten into an accident
    because of this . . .

19. Charles: **Eh bien!**
    Well!

20. Jane: **Qu'est-ce qui se passe?**
What's happening?

21. Le garagiste: **Rien de grave . . . Juste un pneu crevé que je vais vous changer en quelques minutes.**
Nothing serious . . . Just a flat tire that I'm going to change for you in a few minutes.

22. Charles: **Merci monsieur. Je ne sais pas toi, Jane, mais je meurs de faim.**
Thank you, sir. I don't know about you Jane, but I'm starving.

23. Jane: **Oui, moi aussi. Monsieur, connaissez-vous un bon restaurant auquel on puisse aller à pied?**
Yes, I am too. Sir, would you know a good restaurant that we could walk to?

24. Le garagiste: **Ben, oui. Y en a un juste après le prochain croisement à gauche. Vous pouvez pas le rater. *Chez Jeannie*. Vous y mangerez de la bonne cuisine de chez nous.**
Sure. There's one just after the next crossroad on the left. You can't miss it. *Chez Jeannie*. You'll get some good food from the area.

25. Charles: **Merci mille fois. Vous voulez que je vous paie maintenant?**
Thank you so much. Do you want me to pay you now?

26. Le garagiste: **Non, ne vous inquiétez pas. Quand vous viendrez la reprendre. D'ici une à deux heures?**
No, don't worry. When you come and get it. In about one or two hours?

27. Charles: **Très bien. Voici les clés. Et si cela ne vous dérange pas, vérifiez aussi l'huile et . . .**
Great. Here are the keys. And if you don't mind, check out the oil as well, and . . .

28. Le garagiste: **Allez-y! Je vais regarder tout ça. Bon appétit!**
Go ahead! I'm going to look at everything. Enjoy your meal!

B. NOTES

0. *découvrir*: to discover and *la découverte*: discovery

3. Note this colloquial expression: *elle n'est pas si mal, cette voiture*: this car isn't bad; it's not so bad, this car.

4. *le seul truc* (colloquial), *la seule chose*: the only thing
    faire de l'essence: to get gas

5. *la station service* is the gas station. Whoever works there is called *un pompiste* (from *la pompe à essence*: the gas pump) or *un garagiste*, if the place is also *un garage* that fixes cars.

7. *Le plein?* is the colloquial way to ask "would you like me to fill the tank up?" It's the equivalent of "fill it up?"

9. *se rafraîchir*: to freshen up

14. *Dégonflé*, deflated, is used for *les pneus* or balloons and balls. It is also used in the slang expression, *tu es un dégonflé*: you're a chicken, or with the verb form, *tu te dégonfles?* You're giving up, you're

chickening out? The opposite slang adjective *gonflé* means too bold and its non-slang verb *gonfler* means: to fill with air.

The verb *crever* means to burst, but it also has a few idiomatic and slang usages. For instance, *un pneu crevé* is a flat tire. As a colloquial expression, *je suis crevé*: I'm burnt out, I'm exhausted. Also, the slang idioms *je crève de faim*: I'm starving to death, or *je me suis crevé au boulot*: I killed myself at work. The verb *crever* is the slang form of the verb to die.

Il a l'air crevé: (about the tire) it looks flat. *Elle / Il a l'air crevé*: she / he looks very tired.

21. *rien de grave*: nothing serious

14./24. Note the very colloquial expression which drops the subject pronoun: *Y en a un qui* . . . There's one that . . . In the same type of language, one usually drops half the negation ("*ne*") as in, *vous pouvez pas le rater*: you can't miss it.

24. *Ben* is colloquial for *et bien* or *eh bien*.

26. *D'ici une à deux heures* means to "in about one or two hours."

C. GRAMMAR AND USAGE

1. The location pronoun *y* ("there," "in it," "in there," "to there," etc.) is used when a location or destination has previously been expressed and is understood in context.

J'adore la Bretagne. J'y suis allée plusieurs fois. (*y = en Bretagne*)
   I adore Brittany. I've gone there many times.

On va s'y arrêter. (*y = à la station d'essence*)
   We're going to stop there.

Vous y mangerez de la bonne cuisine. (*y = au restaurant*)
> You'll eat some good cooking there.

The pronoun *y* is also used in a few idiomatic expressions.

On y va.
> Let's go.

Allez-y.
> Go ahead.

Il y avait beaucoup de débris de verre.
> There were a lot of pieces of glass.

Il y en a une dans le coffre.
> There's one in the trunk.

Il n'y a plus d'essence.
> There's no more gas.

The pronoun *y* is placed before the verb except in positive imperative sentences, where it comes right after the verb.

Allons-y!
> Let's go there!

2. The phrase composed of the verb *aller* plus the infinitive expresses the immediate future and can be translated by "to be going to."

On va devoir aller faire de l'essence.
> We're going to have to get gas.

Je vais regarder tout ça.
> I'm going to look at all this.

Je vais vous changer ce pneu en quelques minutes.
> I'm going to change this tire for you in a few minutes.

3. Most adjectives take a *-e* in the feminine form, but some adjectives follow irregular but predictable patterns.

Masculine adjectives ending in *-f* change to *-ve* in the feminine.

| active | *actif* | *active* |
| new | *neuf* | *neuve* |

Masculine adjectives ending in *-eux*, take-*euse* in the feminine.

happy	*heureux*	*heureuse*
numerous	*nombreux*	*nombreuse*
wonderful	*merveilleux*	*merveilleuse*

Masculine adjectives ending in *-l*, double the *-l* before adding *-e* in the feminine.

| natural | *naturel* | *naturelle* |
| nice | *gentil* | *gentille* |

Masculine adjectives that end in *-teur* change to *-trice* in the feminine.

| creative | *créateur* | *créatrice* |
| provocative | *provocateur* | *provocatrice* |

Some adjectives have irregular feminine forms that just need to be memorized.

long	*long*	*longue*
beautiful	*beau*	*belle*
good	*bon*	*bonne*
proud	*fier*	*fière*
dry	*sec*	*sèche*
fresh	*frais*	*fraîche*
sweet / soft	*doux*	*douce*
white	*blanc*	*blanche*

EXERCISES

A. Replace the underlined phrases in each of the following sentences with *y, lui,* or *leur*. Write the complete sentence, say it aloud, and translate.

Example: *Je vais à Londres./J'y vais:* I'm going there.

1. *Elle restera <u>à Rome</u>.*

2. *Je passerai mes vacances <u>à la mer</u>.*

3. *Il parle <u>au garagiste</u>.*

4. *J'ai trouvé la roue de secours <u>dans le coffre</u>.*

5. *Il est entré <u>dans la boutique de la station d'essence</u>.*

6. *Elle lit le roman <u>à l'enfant</u>.*

7. *Il a posé une question <u>à ces garagistes</u>.*

8. *Il a passé trois semaines <u>chez sa tante</u>.*

B. Change the affirmative to the negative.

Example: *J'y vais. / Je n'y vais pas.*

1. *J'y suis.*

2. *J'y reste.*

3. *Il y obéit.*

4. *Elle y répond.*

5. *Nous y pensons.*

6. *Allez-y.*

7. *Vas-y.*

8. *Allons-y.*

C. Change the future in the sentences below to a verb phrase with *aller*, and translate.

Example: *Il viendra demain. / Il va venir demain.*: He's going to come tomorrow.

1. *Elle fera de l'essence ce soir.*

2. *Ils sortiront plus tard.*

3. *Elles arriveront à sept heures.*

4. *Nous ferons une promenade en voiture.*

5. *Ils mangeront de la bonne cuisine à ce restaurant.*

6. *Il leur changera le pneu.*

D. Translate the following sentences into French; then say them aloud.

1. I'm going there in three weeks.

2. We stayed there for (*pendant*) a month.

3. Her trip? She thinks about it every day.

4. We're going to leave tomorrow.

5. I'm going to replace the flat tire.

6. It's a long road.

7. What a beautiful rental car!

8. He went to get gas.

E. From among the three choices, select the best translation for the English word or phrase given. Write the complete sentence, and translate.

1. (a spare tire) *Il y a _____ dans le coffre.*

   un pneu neuf / une roue de secours / une roue de rechange

2. (fill it up) _____ *, s'il vous plaît.*

   Remplissez / De l'essence / Le plein

3. (on the French Riviera) *Nous allons faire un voyage*
   _____.

   *sur la Rivière d'Azur / sur la Côte d'Azur /sur la
   côte française*

4. (if possible) *Vérifiez l'huile* _____.

   s'il faut / si possible / si nécessaire

5. (new) *Cette voiture automatique est* _____.

   neuf / nouvelle / neuve

6. (I'll need) _____ *une voiture avec la climatisation.*

   J'aurai besoin de / J'irai au besoin / J'aurai besoin

Answer Key

A. 1. *Elle y restera.* She will stay there. 2. *J'y passerai mes vacances.* I will spend my vacation there. 3. *Il lui parle.* He is speaking to him. 4. *J'y ai trouvé la roue de secours.* I found my spare tire there. 5. *Il y est entré.* He went in there. 6. *Elle lui lit le roman.* She is reading the novel to him (her). 7. *Il leur a posé une question.* He asked them a question. 8. *Il y a passé trois semaines.* He spent three weeks there.

B. 1. *Je n'y suis pas.* 2. *Je n'y reste pas.* 3. *Il n'y obéit pas.* 4. *Elle n'y répond pas.* 5. *Nous n'y pensons pas.* 6. *N'y allez pas.* 7. *N'y va pas.* 8. *N'y allons pas.*

C. 1. *Elle va faire de l'essence ce soir.* She is going to get gas tonight. 2. *Ils vont sortir plus tard.* They are going out later. 3. *Elles vont arriver à sept heures.* They will arrive at seven. 4. *Nous allons faire une promenade en voiture.* We are going to take a ride in the car. 5. *Ils vont manger de la bonne cuisine à ce restaurant.* They are going to eat some good cooking at this restaurant. 6. *Il va leur changer le pneu.* He's going to change the tire for them.

D. 1. *J'y vais dans trois semaines.* 2. *Nous y sommes restés pendant un mois.* 3. *Son voyage? Elle y pense tous les jours.* 4. *Nous allons partir demain.* 5. *Je vais remplacer le pneu crevé.* 6. *C'est une longue route.* 7. *Quelle belle voiture de location!* 8. *Il est allé faire de l'essence.*

E. 1. *Il y a une roue de secours dans le coffre.* There is a spare tire in the trunk. 2. *Le plein, s'il vous plaît.* Fill it up, please. 3. *Nous allons faire un voyage sur la Côte d'Azur.* We are going to take a trip on the French Riviera. 4. *Vérifiez l'huile si possible.* Check the oil if possible. 5. *Cette voiture automatique est neuve.* This automatic car is new. 6. *J'aurai besoin d'une voiture avec la climatisation.* I'll need the car with air conditioning.

LESSON 15

L'EUROTUNNEL
THE CHANNEL TUNNEL

A. DIALOGUE

0. *À la Gare du Nord, Charles, Jane, Michel et Éliane s'apprêtent à prendre l'Eurostar, le train rapide entre Paris et Londres.*
   At the Gare du Nord, Charles, Jane, Michel and Eliane are getting ready to take the Eurostar, the high speed train between Paris and London.

1. Michel: **Et voilà l'escalier roulant qui mène au terminal de l'Eurostar.**
   And here's the escalator that leads to the Eurostar terminal.

2. Éliane: **Tiens, un chariot. Prenons-le, on pourra mettre tous nos bagages dessus. Et regardez, il s'adapte à l'escalier. On n'a plus besoin de les porter.**
   Here's a cart. Let's take it, we'll be able to put all our luggage on it. And look, it fits onto the escalator. We don't need to carry it anymore.

3. Charles: **Ouf! Quel soulagement! Et ils sont gratuits.**
   Whew! What a relief! And they're free.

4. Jane: **Que cette gare est aérée et lumineuse!**
   How airy and bright this station is!

5. Charles: **Oui, il y a vraiment une différence d'atmosphère entre ce hall de gare et le hall de la gare du Nord. Maintenant je comprends pourquoi on en a si souvent entendu parler.**

Yes, there's really a difference in atmosphere between this hall and the hall of Garę du Nord. Now I know why we've heard about it so often.

6. Michel: **Oui, l'Eurostar est très bien conçu. Ils offrent un service excellent à leurs clients, un service moderne et, en même temps, très humain.**
Yes, Eurostar is very well conceived. They offer excellent service to their clients, a modern service, and at the same time very human.

7. Jane: **Oh là là, regardez la queue. On va en avoir pour longtemps.**
Wow, look at that line. It'll take us a long time.

8. Éliane: **Non, au contraire. Vous allez voir comme tout est très rapide et efficace ici.**
No, on the contrary. You'll see how everything here is quick and efficient.

9. *En effet, ils voient les voyageurs défiler devant la police d'immigration et la douane et les contrôles se déroulent sans problème. Plus tard, dans le train.*
Indeed, they see the travelers walk in front of immigration and customs and the checking takes place without any trouble. Later, in the train.

10. Jane: **Vous aviez raison, il ne nous a pas fallu beaucoup de temps. Et là, nous voici bien installés.**
You were right, it didn't take us much time. And here we are all settled in.

11. Charles: **Heureusement. Est-ce que tu te souviens, Jane, de notre dernier voyage en Europe? L'agent d'immigration avait examiné nos passeports comme si nous étions des criminels!**
Fortunately. Do you remember our last trip to Europe, Jane? The immigration officer examined our passports as if we were criminals!

12. Jane: **Et il voulait qu'on ouvre toutes nos valises! J'ai vraiment cru qu'on ne nous laisserait pas partir!**
And he wanted us to open all of our suitcases! I really thought they weren't going to let us leave!

13. Michel: **Oui, ces formalités de douane et d'immigration peuvent parfois agacer.**
Yes, these procedures with customs and immigration can be a pain sometimes.

14. Éliane: **Surtout quand tant de vrais criminels arrivent à passer les frontières.**
Especially when so many real criminals manage to get through the borders.

15. Jane: **Ah, je vois venir une hôtesse avec les journaux. Vous désirez un journal ou un magazine?**
Ah, I see a hostess coming with newspapers. Would you like a newspaper or a magazine?

16. Éliane: **Non, merci, Jane. J'ai un peu de travail à faire.**
No thanks, Jane. I have a bit of work to do.

17. Charles: **Et toi, Michel?**
And you, Michel?

18. Michel: **Je ne sais pas s'ils ont *Le Monde Diplomatique*.**
I don't know if they have *Le Monde Diplomatique*.

19. Jane: **Madame, je voudrais *Le Monde* s'il vous plaît et *Le Monde Diplomatique*. Je te prends le *Herald Tribune*, Charles? Oui, merci. Je vous dois . . . ?**
Ma'am, I'd like a copy of *Le Monde*, please, and *Le Monde Diplomatique*. Should I get you the Herald Tribune, Charles? Yes, thank you. I owe you . . . ?

20. L'hôtesse: **Rien, madame, les journaux sont gratuits dans l'Eurostar.**
Hostess: Nothing, Ma'am, newspapers are free in the Eurostar.

21. Jane: **Ah! Eh bien merci! Maintenant, tout ce qu'il me faut c'est un sandwich et je serai au comble du bonheur.**
Ah! Well, thank you! And now, all I need is a sandwich and I'll be all set.

22. Michel: **Ils passeront plus tard avec de la nourriture et des boissons. Il y a aussi un restaurant dans le train.**
They'll come around later with some food and drinks. There's also a restaurant on the train.

23. Jane: **Tiens, quand on parle du loup . . . Bonjour Monsieur, je voudrais un . . . deux Perrier, un jus d'orange, une bière et donc, juste un sandwich, un jambon-beurre, s'il vous plaît.**
Here, speak of the devil . . . Hello sir, I'd like one . . . two perriers, one orange juice, one beer and then, just one sandwich, ham and butter, please.

24. Charles: **Tu te rends compte, Jane, il faut moins de trois heures pour aller de Paris à Londres, et on ne sera dans le tunnel que pendant trente minutes!**
You realize, Jane, it takes less than three hours to go from Paris to London, and we'll be in the tunnel for only only thirty minutes!

25. Michel: **En fait, cela va très vite. On ne s'aperçoit de rien.**
In fact, it goes by very quickly. You don't notice a thing.

B. NOTES

1. *L'escalier roulant qui mène à* comes from the verb *mener à*: to lead to.

   L'Eurostar, inaugurated in 1994, is the train that runs from the *Gare du Nord* in Paris to Waterloo Station in London in two hours and 35 minutes. The fastest train in the world, it travels at speeds of up to 180 miles per hour. It also travels between London and Brussels, and London and Lille, in the North of France.

7. The idiomatic expression *en avoir pour longtemps* means: to take a long time.

   la queue: the line, as in *faire la queue*: to wait in line. It also means: the tail (of an animal).

10. The expression *falloir beaucoup de temps* means to need a lot of time.

    Nous voilà bien installés means *nous nous sommes bien installés*: We are (comfortably) settled in. The verb is *s'installer*, to settle in, to get comfortable.

13. *agacer, ennuyer*: to bother, to be a pain, to annoy

16. *avoir du travail à faire*: to have some work to do

23. *Quand on parle du loup . . . on voit sa queue* literally means: when you speak of the wolf, you see its tail. It's the equivalent of: "Speak of the devil!"

24. *se rendre compte*: to realize, to understand

C. GRAMMAR AND USAGE

1. The verbs *entendre* (to hear) and *voir* (to see) are followed by the infinitive when expressing another's actions

which are heard or seen. Often, these infinitives can be translated in English by the-*ing* form.

On a entendu une hôtesse annoncer le départ du train.
>We heard a hostess announcing the departure of the train.

Ils voient les voyageurs défiler devant la douane.
>They see the travelers walking in front of customs.

Avez-vous vu ce train passer?
>Have you seen this train passing by?

This construction is used in common idioms.

J'en ai entendu parler.
>I've heard about it. / I've heard it spoken of.

Nous avons entendu dire que ce train est le plus rapide du monde.
>We've heard (it said) that this train is the fastest in the world.

2. The irregular verb *vouloir* (to want) is followed by the subjunctive if the subject of *vouloir* is not the same as the subject of the second verb.

Qu'est-ce que tu veux que je fasse?
>What do you want me to do?

Je voudrais que vous veniez passer le week-end avec nous.
>I'd like you to come and spend the weekend with us.

Le douanier veut que nous ouvrions la valise.
>The customs agent wants us to open the suitcase.

Note that the infinitive is used when the subject of *vouloir* and the subordinate verb is the same. Compare the examples below with those above.

Qu'est que tu veux faire?
  What do you want to do?

Voudriez-vous venir passer le week-end avec nous?
  Would you like to come and spend the weekend with us?

Le douanier veut ouvrir la valise.
  The customs agent wants to open the suitcase.

3. Agreement of the past participle follows different rules depending on whether the main verb takes *être* or *avoir* as an auxiliary. With *avoir*, the participle does not agree unless the direct object is placed before the auxiliary. It then agrees in gender and number with the direct object.

Nous avons vu les hôtesses.
  We saw the hostesses.

Nous les avons vues.
  We saw them.

As-tu mangé les deux sandwiches?
  Did you eat the two sandwiches?

Les as-tu mangés?
  Did you eat them?

La grande voiture? Oui, nous l' avons louée.
  The big car? Yes we rented it.

Note that *que* counts as an object pronoun and triggers this agreement, too.

La voiture que nous avons louée est grande.
  The car we rented is big.

Les trains que vous avez vus sont en provenance de Bordeaux.
  The trains that you saw come from Bordeaux.

However *en* does not cause the participle to agree.

Des trains de Bordeaux? Oui, nous en avons vu cinq.
   Trains from Bordeaux? Yes, we've seen five of them.

With *être*, the participle always agrees in gender and number with the subject.

Charles et Jane sont partis ce matin.
   Charles and Jane left this morning.

Tu es soulagée, Madeleine!
   You're relieved, Madeleine!

Notre chienne est restée avec les enfants.
   Our dog (f.) stayed with the children.

Note that with reflexive and reciprocal verbs, which are always conjugated with *être* in a compound tense, the participle agrees with the subject only when the subject and the direct object are the same. In these first two examples, the subjects and the direct objects are the same, *nous* and *Jane.*

Nous nous sommes amusés tout au long du voyage.
   We had fun the whole trip.

Jane s'est lavée.
   Jane washed herself.

But in the following examples, the subjects are *Jane* and *je* but the direct objects are *les mains* and *les cheveux.*

Jane s'est lavé les mains.
   She washed her hands.

Je me suis coupé les cheveux.
   I cut my hair.

4. Verbs ending in *-cer* and verbs ending in *-ger* have a slight spelling change in their conjugations to conserve

pronunciation of the soft *c* and *g*. Remember that *c* and *g* are pronounced differently, hard before *a*, *o* or *u*, but soft before *e* and *i*. In order to preserve a soft pronunciation, *c* changes to *ç* and *g* changes to *ge* in conjugation before *a, o, u.*

Nous mangeons dans le train.
  We're eating on the train.

Je nageais quand il a commencé à pleuvoir.
  I was swimming when it started to rain.

Nous commençons demain.
  We're starting tomorrow.

Other common *-cer* verbs are: *avancer, menacer, annoncer, placer, prononcer,* and *remplacer,* and other common *-ger* verbs are: *arranger, corriger, songer, changer, nager,* and *partager.*

For all other tenses, see the Regular Verb Charts.

EXERCISES

A. Substitute each of the words in parentheses for the word or expression in the model sentence. Write the complete sentence and say aloud.

  1. *Nous avons entendu parler de cela. (l'Eurostar, la gare du Nord, le train, l'hôtesse)*

  2. *Ils sont partis hier. (rentrés, arrivés, venus, sortis)*

  3. *Nous les avons lus. (vus, écrits, achetés, regardés)*

B. Expand the clauses listed below by placing *J'ai entendu dire* in front of each of the following. Write, say, and translate.

  1. *qu'elle était arrivée.*

2. *que vous étiez à la gare.*

3. *que tu étais parti hier.*

Now place *Il ne veut pas* in front of each of the following, write, say, and translate.

4. *que vous dormiez dans le train.*

5. *que vous partiez en week-end.*

6. *que je fasse ce voyage.*

C. Say the following sentences aloud, and then translate them into English.

1. *Avez-vous entendu parler de ce train?*

2. *Je vois l'hôtesse arriver.*

3. *Il a raté le train.*

4. *Il ne me faut pas beaucoup de temps.*

5. *Je veux que vous partiez en vacances.*

D. Translate the following sentences into French. Then say them aloud.

1. I read them yesterday morning.

2. She arrived late.

3. It didn't take much time.

4. I was beginning to read when the train arrived in the station.

5. The friends we met in London were so nice.

E. From among the three choices, select the best translation for the English word or phrase given, write the complete sentence, and translate.

1. (line) *Regarde cette _____ !*

   ligne / queue / monde

2. (between) *C'est le tunnel _____ la France et l'Angleterre.*

   entre / contre / à travers

3. (leads) *C'est l'escalier roulant qui _____ au terminal.*

   va / guide / mène

4. (heard) *J'ai _____ qu'ils sont efficaces.*

   entendu / entendu dire / entendu parler

5. (settled) *Nous voici déjà _____ .*

   fatigués / installés / arrangés

6. (a long time) *Nous en aurons pour _____ .*

   un instant / longtemps / beaucoup de temps

7. (It took us) *_____ trois heures pour y aller.*

   Nous avons mis / Il nous a mis / Nous avons pris

8. (searched) *Les douaniers les (valises) ont _____ .*

   cherchées / fouillé / fouillées

Answer Key

A. 1. *Nous avons entendu parler de l'Eurostar. Nous avons entendu parler de la gare du Nord. Nous avons entendu parler du train. Nous avons entendu parler de l'hôtesse.* 2. *Ils sont rentrés hier. Ils sont arrivés hier. Ils sont venus hier. Ils sont sortis hier.* 3. *Nous les avons vus. Nous les avons écrits. Nous les avons achetés. Nous les avons regardés.*

B. 1. *J'ai entendu dire qu'elle était arrivée.* I heard that she had arrived. 2. *J'ai entendu dire que vous étiez à la gare.* I've heard that you were at the station. 3. *J'ai entendu dire que tu étais parti hier.* I heard that you had left yesterday. 4. *Il ne veut pas que vous dormiez dans le train.* He doesn't want you to sleep in the train. 5. *Il ne veut pas que vous partiez en week-end.* He doesn't want you to go away for the weekend. 6. *Il ne veut pas que je fasse ce voyage.* He doesn't want me to take this trip.

C. 1. Have you heard of this train? 2. I see the hostess coming. 3. He missed the train. 4. I don't need a lot of time. 5. I want you to go on vacation.

D. 1. *Je les ai lu(e)s hier matin.* 2. *Elle est arrivée en retard.* 3. *Cela n'a pas pris beaucoup de temps.* 4. *Je commençais à lire quand le train est entré en gare.* 5. *Les amis que nous avons rencontrés à Londres étaient si gentils.*

E. 1. *Regarde cette queue!* Look at that line! 2. *C'est le tunnel entre la France et l'Angleterre.* It's the tunnel between France and England. 3. *C'est l'escalier roulant qui mène au terminal.* It's the escalator that leads to the terminal. 4. *J'ai entendu dire qu'ils sont efficaces.* I've heard that they are efficient. 5. *Nous voici déjà installés.*

Here we are already settled in. 6. *Nous en aurons pour longtemps*. We'll be waiting for a long time. 7. *Nous avons mis trois heures pour y aller*. It took us three hours to get there. 8. *Les douaniers les ont fouillées*. The custom agents searched them.

LESSON 16

À LA BANQUE
AT THE BANK

A. DIALOGUE

0. *Charles se trouve au guichet de change d'une banque.*
   Charles is at the exchange window of a bank.

1. Charles: **Est-il possible de changer un chèque de voyage de cent dollars, s'il vous plaît?**
   Is it possible to change a hundred-dollar traveler's check, please?

2. Le caissier: **Certainement, monsieur. Vous n'avez qu'à le contresigner.**
   The cashier: Certainly, sir. You only have to endorse it.

3. Charles: **Quel est le taux du dollar en euros, monsieur?**
   How much is the dollar in euros, sir?

4. Le caissier: **Le taux est de 0,8119 aujourd'hui. Puis-je avoir votre passeport, s'il vous plaît?**
   The exchange rate is 0.8119 today. May I have your passport, please?

5. Charles: **Le voici, monsieur.**
   Here it is, sir.

6. Le caissier: **Avec notre commission en moins, qui est de 4%, cela fait 77,95 euros. Je vous les donne en coupures de 10 euros?**
   Less our commission, which is 4%, that comes to 77.95 euros. Would you like them in 10 euros bills?

7. Charles: **Très bien.**
Very well.

8. Le caissier: **Voilà, monsieur, soixante-dix-sept euros et quatre-vingt-quinze cents. Voici votre reçu.**
Here you are, sir, seventy-seven euros and ninety-five cents. Here's your receipt.

9. Charles: **Et pour un transfert de devises à l'étranger, à qui dois-je m'adresser?**
And for a transfer of funds to a foreign account, to whom should I speak?

10. Le caissier: **Adressez-vous au service international, monsieur.**
Go to international service, sir.

Au service international. At International Service.

11. L'agent de banque: **Que puis-je faire pour vous, monsieur?**
Bank teller: How can I help you, sir?

12. Charles: **Je voudrais faire un transfert de devises de mon compte aux États-Unis, et je voudrais faire payer les frais par ma banque à New York.**
I'd like to transfer some funds from my account in the United States, and I'd like to have the fees paid by my bank in New York.

13. L'agent de banque: **Il y a deux possibilités. Si vous voulez faire un virement en euros, il vous faudra payer une commission aux États-Unis. Si vous préférez faire un virement en dollars, vous la paierez ici. Nous aurons également besoin de renseignements sur votre banque aux États-Unis.**
There are two possibilities. If you want to transfer euros, you'll have to pay a commission in the United

States. If you prefer to transfer dollars, you'll pay it
here. We'll also need information on your bank in
America.

14. Charles: **Quand pourrais-je recevoir cet argent?**
    When could I receive this money?

15. L'agent de banque: **S'il n'y a pas de problème,
    vous devriez avoir votre argent dès demain
    matin.**
    If there's no problem, you should have your money
    as early as tomorrow morning.

16. Charles: **Excellent! Et, autre chose encore, en cas
    de besoin, pourrais-je louer un coffre-fort, ou
    bien ouvrir un compte ici?**
    Excellent! And, one more thing. If I needed to, could
    I rent a safe-deposit box or open an account here?

17. L'agent de banque: **Bien sûr. Nous sommes à votre
    disposition.**
    Of course. We are at your service.

18. Charles: **Que dois-je faire?**
    What do I have to do?

19. L'agent de banque: **Pour ouvrir un coffre-fort, il
    suffit de nous donner votre adresse permanente
    ainsi que vos références bancaires complètes, et
    bien sûr, il nous faut votre passeport.**
    To open a safe-deposit box, all you have to do is
    give us your permanent address as well as all your
    bank references, and of course we'll need your
    passport.

20. Charles: **D'accord. Et pour le compte en banque?**
    All right. And for the bank account?

21. L'agent de banque: **Il nous faut les mêmes renseignements mais, en plus, selon le compte que vous choisissez, vous devrez déposer une somme d'argent minimum.**
We need the same information, but, on top of that, depending on which account you open, you will have to make a minimum deposit.

22. Charles: **Et quelles sortes de comptes particuliers y a-t-il?**
And what types of personal accounts are there?

23. L'agent de banque: **Voici des prospectus qui vous en diront plus sur chaque compte. Le premier compte courant est un compte-chèque qui vous donne accès à un chéquier, un relevé bancaire mensuel gratuit et la possibilité d'obtenir une carte bancaire.**
Here's some literature which will tell you more about each account. The first common account is a checking account, which gives you access to a check book, a free monthly bank statement and the possibility of getting a bank card.

24. Charles: **Et est-ce que je peux avoir accès avec cette carte aux divers distributeurs de billets des grandes villes de France?**
And can I have access with this card to various ATM's in the large cities in France?

25. L'agent de banque: **Oui, bien sûr, nous avons plusieurs succursales répandues dans toutes les villes de France. Et vous pouvez utiliser aussi notre service en ligne.**
Yes, of course, we have several branches spread out in all the cities in France. And you also can use our online banking services.

26. Charles: **Merci beaucoup. Je vais lire tout ça. Commençons par le transfert, s'il vous plaît.**
Thanks a lot. I'm going to read all this. Let's start with the transfer, please.

27. L'agent de banque: **Voici, monsieur, un formulaire. Après l'avoir rempli, adressez-vous au guichet 4. Notre représentant s'occupera de votre transfert.**
Here's a form, sir. After filling it out, go to Window 4. Our representative will take care of your transfer.

28. Charles: **Merci beaucoup, monsieur. Devrai-je m'adresser à vous demain?**
Thank you very much, sir. Should I ask for you tomorrow?

29. L'agent de banque: **Oui, venez me voir directement.**
Yes, come see me directly.

30. Charles: **Alors, à demain!**
Until tomorrow, then!

B. NOTES

1. *Des chèques de voyage*, traveler's checks, can be changed in banks and in many other stores and businesses. Note that the English-derived term *le traveler's check* is often used in French.

3. *Le taux du dollar*, the (dollar) exchange rate, or *le taux de change*, is posted in all *banques et bureaux de change* and in most newspapers. The rate fluctuates daily, but it also varies from place to place on any given day.

4./6. Notice the use of *de* with rates, commissions, etc., as in *le taux est de . . .*

6. On top of the fluctuating exchange rate, most establishments will charge *une commission,* a commission for exchanging your currency. This varies from place to place, and again, it is wise to compare.

9./10. The verb *s'adresser à* means "to go to," "to report to," "to inquire at," or "to see" when referring to official capacities or situations. The expression *adresser la parole à quelqu'un* means "to address someone."

17. *être à la disposition de quelqu'un*, as in, *je suis à votre disposition*: to be at someone's service.

23. *Un prospectus* is a commercial information pamphlet.

25. *une succursale*: a branch
   répandu from the verb *répandre*: to spread out
   If you make use of *services bancaires en ligne*, online banking services, you'll be able to set up an account, *un compte bancaire*, where you can check on balances, *vérifier votre solde*, see if checks have cleared, *si les chèques ont été encaissés*, and do other transactions. You'll need a password, *un mot de passe*, to access it. And if you have direct deposit, *vous êtes payé par virement*, you may never need to go to the bank!

27. The reflexive verb *s'occuper de* means to handle, to deal with, to take care of.

C. GRAMMAR AND USAGE

1. French uses the expression *avant de* followed by the infinitive, which corresponds to the English "before" followed by an -ing verb.

Avant de me décider, je vais lire ces prospectus.
Before deciding, I'm going to read this literature.

Avant de faire quoi que ce soit, nous voudrions avoir des renseignements.
Before doing anything, we'd like to get some information.

Avant d'aller changer des devises à la banque, ils auraient dû se renseigner dans les bureaux de change du quartier.
Before changing currencies at the bank, they should have gotten some information in the exchange offices in the neighborhood.

2. Similarly, French uses the past infinitive after *après*. That is: *après* + (*avoir* or *être*) + past participle. If the verb is reflexive, the reflexive pronoun is kept. Don't forget the agreement with *être* or the direct object if it comes before *avoir*.

Après s'être décidée, Jane a ouvert un compte dans cette banque.
After deciding (having decided), Jane opened an account in this bank.

Après l'avoir vue, ils sont entrés dans la banque.
After seeing (having seen) her, they went into the bank.

Après avoir discuté avec Jane, Charles a décidé de faire un transfert.
After speaking (having spoken) with Jane, Charles decided to make a transfer.

Après avoir rempli ce formulaire, adressez-vous au guichett.
After filling (having filled) out this form, go to the window.

3. The perfect conditional is formed by using the conditional of *avoir* or *être* as appropriate, plus the past participle of the verb. Remember that the future / conditional stems of *avoir* and *être* are *aur-* and *ser-*.

j' aurais fait	I would have done / made
tu aurais fait	you would have done / made
il, elle, on aurait fait	she, he, it, one, we, they would have done / made
nous aurions fait	we would have done / made
vous auriez fait	you would have done / made
ils, elles auraient fait	they would have done / made
je serais entré(e)	I would have come in
tu serais entré(e)	you would have come in
il, on serait entré	he, it, one, we, they would have come in
elle serait entrée	she, it would have come in
nous serions entré(e)s	we would have come in
vous seriez entré(e)(s)	you would have come in
ils seraient entrés	they would have come in
elles seraient entrées	they would have come in

Note that the conditional perfect is generally used in French as it is in English.

Il aurait ouvert un compte dans cette banque.
    He would have opened an account in this bank.

Elle serait allée avec lui, mais elle est arrivée en retard.
    She would have gone with him, but she arrived late.

Ils se seraient entretenus avec le banquier, mais il n' était pas là.
    They would have spoken with the banker, but he wasn't there.

Note the special use of the conditional perfect of the verb *devoir*, which translates as "should have."

Il aurait dû payer la commission.
  He should have paid the commission.

Vous auriez dû apporter votre passeport.
  You should have brought you passport.

4. Both the conditional and the conditional perfect are often preceded by a clause introduced by *si*, that is "if", to express a hypothetical situation. If the main clause is in the conditional present, the clause with *si* is in the imperfect.

S'il avait sa carte de crédit, il retirerait de l'argent.
  If he had his credit card, he would withdraw some money.

Si j'avais le temps, j'irais à la banque.
  If I had time, I'd go to the bank.

If the main clause is in the conditional perfect, the clause with *si* is in the past perfect.

Si sa femme avait été là, elle l'aurait conseillé.
  If his wife had been here, she would have advised him.

S'il avait su les conditions, il aurait ouvert un compte dans cette banque.
  If he had known the conditions, he would have opened an account in this bank.

Notice that, just as in English, the present tense may be used in the clause introduced by *si*, followed by the present or future in the main clause. This expresses an if-then relationship that's not hypothetical or untrue.

S'il n'est pas trop tard, j'irai à la banque.
  If it's not too late, I'll go the bank.

Si on est dimanche, la banque est fermée.
  If it's Sunday today, the bank is closed.

Si tu veux, je t'y conduis.
  If you want, I'll take you there.

5. Most adverbs in French end in *-ment*, which corresponds to the English endings -ly or -ally. Many are based on the feminine form of the adjective, which simply adds *-ment*:

rapide	quick (f.)	*rapidement*	quickly
facile	easy (f.)	*facilement*	easily
heureuse	fortunate (f.)	*heureusement*	fortunately
certaine	certain (f.)	*certainement*	certainly
réelle	real, actual (f.)	*réellement*	really, actually

Some adverbs add an accent on the last *-e* on the feminine adjectives before adding *-ment*.

précise	precise (f.)	*précisément*	precisely
énorme	enormous (f.)	*énormément*	enormously
profonde	profound (f.)	*profondément*	profoundly

Adjectives ending in *-ant* or *-ent*, take *-amment* or *-emment* for their adverb form.

suffisant	sufficient (m.)	*suffisamment*	sufficiently
prudent	prudent (m.)	*prudemment*	prudently
évident	evident (m.)	*évidemment*	evidently
intelligent	intelligent (m.)	*intelligemment*	intelligently

Adjectives ending in a vowel simply take the suffix *-ment* directly onto the masculine form.

poli	polite	*poliment*	politely
vrai	real	*vraiment*	really
absolu	absolute	*absolument*	absolutely
véritable	true	*véritablement*	truly

Finally, they are a few adverbs that do not correspond to any of the above mentioned patterns.

gentil	kind	*gentiment*	kindly
bref	brief	*brièvement*	briefly

EXERCISES

A. Substitute each of the words or expressions in parentheses for the underlined word or expression in the model sentence. Write the complete sentence and say it aloud.

1. *Mangez avant de <u>partir</u>. (sortir, travailler, téléphoner, y aller)*

2. *Après avoir <u>mangé</u>, elle est partie. (étudié, travaillé, bu, dit "Au revoir")*

3. *Après être <u>rentrée</u>, elle m'a téléphoné. (arrivée, revenue, retournée, montée)*

4. *S'il avait fait beau, je serais <u>sorti</u>. (parti plus tôt, resté encore trois jours, arrivée à l'heure, allée à la banque à pied)*

B. Expand the following expressions by placing *avant de commencer* in the position indicated by the line. Say, write, and translate.

1. *Reposez-vous _____ .*

2. *Il faut réfléchir _____ .*

3. *_____ , je viendrai vous voir.*

4. *_____ , elle a téléphoné à son banquier.*

C. Expand the following by placing *Il parle* in front of each. Say and write each sentence.

1. _____ *constamment.*

2. _____ *prudemment.*

3. _____ *poliment.*

4. _____ *intelligemment.*

D. Translate the following sentences into French, then say them aloud.

1. She said good-bye to the director before leaving the bank.

2. Before saying no, make an effort.

3. After reading the literature, I decided to open an account.

4. After seeing my passport, they exchanged my traveler's check.

5. If she gives him enough information, he'll be able to fill out the form.

6. I'd give you all the details if I had the time for (*de*) it.

7. Fortunately, we have enough money.

8. You should have spoken to him before making a transfer.

9. If I wanted to transfer funds, I'd have spoken to the bank agent.

10. If we had known the rate was so low, we would not have taken any traveler's checks in dollars.

E. From among the three choices, select the best translation for the English word or phrase given, write the complete sentence, and translate.

1. (You need only to) _____ le contresigner.

   Vous devez absolument / Vous avez à / Vous n'avez qu'à

2. (show me) *Il faudra* _____ *une pièce d'identité.*

   montrez-moi / me montriez / me montrer

3. (Give them to me) _____ *en grosses coupures.*

   Donnez-les-moi / Donnez-le-lui/ Donnez-moi-le

4. (I'd like to) _____ *faire un transfert de devises.*

   Je voudrais / Je voulais / J'ai voulu

5. (computerized) *Toutes les transactions sont* _____.

   régularisées / comptées / informatisées

6. (as soon as) *Vous aurez votre argent* _____ *lundi.*

   bientôt / dès / aussi

7. (at your service) *Nous sommes* _____.

   à votre disposition / à votre servitude / à votre utilité

8. (It's enough to) _____ *nous donner vos références bancaires.*

   Il suffit de / Tout ce que vous avez faire / Tout que vous avez à faire, c'est de

Answer Key

A. 1. *Mangez avant de sortir. Mangez avant de travailler. Mangez avant de téléphoner. Mangez avant d'y aller.* 2. *Après avoir étudié, elle est partie. Après avoir travaillé, elle est partie. Après avoir bu, elle est partie. Après avoir dit "Au revoir", elle est partie.* 3. *Après être arrivée, elle m'a téléphoné. Après être revenue, elle m'a téléphoné. Après être retournée, elle m'a téléphoné. Après être montée, elle m'a téléphoné.* 4. *S'il avait fait beau, je serais parti plus tôt. S'il avait fait beau, je serais resté encore trois jours. S'il avait fait beau, je serais arrivée à l'heure. S'il avait fait beau, je serais allée à la banque à pied.*

B. 1. *Reposez-vous avant de commencer.* Rest before you begin. 2. *Il faut réfléchir avant de commencer.* It's necessary to reflect before beginning. 3. *Avant de commencer, je viendrai vous voir.* Before beginning, I'll come to see you. 4. *Avant de commencer, elle a téléphoné à son banquier.* Before beginning, she telephoned her banker.

C. 1. *Il parle constamment.* 2. *Il parle prudemment.* 3. *Il parle poliment.* 4. *Il parle intelligemment.*

D. 1. *Elle a dit au revoir au directeur avant de quitter la banque.* 2. *Avant de dire "non," faites un effort.* 3. *Après avoir lu les prospectus, j'ai décidé d'ouvrir un compte.* 4. *Après avoir vu mon passeport, ils ont échangé mon chèque de voyage.* 5. *Si elle lui donne assez d'informations, il pourra remplir le formulaire.* 6. *Je vous donnerais tous les détails, si j'(en) avais le temps.* 7. *Heureusement, nous avons assez d'argent.* 8. *Vous auriez dû lui parler avant de faire un transfert.* 9. *Si je voulais faire un transfert, j'aurais parlé à l'agent de banque.* 10. *Si nous avions su que le taux était si bas, nous n'aurions pas pris de chèques de voyage en dollars.*

E. 1. *Vous n'avez qu'à le contresigner.* You need only to countersign it. 2. *Il faudra me montrer une pièce d'identité.* You will have to show me some identification. 3. *Donnez-les-moi en grosses coupures.* Give them to me in large bills. 4. *Je voudrais faire un transfert de devises.* I'd like to transfer some funds. 5. *Toutes les transactions sont informatisées.* All transactions are computerized. 6. *Vous aurez votre argent dès lundi.* You'll have your money as soon as Monday. 7. *Nous sommes à votre disposition.* We're at your service. 8. *Il suffit de nous donner vos références bancaires.* It's enough to give us your bank references.

LESSON 17

À LA POSTE
AT THE POST OFFICE

A. DIALOGUE

0. *Jane se trouve à La Poste.*
   Jane is at the Post Office.

1. Jane: **Bonjour, madame. Je voudrais envoyer ces trois lettres aux États-Unis.**
   Hello, ma'am. I'd like to send these three letters to the United States.

2. Un agent de La Poste: **Vous avez un distributeur de timbres où vous pouvez peser votre courrier et acheter les timbres nécessaires. Ou bien, vous pouvez faire la queue pour les guichets.**
   Postal Clerk: There's a stamp machine, where you can weigh your mail and buy the necessary stamps. Or you can wait on line for the windows.

3. Jane: **Oui, je crois que je vais faire la queue car j'ai aussi d'autres choses à poster.**
   Yes, I think I'm going to wait on line because I also have other things to send.

4. L'agent 2: **Oui, madame?**
   Clerk #2: Yes, madam?

5. Jane: **Bonjour, j'ai trois lettres et aussi un colis à envoyer à New York.**
   Hello, I have three letters and also a package to send to New York.

6. L'agent 2: **Par avion?**
   By air mail?

7. Jane: **Oui, s'il vous plaît.**
   Yes, please.

8. L'agent 2: **Pour les lettres, 1,20 euro chacune.
   Pour le colis, il faut d'abord que je le pèse.
   Veuillez remplir cette fiche de douane.**
   For the letters, 1.20 euros each. For the package, I
   have to weigh it first. Please fill out this customs slip.

9. Jane: **En fait, je voudrais l'envoyer en recommandé.**
   In fact, I'd like to send it by registered mail.

10. L'agent 2: **D'accord. Avec accusé de réception?
    Bien. Voyons. 2 kilos. Cela fait 25,80 euros. Quel
    en est le contenu et la valeur?**
    Okay. With a return receipt? Yes. Let's see. 2 kilos.
    That comes to 25.80 euros. What are the contents,
    and the value?

11. Jane: **Des DVDs, des CDs, et de la confiserie. À
    peu près 100 euros.**
    DVDs, CDs, and some sweets. It's about 100 euros.

12. L'agent 2: **Bien. Indiquez tout cela sur cette fiche.**
    Okay. Indicate all that on this form.

13. Jane: **Voici. Et j'ai une lettre à envoyer qui doit
    absolument arriver demain.**
    Here it is. And I have a letter to send that absolutely
    has to get there tomorrow.

14. L'agent 2: **Est-ce pour New York? Ah, non, pour
    Paris . . .**
    Is it for New York? Ah no, for Paris . . .

15. Jane: **Oui, monsieur.**
    Yes, sir.

16. L'agent 2: **Pourquoi ne l'envoyez-vous pas en Chronopost? Ainsi, la lettre parviendra au destinataire en vingt-quatre heures.**
Why don't you send it by Chronopost? That way it'll reach the addressee within twenty-four hours.

17. Jane: **Oui, c'est parfait.**
Yes, that's fine.

18. L'agent 2: **Donc, pour le Chronopost, 24 euros. Ce sera tout? D'accord, cela vous fait en tout 52 euros et vingt centimes.**
So, for the Chronopost, 24 euros. Will that be all? Okay, all together, it's 52 euros and 20 cents.

19. Jane: **Voici. Merci. Et où dois-je m'adresser pour savoir si j'ai reçu du courrier?**
Here it is. Thanks. And where do I have to inquire to find out if I've gotten any mail?

20. L'agent 2: **Adressez-vous au guichet poste restante, madame.**
Inquire at the General Delivery window, ma'am.

21. *Au guichet poste restante.*
At the General Delivery window.

22. Jane: **Bonjour, madame. Y a-t-il du courrier pour moi, s'il vous plaît? Mon nom est Jane Lewis**.
Good day, ma'am. Is there any mail for me, please? My name is Jane Lewis.

23. L'agent 3: **Voyons. Oui, madame. Je vois que vous avez plusieurs cartes postales, un mandat-poste, et une lettre recommandée. Vous avez une pièce d'identité?**
Clerk #3: Let's see. Yes, Ma'am. I can see that you have several postcards, a postal money order, a registered letter. Do you have a piece of ID?

24. Jane: **Oui, j'ai mon passeport.**
Yes, I have my passport.

25. L'agent: **Oui. Merci. Cela fait 2,50 euros. Voici votre courrier.**
Yes, thank you. That's 2.50 euros. Here's your mail.

B. NOTES

Title: Apart from buying stamps, mailing letters, and using the Minitel, it's also possible to open an account at the French Post Office, *La Poste*, which offers banking services.

3. *poster, expédier* or *envoyer*: to send, to mail

5. *un colis*: a package, *une carte postale*: a postcard, *une lettre*: a letter, *un télégramme*: a telegram, *peser*: to weigh, *le poids*: the weight, *un timbre*: a stamp and *timbrer*: to stamp, to put a stamp on, *un carnet de timbres*: a book of stamps.

9. *envoyer une lettre en recommandé avec accusé de réception*: to send a registered letter with receipt.

16. *Chronopost* is an express mail service attached to *La Poste* in France.

20. *la poste restante*: General Delivery. Many travelers to larger cities abroad have their mail sent to the local post office.

23. *Un mandat* is a money order, *un mandat-poste*: a postal money order

C. GRAMMAR AND USAGE

1. The prepositions *en* and *dans* can both be used in time expressions. *En* means within a given period of time, and *dans* means at the end of a given period of time.

   Avec Chronopost, votre courrier arrivera en 24 heures.
   > With Chronopost, your mail will arrive within / in 24 hours.

   Dans une semaine, ils recevront votre colis.
   > In/After one week, they'll receive your package.

2. The idiomatic expression *avoir à* followed by the infinitive corresponds to "to have to" + infinitive.

   J'ai un colis à envoyer en recommandé.
   > I have a package to send by registered mail.

   Il a aussi quatre lettres à poster.
   > He also has four letters to mail.

   Nous avons beaucoup à faire.
   > We have a lot to do.

   Vous n'avez donc rien à faire?
   > Don't you have anything to do?

3. Object pronouns can be used with infinitive verbs as much as with conjugated ones. They usually precede the infinitives. If there are several pronouns, the rules for the order of the object pronouns are the same as for use after conjugated verbs.

   Je dois d'abord le peser.
   > I have to first weigh it.

   Il faut l'envoyer avant demain.
   > We must send it before tomorrow.

   Il veut me conduire à la Poste.
   > He wants to drive me to the Post Office.

Nous allons le lui envoyer.
     We're going to send it to him.

EXERCISES

A. Substitute each of the words in parentheses for the underlined word or expression in the model sentence. Write the complete sentence and say it aloud.

1. *Nous avons <u>une lettre</u> à écrire. (un livre, une carte postale, une invitation, un télégramme)*

2. *J'ai ce colis à <u>faire</u>. (commencer, finir, envoyer)*

3. *Il faut l'<u>envoyer</u>. (comprendre, lire, timbrer)*

4. *Elles <u>veulent</u> nous parler. (peuvent, doivent, vont)*

B. Expand the following by placing *l'envoyer en recommandé* at the end of each sentence. Say, write, and translate.

1. *Il veut* _____.

2. *Il voulait* _____.

3. *Il voudra* _____.

4. *Il voudrait* _____.

5. *Il a voulu* _____.

6. *Il avait voulu* _____.

7. *Il aurait voulu* _____.

C. Translate the following sentences into French; then say them aloud.

1. I'll see you again in three weeks.

2. Can you finish the work within an hour?

3. I have a money order to send you.

4. Do you have a package to send by registered mail with receipt?

5. We have to write several letters in one hour.

6. I can sell you three books of stamps.

7. She's going to mail it later.

8. Could you weigh this package for me?

D. From among the three choices, select the best translation for the English word or phrase given, write the complete sentence, and translate.

1. (I'd like) _____ envoyer ces lettres.

   Je voulais / Je me plais / Je voudrais

2. (Airmail?) _____?

   Avion courrier / En avion / Par avion

3. (within) *Il lui parviendra* _____ *vingt-quatre heures.*

   en / dans / dedans

4. (me) *Y a-t-il du courrier pour* _____?

   me / moi / je

5. (Weigh them) *Elle doit* _____.

   les peser / peser les / leur peser

6. (in/after) *La lettre arrivera* _____ *cinq jours.*

   en / dans / dedans

7. (to send) *J'ai aussi un colis* _____.

   expédier / pour expédier / à expédier

8. (registered) *Je voudrais aussi l'envoyer* _____.

   en commande / recommander / en recommandé

Answer Key

A. 1. *Nous avons un livre à écrire. Nous avons une carte postale à écrire. Nous avons une invitation à écrire. Nous avons un télégramme à écrire.* 2. *J'ai ce colis à commencer. J'ai ce colis à finir. J'ai ce colis à envoyer.* 3. *Il faut le comprendre. Il faut le lire. Il faut le timbrer.* 4. *Elles peuvent nous parler. Elles doivent nous parler. Elles vont nous parler.*

B. 1. *Il veut l'envoyer en recommandé.* He wants to send it by registered mail. 2. *Il voulait l'envoyer en recommandé.* He wanted to send it by registered mail. 3. *Il voudra l'envoyer en recommandé.* He will want to send it by registered mail. 4. *Il voudrait l'envoyer en recommandé.* He would like to send it by registered mail. 5. *Il a voulu l'envoyer en recommandé.* He wanted to send it by registered mail. 6. *Il avait voulu l'envoyer en recommandé.* He had wanted to send it by registered mail. 7. *Il aurait voulu l'envoyer en recommandé.* He would have wanted to send it by registered mail.

C. 1. *Je vous reverrai dans trois semaines.* 2. *Pouvez-vous finir le travail en une heure?* 3. *J'ai un mandat à vous envoyer.* 4. *Avez-vous un colis à envoyer en recommandé avec accusé de réception?* 5. *Nous avons à écrire plusieurs lettres en une heure.* 6. *Je peux vous vendre trois carnets de timbres.* 7. *Elle va le/la poster plus tard.* 8. *Pouvez-vous peser ce paquet pour moi?*

D. 1. *Je voudrais envoyer ces lettres.* I would like to send these letters. 2. *Par avion?* By airmail? 3. *Il lui parviendra en vingt-quatre heures.* It will reach him within twenty-four hours. 4. *Y a-t-il du courrier pour moi?* Is there some mail for me? 5. *Elle doit les peser.* She has to weigh them. 6. *La lettre arrivera dans cinq jours.* The letter will arrive in five days. 7. *J'ai aussi un colis à expédier.* I also have a package to send. 8. *Je voudrais aussi l'envoyer en recommandé.* I'd also like to send it by registered mail.

LESSON 18

ON FAIT DU SHOPPING
WE DO SOME SHOPPING

A. DIALOGUE

0. *Jane, en compagnie de Marianne, vient de déjeuner avec Frédérique, la sœur de Marianne. Alors que Frédérique va prendre le métro, les deux amies se baladent aux Halles, en vue d'acheter des vêtements pour la fille de Jane. Par hasard, elles rencontrent Étienne, le mari de Frédérique.*

   Jane, along with Marianne, has just had lunch with Frédérique, Marianne's sister. While Frédérique is going to get the metro, the two friends are walking around the Halles, with an eye toward buying some clothes for Jane's daughter. By chance, they meet Étienne, Frédérique's husband.

1. Marianne: **Salut! C'est marrant, on vient juste de laisser Fréd. Étienne, tu connais Jane, en visite des États-Unis?**

   Hi! That's funny, we just left Fred. Étienne, I'm not sure if you know Jane, visiting from the U.S.

2. Étienne: *(Il serre la main à Jane)* **Non. Par contre, Frédérique m'a beaucoup parlé de vous. Enchanté. Qu'est-ce que vous faites de beau par ici?**

   (He shakes Jane's hand) No. But Frédérique has talked to me a lot about you. Pleased to meet you. What are you doing around here?

3. Jane: **Nous venons de déjeuner avec votre femme et Marianne me fait le plaisir de m'accompagner pour faire quelques courses.**

We've just had lunch with your wife and Marianne is nice enough to come along with me to run a few errands.

4. Marianne: **Jane désire acheter des vêtements à sa fille. Tu peux nous conseiller quelques boutiques? La fille de Jane a l'âge de ta fille.**
Jane wants to buy some clothes for her daughter. Can you recommend some stores? Jane's daughter is your daughter's age.

5. Étienne: **Tu me demandes ça à moi? Des restos, peut-être . . . Bon, je file car je dois finir mes livraisons avant seize heures. Bonne après-midi et à la prochaine!**
You're asking me that? Restaurants, maybe . . . Anyway, I have to run, because I have to finish my deliveries before 4 p.m. Have a good afternoon and see you soon!

6. Marianne: **À toi aussi. Ciao. Bon, voyons, voyons . . . Tu sais, Jane, moi aussi, je devrais faire des achats. Ma fille fête ses douze ans le mois prochain. Que le temps passe vite!**
You, too. Ciao. Well, let's see. You know Jane, I should do some shopping, too. My daughter's celebrating her twelfth birthday next month. How quick time goes by!

7. Jane: **Et bien, unissons nos efforts, et amène-moi aux boutiques préférées de Sonja.**
Well, let's combine our efforts, and bring me to Sonja's favorite stores.

8. *Dans une boutique de vêtements.*
In a clothing store.

9. Le vendeur: *(à Jane)* **Quelle taille fait-elle?**
Salesman: (to Jane) What size is she?

10. Jane: **Je crois que cela correspond à votre 36.**
    I think it corresponds to your 36.

11. Le vendeur: **Tenez, voici ce pantalon en 36, mais
    dans d'autres coloris. Il est en coton spandex. Il a
    beaucoup de succès . . . Il peut se porter habillé
    ou décontracté.**
    Here is this pair of pants in 36, but in other colors.
    It's in cotton and spandex. It's very popular. It can
    be worn dressed-up or casual.

12. Marianne: **Il n'est pas mal du tout. Il est bien
    coupé et c'est un modèle bien à la mode ici.**
    It's not bad at all. It's nicely cut and this is quite a
    fashionable style here.

13. Jane: **Oui, je crois que cela devrait lui plaire. En
    plus, il est en solde. Je vais le prendre.**
    I think she should like it. Plus, it's on sale. I'm going
    to take it.

14. Marianne: **Regarde ces robes à pois. Elles sont
    plutôt jolies, non? En soie.**
    Look at these polka-dot dresses. They're pretty nice,
    aren't they? In silk.

15. Jane: **Oui, c'est joli . . . Quelles couleurs avez-
    vous?**
    Yes, it's nice . . . What colors do you have?

16. Le vendeur: **Tout est là, Madame. Vous les avez en
    noir, rouge, bleu et marron.**
    Everything's here, Ma'am. They come in black, red,
    blue and brown.

17. Marianne: **Voyons le bleu en . . . Cela taille petit,
    on dirait, non?**
    Let's see the blue one in . . . It runs small, right?

18. Le vendeur: **Un peu. Il vaut toujours mieux prendre une taille au-dessus.**
    A little. It's always better to take a larger size.

19. Marianne: **Hmm . . . Donnez-moi un 14 ans, s'il vous plaît. Je crois que cela devrait aller pour Sonja. Elle est si mince.**
    Hmm . . . Give me a 14-years, please. I think this should be fine for Sonja. She's so skinny.

20. Jane: **Oui, ça a l'air bien . . . En plus, cela lui ira bien au teint.**
    Yes, it looks good . . . Besides, it will go well with her complexion.

21. Marianne: **C'est vrai. Mais j'ai quand même peur qu'elle soit un peu trop étriquée. Bon, au cas où il y aurait un problème, il est possible d'échanger, n'est-ce pas?**
    That's true. But I'm still afraid it's a bit too tight. Well, in case there's a problem, it's possible to exchange, isn't it?

22. Le vendeur: **Oui, madame, mais il faut conserver le ticket de caisse et ramener l'article dans les quinze jours. Aussi, nous pouvons échanger mais pas rembourser.**
    Yes, Ma'am, but you have to keep the receipt and bring back the article within fifteen days. Also, we can exchange but not reimburse.

24. Marianne: **Bon, je prends le 14 ans. Vous acceptez les chèques?**
    Well, I'll take this one for 14-year-olds. Do you accept checks?

Plus tard, après plusieurs achats et une pause-café . . .
Later, after several purchases and a coffee break . . .

25. Jane: **Eh bien, il ne me reste plus qu'à trouver des gants pour moi et tout sera fait.**
Well, I just need to find some gloves for myself and that will take care of everything.

26. Marianne: **En fait, je connais un magasin de chaussures qui vend d'autres articles en cuir. Allons-y!**
In fact, I know a shoe store that sells other leather goods, Let's go!

27. Jane: **Je voudrais des gants, de couleur foncée de préférence et plutôt habillés. Ceux qui sont présentés en vitrine semblent très bien. Puis-je les voir? Non, je ne connais pas ma pointure.**
I'd like some gloves, preferably in a dark color, and rather dressy. The ones that are on display in the window seem to be nice. May I see them? No, I don't know my size.

28. Le vendeur: **Voici Madame, essayez cette pointure. Ils existent en deux couleurs: marron et noir. Vous avez aussi cette paire en daim ou en cuir. Nous venons juste de les recevoir en beige et bleu marine pour le modèle en cuir et en fauve et en noir pour celui en daim. Ils sont tous doublés.**
Salesman: Here they are, Ma'am. Try this size. They come in two colors, brown and black. You also have this pair in suede or leather. We've just got them in beige and dark blue for the model in leather, and in fawn and black for the one in suede. They all have a lining.

29. Jane: **Ils sont très beaux. Le cuir est très souple. Je choisis ceux-là en noir. Cela fera merveilleusement l'affaire.**
They're very beautiful. The leather is so soft. I'll take those in black. This will be great.

30. Marianne: **Bon, il semble que tout le monde ait trouvé son bonheur.**
Well, it seems that everyone has found what they were looking for.

B. NOTES

0. *Faire du shopping, faire les boutiques*, and *faire des achats* all mean: to do some shopping, while *faire des courses* means: to run some errands or to shop.

Les Halles is a famous neighborhood in the *premier arrondissement*. It is also *une galerie marchande souterraine*, which is a type of underground mall.

en vue de: in view of, in order to, with an eye toward. There are many expressions starting with *en*: *en compagnie de*: in the company of, along with, *en bleu*: in blue, *en cuir*: in leather, *en haut*: on the top, *en français*: in French, *en visite*: visiting, *en vitrine*: in the display window, etc.

des vêtements or *des habits*: clothing. In slang, *des fringues*. The corresponding verbs are *s'habiller*: to dress or *porter un vêtement*: to wear a piece of clothing.

par hasard: by chance

la sœur de Fred, la fille de Jane, le mari de . . . Note that the possessive case in French is like the English possessive case for objects, using the preposition *de*, that is "of."

2. *par contre:* on the other hand

4. *Comme vêtements,* as clothes, there are: *le chapeau*: hat, *le manteau*: coat, *l'imperméable*: raincoat, *la veste*: jacket, *le chemisier*: blouse, *la chemise*: shirt, *le pull-over*:

sweater, *la jupe*: skirt, *le pantalon*: pants, *la robe*: dress, *le short*: shorts, *le survêtement*: jogging or track suit, *la salopette*: overalls, *les chaussures*: shoes, *les bottes*: boots, *la ceinture*: belt, *le chapeau*: hat, *les gants*: gloves, *les sous-vêtements*: underwear, *le soutien-gorge*: bra, *le tricot de peau*: undershirt, *les chaussettes*: socks, *les collants*: tights, stockings, *le foulard*, *l'écharpe*: scarf, etc.

6. *célébrer ses douze ans*: to celebrate her twelfth year's birthday and *avoir douze ans*: to be twelve years old. From the verb *célébrer*, the adjective *célèbre* is famous. Also: *Quel âge a-t-il? Quel âge a-t-elle?*: How old is he? How old is she? Note that French uses the verb *avoir* (to have).

7. *une boutique*: a shop or *un magasin*: a store, as in *une boutique de vêtements, un magasin de chaussures*.

9. *le vendeur, la vendeuse*: the salesman, the saleswoman, *la vente*: the sale, the verb is *vendre*, to sell. Also, the expressions: *les soldes*: articles on sale.

   Quelle taille fait-elle? What size is she? Regarding the sizes, French uses *la taille* for all clothing but gloves, hat and shoes, which use: *la pointure*.

11. *Il est en coton spandex*: It's in cotton-spandex. *Le coton*, like *la laine* (wool), *la soie* (silk) are called *des tissus*, fabrics. Some other fabrics are: *le lin* (linen), *le velours* (velvet), *le velours côtelé* (corduroy), *l'acrylique*, *le nylon*, etc.

   Un vêtement peut faire habillé ou décontracté: A piece of clothing can look dressy or casual.

14. *à pois*: with polka-dots, *à rayures*: with stripes, *uni*: solid (color).

19./20. *Cela devrait lui aller*: It should fit her. The verb *aller bien* or *aller mal* corresponds to "to fit", but also "to match": *Cela lui va bien au teint*. It matches her complexion.

21. *Étriqué* or *serré* means tight. The opposite is *grand*: large, loose.

27. *une couleur foncée*: a dark color and *une couleur claire*: a light color.

C. GRAMMAR AND USAGE

1. As you saw in the first lesson, some verbs are followed by a preposition when introducing a second verb in the infinitive form. Since there is no rule about which verbs use which preposition, it's best to study the forms as they come.

Some verbs are followed by *de*: *venir de, décider de, recommander de, demander de, finir de*, etc.

Elles viennent de faire des achats.
   They have just run some errands.

Elles ont décidé d'acheter des vêtements pour leurs filles.
   They have decided to buy some clothes for their daughters.

La sœur de Frédérique leur recommande d'aller dans cette boutique.
   Frédérique's sister advises them to go in this shop.

On lui demande de nous montrer une petite taille.
   We ask her to show us a small size.

Elles ont fini de faire leurs courses.
   They finished shopping.

Others are followed by *à*: *aider à, réussir à, commencer à, tenir à, apprendre à*, etc.

Mon amie m'aide à choisir une chemise pour ma fille.
My friend helps me choose a shirt for my daughter.

On a réussi à tout faire en quelques heures.
We managed to do it all in a few hours.

Il a commencé à pleuvoir dès que nous sommes sortis.
It started to rain as soon as we went out.

Elle tient à acheter des vêtements pour son anniversaire.
She really wants to buy some clothing for her birthday.

Ils ont appris à parler français.
They learned how to speak French.

2. The verbs *mener* and *préférer* take an accent in their conjugation in the present tense. Study these forms and notice the places that take an accent.

mener (to lead)
je mène	*nous menons*
tu mènes	*vous menez*
il/elle/on mène	*ils/elles mènent*

préférer (to prefer)
je préfère	*nous préférons*
tu préfères	*vous préférez*
il/elle/on préfère	*ils/elles préfèrent*

Note that other verbs derived from *mener* follow the same pattern: *amener* (to bring), *emmener* (to take someone somewhere), *ramener* (to bring back). So does *acheter* (to buy). Other common verbs conjugated like *préférer* are: *espérer* (to hope), *protéger* (to protect), *répéter* (to repeat)

3. Past participles used as adjectives are common in French. Like adjectives, these past participles agree in number and gender with the nouns they modify.

Ils sont tous doublés.
They all have a lining.

Ce pantalon est bien coupé.
These pants are nicely cut.

J'ai acheté des vêtements habillés.
I bought some dressy clothes.

Voici la boutique préférée de ma fille.
Here's my daughter's favorite store.

EXERCISES

A. Substitute each of the words or expressions in parentheses for the underlined word or expression in the model sentence. Write the complete sentence and say it aloud.

1. *Il a décidé de __partir__. (rentrer, étudier, m'aider, le faire)*

2. *J'ai appris à __conduire__. (danser, jouer aux cartes, jouer au tennis, jouer du piano)*

B. Change these sentences to the negative. Say, write, and translate.

1. *Je préfère ces gants-ci.*

2. *Ils préfèrent les autres chemises.*

3. *Nous essayons les vêtements.*

4. *Ma sœur nous amène dans des boutiques à la mode.*

5. *Elle mène une vie heureuse.*

6. *Nous achetons des robes en soie.*

C. Translate the following sentences into French; then say them aloud.

    1. I'll ask her to come along with me to run some errands.

    2. They began to walk quickly in the mall.

    3. Don't leave without paying for the clothes.

    4. She brings her daughter a pair of pants from France.

    5. Which fabric do you prefer?

    6. This overall looks too casual.

    7. This size of sweater is too big.

    8. This dress is well cut.

D. From among the three choices, select the best translation for the English word or phrase given. Write the complete sentence, and translate.

    1. (relaxed) *Elle veut une tenue* _____.

    fatiguée / décontractée / serrée

    2. (What kind of fabric) *Qu'est-ce que c'est* _____?

    tissu / de tissu / comme tissu

    3. (would be better) *Le coton* _____ *que la soie.*

    ferait mieux / ferait mieux l'affaire / serait une meilleure affaire

    4. (He's a size) _____ *38.*

    C'est une taille / Il fait de la taille / Il fait du

    5. (polka-dotted overall) *J'aimerais acheter une* _____.

    salopette à rayures / salopette à pois / salopette tachée

6. (to buy) *Elle nous a demandé* _____ *des bottes.*

   acheter / à acheter / d' acheter

7. (prefer) *Je* _____ *celui-ci.*

   prefere / préfére / préfère

8. (on sale) *Cette jupe est* _____.

   à vendre / en vente / en solde

Answer Key

A. 1. *Il a décidé de rentrer. Il a décidé d'étudier. Il a décidé de m'aider. Il a décidé de le faire.* 2. *J'ai appris à danser. J'ai appris à jouer aux cartes. J'ai appris à jouer au tennis. J'ai appris à jouer du piano.*

B. 1. *Je ne préfère pas ces gants-ci.* I don't prefer these gloves. 2. *Ils ne préfèrent pas les autres chemises.* They don't prefer the other shirts. 3. *Nous n'essayons pas les vêtements.* We don't try the clothes. 4. *Ma sœur ne nous amène pas dans des boutiques à la mode.* My sister does not bring us into some fashionable stores. 5. *Elle ne mène pas une vie heureuse.* She doesn't lead a happy life. 6. *Nous n'achetons pas les robes en soie.* We are not buying the dresses in silk.

C. 1. *Je lui demanderai de venir avec moi faire des courses.* 2. *Ils ont commencé à marcher rapidement dans la galerie marchande.* 3. *Ne partez pas sans payer les vêtements.* 4. *Elle ramène un pantalon de France à sa fille.* 5. *Quel tissu préférez-vous?* 6. *Cette salopette fait trop décontracté.* 7. *Cette taille de pull est trop grande.* 8. *La robe est bien coupée.*

D. 1. *Elle veut une tenue décontractée.* She wants a casual outfit. 2. *Qu'est-ce que c'est comme tissu?* What kind of fabric is it? 3. *Le coton ferait mieux l'affaire que la soie.* Cotton would be better than silk. 4. *Il fait du 38.* He's a size 38. 5. *J'aimerais acheter une salopette à pois.* I would like to buy a polka-dotted jumper. 6. *Elle nous a demandé d'acheter des bottes.* She asked us to buy some boots. 7. *Je préfère celui-ci.* I prefer this one. 8. *Cette jupe est en solde.* This skirt is on sale.

LESSON 19

QUELQUES PROBLÈMES DE SANTÉ
A FEW HEALTH PROBLEMS

A. DIALOGUE

0. *Frédérique amène Jane chez son dentiste, car elle a très mal aux dents. Arrivées au cabinet du dentiste, elles suivent les instructions affichées à la porte: "Sonnez et entrez."*

    Frédérique brings Jane to her dentist's, because she has a bad toothache. Once they arrive at the dentist's office, they follow the instructions posted on the door: "Ring and come in."

1. Le réceptioniste: **Bonjour Mesdames. Est-ce que vous avez rendez-vous?**

    Receptionist: Hello, ladies. Do you have an appointment?

2. Frédérique: **Oui, je suis Madame Montès et je vous ai téléphoné hier après-midi pour prendre un rendez-vous d'urgence pour madame Jane Lewis. Son rendez-vous est à trois heures. Nous sommes un peu en avance.**

    Yes, I am Mrs. Montès and I called you yesterday afternoon to make an emergency appointment for Mrs. Jane Lewis. Her appointment is at 3 p.m. We're a bit early.

3. Le réceptioniste: **Ah oui. Je vais avertir le Docteur Signoret qui est avec un client en ce moment. En attendant, veuillez patienter s'il vous plaît, dans la salle d'attente. Nous vous appellerons dès que c'est à vous.**

Ah yes, I'll tell Doctor Signoret, who is with a client right now. In the meantime, please have a seat in the waiting room. We'll call you as soon as it's your turn.

4. *Un quart d' heure plus tard.*
   Fifteen minutes later.

5. Le dentiste: **Ah, bonjour Madame Montès, comment allez-vous? Ah, oui, enchanté Madame Lewis, enfin, même si ce n'est pas la meilleure des occasions pour faire connaissance!**
   Dentist: Good afternoon, Mrs. Montès, how are you? Ah yes, pleased to meet you, Mrs. Lewis, well, even if it's not the best occasion to make an acquaintance!

6. Jane: (*avec difficulté*) **Enchantée, Docteur.**
   (with difficulty) Pleased to meet you, Doctor.

7. Le dentiste: **Bien, entrez et asseyez-vous, on va voir ça de près.**
   Well, come in and sit down, we'll take a closer look.

8. Jane: **J'ai une dent qui me fait terriblement mal depuis deux jours. Elle me faisait mal aussi il y a trois semaines, mais pas autant. C'est celle du fond à droite.**
   I have a tooth that's been hurting me terribly for two days. It also hurt me three weeks ago, but not so much. It's the one in the back on the right.

9. Le dentiste: **Oui, je vois. Les gencives sont enflées et elles saignent un peu.**
   Yes, I see. The gums are swollen and they're bleeding a little.

10. Jane: **Oui, quand je me brosse les dents aussi.**
    Yes, when I brush my teeth, too.

11. Le dentiste: **Ah! Je vois maintenant ce dont vous vous plaignez. C'est une des molaires inférieures, à droite. Je ne pense pas que ce soit très grave, mais on va faire une radio pour s'en assurer.**
Ah! Now I see what you're complaining about. It's one of the lower right molars. I don't think it's very serious, but we're going to do an X-ray to make sure.

12. Jane: **D'accord.**
Okay.

13. Le dentiste: **Penchez la tête en arrière et ouvrez la bouche, s'il vous plaît. Fermez-la bouche. Un, deux, trois, quatre . . . Voilà!**
Lean your head back and open your mouth, please. Close your mouth. One, two, three, four . . . There we go!

15. Jane: **Déjà?**
Already?

16. Le dentiste: **Et oui! Les radios seront prêtes dans quelques minutes. En attendant, je vais examiner les autres dents. Non, le reste semble aller. Vous pouvez vous rincer la bouche si vous voulez. Je reviens aussitôt.**
Yes! The X-rays will be ready in a few minutes. In the meantime, I'm going to examine the other teeth. No, the rest seem fine. You can rinse your mouth out if you want. I'll be right back.

17. Le dentiste: **Bon, regardons la radiographie. Mmmm. Vous avez une bonne carie, mais la racine paraît saine.**
Let's look at the X-ray. Mmmm. You have a nice cavity, but the root seems healthy.

18. Jane: **Alors, ce n'est qu'une dent cariée? Va-t-il falloir l'arracher?**

It's only a decayed tooth, then? Is it going to be necessary to pull it out?

19. Le dentiste: **Non, il ne faudra pas l'arracher. Il va juste falloir nettoyer la dent et faire un plombage.**
No, it won't be necessary to pull it out. We'll just need to clean the tooth and do a filling.

20. Jane: **Allez-vous me faire une anesthésie? Je suis très sensible. Je ne peux pas supporter la douleur. Il y a deux ans, je me suis évanouie chez le dentiste!**
Are you going to give me an anesthetic? I'm very sensitive. I can't take any pain. Two years ago, I fainted at the dentist's!

21. Le dentiste: **Bien sûr, Madame. Ne vous inquiétez pas. Je vais vous faire une petite anesthésie locale et vous ne sentirez rien.**
Of course, Madam. Don't worry. I'm going to give you a slight local anesthetic and you won't feel anything.

22. *Après sa visite chez le dentiste, Jane se rend à la pharmacie.*
After her visit at the dentist's, Jane goes to the pharmacy.

23. Jane: **Voici l'ordonnance que m'a prescrite le dentiste.**
Here's the prescription the dentist filled out for me.

24. La pharmacienne: **Oui. Je vais vous chercher ces médicaments tout de suite. Voilà. Vous devez prendre deux de ces cachets trois fois par jour, avant les repas. Pour ceux-ci, un à midi et un le soir, avant les repas aussi. Et vous devez faire un bain de bouche à chaque fois que vous mangez quelque chose.**

The pharmacist: Yes. I'll get the medication for you right away. Here we go. You have to take two of these pills three times a day before meals. These, one at noon and one in the evening, before meals as well. And you have to wash your mouth out each time you eat something.

25. Jane: **Merci bien. Puisque je suis ici, je vais en profiter. Ah, voici ma liste. J'ai une amie française à New York, qui m'a demandé de lui ramener quelques produits. Alors, allons-y . . . Du talc, une boîte de bicarbonate, un flacon d'eau de rose et une crème de jour au beurre de karité. Aussi, trois tubes de dentifrice de cette marque-là.**
Thank you very much. Since I'm here, I'm going to take advantage of it. Ah, here's my list. I have a French friend in New York who asked me to bring her back a few products. So, let's see . . . Some talcum powder, a box of baking soda, a bottle of rose water and a day cream with shea butter. Also, three tubes of toothpaste of this brand right there.

26. La pharmacienne: **Bien voilà, je crois que tout y est. Vos médicaments sont dans ce petit sac en papier. Et les produits pour votre amie sont dans cette grande bourse.**
Well, that's it I think. Your medicines are in this small paper bag. And the products for your friend are in this large one.

27. Jane: **Et je vais prendre aussi deux boîtes de pastilles au miel pour la gorge. Oui, ce sera tout merci.**
And I'm also going to take two boxes of honey lozenges for the throat. Yes, that'll be all thank you.

28. La Pharmacienne: **Alors, vous êtes américaine. Je ne suis pas allée à New York depuis trois ans.**

Mais il se peut que j'y aille avec mes enfants en
août. Si ça ne tenait qu'à moi! je ne peux pas
rester longtemps sans voyager.

So you're American. I haven't been to New York for
three years. But I might go there with my children in
August. If it were only up to me! I can't go for very
long without traveling.

29. Jane: **New York a pas mal changé en trois ans.
Enfin, vous verrez. En tous cas, merci Madame.
Au revoir.**
New York has changed quite a bit in three years.
Well, you'll see. In any case, thank you, Ma'am.
Goodbye.

B. NOTES

0. *chez le dentiste, chez le docteur* . . . but *à la pharmacie.*
Note the difference of use between *chez le / la*, used
when there is an actual office, *un cabinet* and *à la / le*
otherwise.

Elle a très mal aux dents means: her teeth are really
hurting. In the same way, *j'ai mal aux dents*: I have a
toothache, *mal à la tête*: a headache, *mal à l' estomac*: a
stomach ache, *mal à la gorge*: a sore throat. Also, from
mal, être malade: to be sick, to be ill.

1. *avoir rendez-vous* or *avoir un rendez-vous*: to have an
appointment and *prendre (un) rendez-vous*: to make an
appointment. *une visite médicale, une visite chez le dentiste, une visite chez le docteur*: a medical appointment,
a dentist's visit, a doctor's visit.

2. *d'urgence*: an emergency and in the hospital, *les
urgences*: the emergency room.

3. *C'est à vous*: It's your turn, it's yours.

10. *se brosser les dents*: to brush one's teeth

11. *pour s'en assurer*, or *pour être sûr*, means to make sure

16. *se rincer* is to rinse (out) and *faire un bain de bouche*: to wash one's mouth

20. *s'évanouir*: to faint; *un évanouissement*: the state of fainting

23. *une ordonnance*: a prescription

24. *un médicament*: a medicine but *un médecin* or *un docteur*: a practioner. *Les honoraires* describes the fee received by a doctor or dentist.
    Un cachet or *un comprimé* is a pill, a tablet and *une gélule* is a gel tab. As for *la pillule*, it is rarely used to mean a general pill because it refers to the birth control pill.
    à chaque fois que vous . . . : each time you . . .

28. *si ça ne tenait qu'à moi*: if it were only up to me.

C. GRAMMAR AND USAGE

1. The preposition *depuis,* which introduces a time expression, is used with the present tense. It is the equivalent of the English "since" and "for," used with the present perfect.

    Depuis ce matin, j'ai mal à la tête.
        Since this morning, I've had a headache.

    Il a mal aux dents depuis deux mois.
        He has had a toothache for two months.

Ils discutent depuis deux heures.
> They've been talking for two hours. They've talked for two hours.

Vous n'êtes pas allé chez le dentiste depuis cinq ans?
> You haven't been to the dentist for five years?

Note that another way of expressing the same idea of length of time (and not a specific time, such as: *depuis lundi*) is to use *il y a* or *cela fait* followed by the length of time expression, then *que*.

Il y a deux mois qu'il a mal aux dents.
Cela fait deux mois qu'il a mal aux dents.
> He has had a toothache for two months.

Il y a cinq ans que vous n'êtes pas allé chez le dentiste?
Cela fait cinq ans que vous n'êtes pas allé chez le dentiste?
> You haven't been to the dentist for five years?

Finally, the correponding questions are introduced by *depuis combien de temps* or *depuis quand*.

Depuis combien de temps avez-vous mal à cette dent?
> For how long has this tooth been hurting?

J'ai mal à cette dent depuis trois jours.
> This tooth has been hurting for three days.

But:

Depuis quand avez-vous mal à cette dent?
> Since when has this tooth been hurting?

J'ai mal à cette dent depuis hier.
> This tooth has been hurting since yesterday.

2. To express a past and completed action, French uses the *passé composé* and *il y a* with a length of time expression. It is the equivalent of "ago" with a time expression.

Here again, *il y a* can be used with *que* or without (which is more common).

La pharmacienne est allée aux États-Unis il y a trois ans.
(Il y a trois ans que la pharmacienne est allée aux États-Unis.)
> The pharmacist went to the United States three years ago.

J'ai vu mon dentiste il y a une semaine.
(Il y a une semaine que j'ai vu mon dentiste.)
> I saw my dentist a week ago.

3. *Il se peut que* is followed in French by the subjunctive, because it expresses a possibility. Notice that the English equivalents use "it's possible that . . ." or "may" or "might."

Il se peut que nous voyagions au mois d'août.
> It's possible that we'll travel in August. / We might travel in August.

Il se peut que vous ayez une dent cariée.
> It's possible that you have a cavity. / You may have a cavity.

Il se peut qu'il faille aller aux urgences.
> It's possible that we have to go to the emergency room. / We might have to go to the emergency room.

4. In French, as you've already seen, the definite article is used before parts of the body, although English uses the possessive adjectives.

J'ai mal aux dents.
> My teeth hurt.

Penchez la tête en arrière et ouvrez la bouche.
> Lean your head back and open your mouth.

Vous devez vous rincer la bouche chaque fois que vous mangez.
 You have to rinse out your mouth each time you eat.

In the same way, when French uses the definite article before the particular features of a person, English uses no article or possessive adjectives at all.

Elle a les yeux bleus.
 She has blue eyes.

Il a les cheveux noirs.
 He has black hair.

Ils ont les dents blanches.
 They have white teeth.

The article may also be found in front of the language one is studying or speaking. Note that with *parler*, the article is not obligatory.

J'étudie le français.
 I study French.

Jane parle (l') anglais.
 Jane speaks English.

EXERCISES

A. Substitute each of the words or expressions in parentheses for the underlined word or expression in the model sentence. Write the complete sentence and say it aloud.

1. *Ils étudient <u>le français</u> depuis sept mois. (l'italien, l'espagnol, l'allemand, le japonais)*

2. *J'étudie le français depuis <u>sept mois</u>. (trois ans, huit jours, six semaines, juillet)*

3. *Il y a <u>trois ans</u> que j'habite ici. (deux ans, six mois, huit semaines, une quinzaine d'années)*

4. *Il se peut qu'elle soit <u>malade</u>. (fâchée, fatiguée, triste, partie)*

5. *Elle a les cheveux <u>noirs</u>. (blonds, blancs, roux, châtains)*

B. Change the sentences with *il y a* into sentences with *depuis*. Say, write, and translate.

Example: *Il y a un an que je suis ici. / Je suis ici depuis un an*: It've been here for one year.

1. *Il y a deux jours que j'ai mal.*

2. *Il y a un mois qu'elle est malade.*

3. *Il y a trois semaines que je veux prendre rendez-vous.*

4. *Il y a quatre ans qu'il est dentiste.*

C. Translate the following sentences into French. Then say them aloud.

1. She's been working since four o'clock.

2. He's been waiting for me for five minutes.

3. It's possible that she doesn't know him.

4. He might have a cavity.

5. Do you have a headache?

6. She has blond hair and brown eyes.

7. He might have a sore throat.

8. She went to her dentist two days ago.

9. I made an appointment an hour ago.

10. Do you have the doctor's prescription?

D. From among the three choices, select the best translation for the English word or phrase given. Write the complete sentence, and translate.

1. (It may be) _____ *que vous ayez une carie.*

   Il se peut / Il peut / Qu'il puisse être

2. (back) *Penchez la tête* _____.

   au dos / derrière / en arrière

3. (I'm not well) _____, *docteur.*

   Ce n'est pas bon / Je ne vais pas bien / Je ne suis pas bon

4. (medicines) *Il doit prendre des* _____.

   médecins / médicaments / pillules.

5. (your fee) *Quels sont* _____?

   votre prix / vos honoraires / les heures

6. (Make an appointment) _____ *pour demain.*

   Faites un meeting /Prenez un rendez-vous / Organisez un rendez-vous

Answer Key

A. 1. *Ils étudient l'italien depuis sept mois. Ils étudient l'espagnol depuis sept mois. Ils étudient l'allemand depuis sept mois. Ils étudient le japonais depuis sept mois.* 2. *J'étudie le français depuis trois ans. J'étudie le français depuis huit jours. J'étudie le français depuis six semaines. J'étudie le français depuis juillet.* 3. *Il y a deux ans que j'habite ici. Il y a six mois que j'habite ici. Il y a huit semaines que j'habite ici. Il y a une quinzaine d'années que j'habite ici.* 4. *Il se peut qu'elle soit fâchée. Il se peut qu'elle soit fatiguée. Il se peut qu'elle soit triste. Il se peut qu'elle soit partie.* 5. *Elle a les cheveux noirs. Elle a les cheveux blonds. Elle a les cheveux roux. Elle a les cheveux châtains.*

B. 1. *J'ai mal depuis deux jours.* I've been hurting (in pain) for two days. 2. *Elle est malade depuis un mois.* She's been sick for a month. 3. *Je veux prendre rendez-vous depuis trois semaines.* I've wanted to make an appointment for three weeks. 4. *Il est dentiste depuis quatre ans.* He's been a dentist for four years.

C. 1. *Elle travaille depuis quatre heures.* 2. *Il m'attend depuis cinq minutes.* 3. *Il se peut qu'elle ne le connaisse pas.* 4. *Il se peut qu'il ait une carie.* 5. *Avez-vous mal à la tête?* 6. *Elle a les cheveux blonds et les yeux marron.* 7. *Il se peut qu'il ait mal à la gorge.* 8. *Elle est allée chez son dentiste il y a deux jours.* 9. *J'ai pris rendez-vous il y a une heure.* 10. *Est-ce que vous avez l'ordonnance du médecin?*

D. 1. *Il se peut que vous ayez une carie.* It's possible that you have a cavity. 2. *Penchez la tête en arrière.* Put your head back. 3. *Je ne vais pas bien, docteur.* I'm not well, Doctor. 4. *Il doit prendre des médicaments.* He must take some medicine. 5. *Quels sont vos honoraires?* What is your fee? 6. *Prenez un rendez-vous pour demain.* Make an appointment for tomorrow.

LESSON 20

UN DÉJEUNER ENTRE AMIS
A LUNCH AMONG FRIENDS

A. DIALOGUE

0. *Michel et Éliane ont organisé un déjeuner à leur maison de campagne et ils y ont invité plusieurs personnes: des amis, de la famille, et bien sûr, Jane et Charles, dont c'est la dernière semaine en France. Pour l'occasion, Éliane a cuisiné son fameux couscous. Autour de la table, le dialogue est animé . . .*
Michel and Éliane have put together a lunch at their country house, and they have invited several people: friends, family, and of course, Jane and Charles, who are spending their last week in France. For the occasion, Éliane has made her famous couscous. Around the table, the dialogue is lively . . .

1. Éliane: **Non, je n'ai pas le temps de cuisiner régulièrement. C'est qu'il y a tant à faire dans ce monde. À tous les niveaux. Cependant, un bon repas en famille est toujours très agréable.**
No, I don't have time to cook regularly. There's so much to do in this world. At all levels. However a nice meal surrounded by family is always very pleasant.

2. Marianne: **Eh bien, Éliane, le plaisir est d'autant plus partagé que ton couscous est dé-li-cieux!**
Well, Éliane, the pleasure is ours, and your couscous is de-li-cious!

3. Charles: **Absolument . . . Il faut que vous nous donniez cette recette! D'où vous vient-elle?**
Absolutely! You have to give to us this recipe! Where did you get it from?

4. Éliane: **Ma famille vient d'Afrique du Nord, d'Algérie. Et le couscous est un des plats traditionnels de ce pays.**
My family comes from North Africa, from Algeria. And couscous is one of the traditional dishes of that country.

5. Charles: **Y êtes-vous retournée?**
Have you gone back there?

6. Éliane: **Non, toujours pas. Mais c'est dans mes projets.**
No, not yet. But it's a plan of mine.

7. Cajo: **J'adore ce pays. Les Algériens ont toujours le sens de l'hospitalité, après tout ce qui leur est arrivé.**
I love that country. Algerians always have a sense of hospitality, in spite of everything that happened to them.

8. Éliane: **En effet, c'est un très beau pays. Et c'est malheureux de voir que son histoire a souvent été mêlée de grandes violences.**
That's true, it's a very beautiful country. And it's unfortunate to see that its history has often been mixed with great violence.

9. Marianne: **C'est la paix qu'il faut désormais leur souhaiter.**
Peace is what we have to wish them from now on.

10. Cajo: **Oui, espérons que les choses s'améliorent; et cela semble être le cas. Est-ce que vous connaissez l'art algérien ou la littérature de ce pays?**
Yes, let's hope things are getting better; and that seems to be the case. Are you familiar with Algerian art or literature?

11. Marianne: **Oui, pour ce qui est de la litérature francophone, j'ai lu de très bons livres d'auteurs algériens.**
Yes, as far as French speaking literature goes, I've read some very good books by Algerian authors.

12. Charles: **Excusez-moi, mais . . . Est-ce que je peux avoir de la semoule?**
I'm sorry, but . . . May I have some semolina?

13. Cajo: **Ah, ces Français, ils ont tellement la tchatche qu'ils en oublient leurs invités!**
Ah, these French, they chat so much that they forget about their guests!

14. *Tout le monde rit . . .*
Everyone laughs . . .

15. Marianne: **Voici, Charles. Jane, un peu plus de bouillon? Tenez . . . Mais dis-nous Éliane, sur quoi travailles-tu en ce moment?**
Here, Charles, Jane, a little more broth? Here you go . . . But tell us Éliane, what are you working on right now?

16. Éliane: **En fait, je travaille sur plusieurs projets: je viens de commencer un projet éducatif sur la Cour pénale internationale et je travaille sur une série au sujet de l'évolution de l'éducation nationale en France depuis les années 60.**
Actually I'm working on several projects: I've just started an educational project on the International Criminal Court and I'm working on a series on the evolution of national education in France since the 60's.

17. Marianne: **Une série pour la télévision?**
A television series?

18. Éliane: **Oui, en effet. Tous les gouvernements, les professions académiques, les parents et les élèves savent que des changements sont nécessaires.**
Yes, indeed. All the governments, the academic professions, parents and children know that changes are necessary.

19. Marianne: **C'est évident, le niveau de l'éducation ne cesse de baisser, les classes sont surpeuplées . . .**
It's obvious, the level of education keeps getting lower, classes are over-crowded . . .

20. Cajo: **Et il faut aussi qu'on prenne en compte la composition du corps des élèves et ce nouveau cadre de l'Union Européenne. Éliane, c'est un délice!**
And it's necessary that we take into account the diversity of the student body and this new framework of the European Union. Éliane, it's a delight!

21. Charles: **Il y a au moins une bonne chose, c'est que l'école en France est gratuite.**
There's at least one good point, that school is free in France.

22. Éliane: **Oui, sauf pour les écoles privées, bien sûr; et les droits d'université restent abordables.**
Yes, except for private schools of course; and university fees remain affordable.

23. Marianne: **Heureusement, car les Français n'accepteraient jamais que ce principe soit inversé.**
Fortunately, because the French would never accept this principle being changed.

24. Charles: **C'est vrai, c'est un grand et noble privilège. Jane, tu peux me passer l'eau? Merci. Je crois que j'ai mis trop de sauce piquante . . .**

It's true, it's a great and noble privilege. Jane, can you give me some water? Thanks. I think I put too much hot sauce . . .

25. Cajo: **Il faut que vous repreniez plus de semoule! C'est simple: du couscous, de la harissa, du bouillon. Oh, c'est trop piquant! Et du couscous . . .**
You have to take more semolina. It's simple: some couscous, some harissa, some broth. Oh it's too spicy! And some couscous . . .

26. Marianne: **On vous dira que le secret pour manger ces grands repas, c'est de prendre son temps, de boire modérément et de . . . beaucoup tchatcher!**
One will tell you that the secret to eating these large meals is to take your time, to drink moderately and to . . . chat a lot!

27. Éliane: **Oui . . . Mais avant tout, il faut apprécier!**
Yes . . . But before everything else, you've got to enjoy the time!

28. Charles: **Cela reste une de mes expériences préférées quand nous venons en France. Partager un bon repas avec des amis en toute tranquillité! Dire que mardi prochain, nous aurons repris notre rythme à New York! Nous partons samedi.**
It remains one of my favorite experiences when we come to France. To share a good meal with friends in total peace! Hard to believe that by next Tuesday, we'll have gotten back to our New York rhythm! We leave on Saturday.

29. Cajo: **Ah, il faut que nous trinquions à cette dernière semaine et à votre retour! Eh Frédérique, tu veux mettre de la musique? Étienne, il nous reste de ce vin? Merci!**

Ah! We must drink to your last week and your return! Hey Frédérique, do you want to put on some music? Étienne, do we still have any of this wine? Thanks!

B. NOTES

0. *Les repas, déjeuners* or *dîners* still remain important moments of social life where people share a meal, ideas, and have discussions. But as Éliane explains, fewer and fewer people, especially women, have time to cook extensive meals.

   Le couscous is a specialty from North Africa, where many French people once lived. It is made of durum (a type of wheat) semolina, and is served in various ways according to the region it comes from.

1. *Je n'ai pas le temps de* + infinitive means I don't have time to.

   Il y a tant à faire: there's so much to do. Note that *tant* and *temps* have the same pronunciation but are two different words.

2. *Le plaisir est partagé* is the idiomatic expression corresponding to "the pleasure is ours."

   d'autant plus que: as much as

7. *après tout ce que*: after all that

13. *Tchatcher* is a colloquial term, equivalent to "to chat, to yak", *la tchatche* is the noun.

16. *La Cour pénale internationale* is the International Criminal Court, founded in July 1998, originally adopted by 120 heads of state, among them President Clinton. The organization is the first international

criminal court established to promote international law and ensure that no international crime go unpunished. Before its entry in force, at least 60 nations were to ratify the statute, which happened in 2002. By 2004, 97 countries had joined this institution, although the U.S. was not one of them. The Court will have its seat in the Hague (*La Haye*) in the Netherlands.

L'Éducation nationale refers to the government institution that is responsible for education in France, similar to what would be a federal Board of Education.

22. *abordable*: affordable. The verb *aborder quelqu'un* is to approach someone.

23. *être inversé*: to be inversed, switched

24. *Passer quelque chose à quelqu'un* is the familiar form for to give something to someone.

28. *Dire que . . .* is the rough equivalent of "hard to believe that . . ."

29. *Il nous reste du . . . ?* Do we still have any/some . . . ?

C. GRAMMAR AND USAGE

1. Remember that the verb *falloir* is followed by the subjunctive when it is used with the conjunction *que*. The verb *falloir* is used impersonally, that is, always with the subject *il*. The "actual" subject follows *que*: *il faut que . . .*

   Il faut que vous repreniez de la semoule.
       You have to take some semolina again.

   Il faut que tu m'expliques ton secret!
       You have to explain your secret to me!

Il faut que nous partions samedi.
> We have to go back on Saturday.

Il faut qu'on trouve une solution.
> One has to find a solution.

2. *Les jours de la semaine*, or the days of the week are used differently in French. The first difference is that they're not capitalized.

Il vient dimanche à trois heures.
> He's coming on Sunday at three o'clock.

Without an article, the reference is to the next (or last) day.

On part samedi.
> We leave on Saturday.

J'ai commencé mon nouveau travail lundi.
> I started my new job on Monday.

Jeudi, on est invité chez nos amis.
> Thursday, we're invited to our friends'.

The days can be used with a definite article to indicate a regularity, when English uses "on" with a plural.

Elle vient le dimanche (or *tous les dimanches*).
> She comes on Sundays (or every Sunday).

Le lundi, je vais à la gym.
> On Monday, I go to the gym.

3. The difference between *c'est* and *il est* (in some cases, *elle est*) has to do with usage. Both *c'est* and *il est* can mean "it is", and "he is" or "she is" may be translated in French as *c'est* or *il est / elle est* depending on context. With professions or nationalities, note that *c'est* uses an article when necessary, but not *il est* or *elle est*.

Elle est cinéaste.
C'est une cinéaste.
> She is a filmmaker.

Ils sont Algériens.
Ce sont des Algériens.
> They are Algerian.

If an adjective is added, *c'est* alone is used.

C'est une cinéaste intéressante.
> She's an interesting filmmaker.

C'est un Algérien célèbre.
> He's a famous Algerian.

When there is an object introduced by the preposition *à*, only *c'est* is used. The pronoun *ce* refers to something that has been talked about already and is understood in context.

C'est difficile à expliquer.
> It's difficult to explain.

C'est à moi.
> It's mine. / That's mine.

C'est is also used in the context when it is followed just by an adjective.

Ce n'est plus acceptable.
> It's no longer acceptable.

C'est vrai.
> It's true.

C'est fou, ça!
> That's crazy!

But *il est* is used when it is followed by an adjective and a whole clause. The pronoun *il* introduces a new idea in this case.

Il est important de coopérer.
> It's important to cooperate.

Il est nécessaire que les institutions internationales soient respectées.

It's necessary that international institutions be respected.

Note that in this last example, the conjugated verb of the clause is in the subjunctive.

Il n'est plus acceptable d'ignorer la misère du monde.

It's no longer acceptable to ignore the world's misery.

Il est difficile d'expliquer ce livre en quelques mots.

It's difficult to explain this book in a few words.

But if an adjective is used alone, "it" can be translated as *il* or *elle* if "it" refers specifically to a particular noun.

Ce couscous? Oui, il est délicieux.

This couscous? Yes, it's delicious.

(la ville) Elle est grande et belle.

(the city) It's big and beautiful.

Finally, when showing, indicating, or defining, use *c'est.*

C'est elle.

It's she. / That's her.

C'est un grand privilège.

It's a great privilege.

C'est blanc.

It's white.

C'est Éliane au téléphone.

It's Éliane on the phone.

C'est notre maison de campagne.

It's our country house.

C'est tout.

That's all.

C'est ça.

That's it.

D. EXERCISES

A. Substitute each of the words or expressions in parentheses for the underlined word or expression in the model sentence. Write the complete sentence and say it aloud.

1. *Il faut que j'y aille.* (que je change, nous respections les autres, on trouve une solution)

2. *Il faut qu'il apprenne le français.* (le droit, l'histoire, l'humilité)

3. *Il est médecin.* (avocat, professeur, comédien)

4. *C'est facile à voir.* (faire, comprendre, dire)

5. *Il est incroyable que cela se passe de nos jours.* (regrettable, triste, étonnant)

B. Translate the following sentences into French. Then say them aloud.

1. We have to think differently.

2. It's important to enjoy everything you do.

3. It is unthinkable to ignore misery.

4. They have to learn to respect others.

5. On Monday, we had lunch together.

6. Every Sunday, we go to our country house.

7. He's a great author.

8. It would be too difficult to explain in details.

9. Is that it?

10. Isn't it from your country?

C. From among the three choices, select the best translation for the English word or phrase given, write the complete sentence, and translate.

1. (It is) _____ *impensable de se conduire de la sorte.*

   Est-ce / Ce n'est / Il est

2. (so much) *Il y a* _____ *à faire.*

   beaucoup / temps / tant

3. (right) *Vous avez* _____.

   raison / droit / vrai

4. (rests) *La paix dans ce monde* _____ *sur le respect de tous.*

   reste / dort / repose

5. (hard to believe) _____ *nous serons chez nous mardi prochain.*

   C'est difficile / Dur que / Dire que

6. (after all that) _____ *s'est passé, les gens sont toujours accueillants.*

   Après tout / Tout ce que / Après tout ce qui

Answer Key

A. 1. *Il faut que je change. Il faut que nous respections les autres. Il faut qu'on trouve une solution.* 2. *Il faut qu'il apprenne le droit. Il faut qu'il apprenne l'histoire. Il faut qu'il apprenne l'humilité.* 3. *Il est avocat. Il est professeur. Il est comédien.* 4. *C'est facile à faire. C'est facile à comprendre. C'est facile à dire.* 5. *Il est regrettable que cela se passe de nos jours. Il est triste que cela se passe de nos jours. Il est étonnant que cela se passe de nos jours.*

B. 1. *Il faut que nos pensions différemment.* 2. *Il est important d'apprécier tout ce qu'on fait.* 3. *Il est impensable d'ignorer la misère.* 4. *Il faut qu'ils apprennent à respecter les autres.* 5. *Lundi, nous avons déjeuné ensemble.* 6. *Tous les dimanches, nous allons à notre maison de campagne.* 7. *C'est un grand auteur.* 8. *Ce serait trop difficile à expliquer en détail.* 9. *C'est ça?* 10. *N'est-ce pas de ton pays?*

C. 1. *Il est impensable de se conduire de la sorte.* It's unthinkable to behave in such a way. 2. *Il y a tant à faire.* There's so much to do. 3. *Vous avez raison.* You're right. 4. *La paix dans ce monde repose sur le respect de tous.* Peace in the world rests on the respect of all. 5. *Dire que nous serons chez nous mardi prochain.* Hard to believe that we'll be home next Tuesday. 6. *Après tout ce qui s'est passé, les gens sont toujours accueillants.* After all that has happened, people are still welcoming.

SUMMARY OF FRENCH GRAMMAR

1. ABOUT THE SOUNDS

Very few sounds are exactly alike in both English and French. The pronunciation equivalents given below can therefore be only approximate. Although exceptions exist for almost every pronunciation rule, the guidelines in this section should prove useful to the student.

The Consonants. French consonant sounds are generally softer than those of English. A number of them are produced by bringing the tongue in contact with different parts of the mouth cavity from those used for the equivalent English consonant, or by changing the pressure of the airstream. For example, the English speaker produces the sound of *d, t,* or *n* by placing the tip of the tongue against the gum ridge behind the upper teeth. The French speaker produces these sounds by placing the tip of the tongue against the back of the upper teeth.

In pronouncing a *p* at the beginning of a word such as "pat" or "pen," the English speaker produces a puff of air, whereas the French speaker does not. Try holding your hand in front of your mouth and saying the words "pit," "pack," and "punch." You will feel the puff of air each time you say the *p* at the beginning of each of these words. The French speaker, on the other hand, produces the *p* at the beginning of words *without* the puff of air. The French *p* is close in sound to the English *p* in words like "speak" or "spot."

The pronunciation of the sound *l* also varies in the two languages. American English has two *l* sounds— one which is used at the beginning of a word (the "light" *l*), and another which is used in the middle or at the end of a word (the "dark" *l*). Contrast the *l* sound in the words "like" and "beautiful." The *l* in "like" is a "light" *l*, and this is the *l* sound pronounced in French.

The Vowels. Some of the vowel sounds of French resemble the vowels in English. Many vowel sounds, however, are quite different, and some do not exist in English at all. For example, the sound represented by *é* resembles the English *ay* in the word "day," but the two sounds are not the same. When an English speaker says "day," he is actually pronouncing two sounds: an *a* and a *y*, which glide together to form a diphthong. Try holding your hand on your jaw and saying the words listed below. As you do so, notice how your jaw closes up a bit toward the end of the *ay* sound:

day   say   may   ray   nay   tray   jay

In French, however, the jaw does not move as you say the *é* sound; it remains steady. Pronounce the following French words, while holding the jaw still.

des   *bébé*   *fâché*   *mes*   *réalité*

A similar phenomenon occurs with the sound *o*. Say the following words in English:

bow   tow   know   so

Note that the jaw rises at the end of the sound as though to close on the sound *w*. Hold your hand on your jaw and say the above words "in slow motion." Now, leaving off the *w* sound at the end by holding the jaw steady, say the following words in French:

beau tôt nos sot
(the final consonants are silent)

Space does not permit us to compare every English sound with its French counterpart, but the charts below will help to clarify the sounds. Repeated imitation of the speakers on the recordings is the best way to learn how to pronounce French correctly.

2. THE ALPHABET

LETTER	NAME	LETTER	NAME	LETTER	NAME
a	*a*	j	*ji*	s	*esse*
b	*bé*	k	*ka*	t	*té*
c	*cé*	l	*elle*	u	*u*
d	*dé*	m	*emme*	v	*vé*
e	*e*	n	*enne*	w	*double vé*
f	*effe*	o	*o*	x	*iks*
g	*gé*	p	*pé*	y	*i grec*
h	*ache*	q	*ku*	z	*zède*
i	*i*	r	*erre*		

3. THE CONSONANTS

The letters *b, d, f, k, l, m, n, p, s, t, v,* and *z* are pronounced approximately as in English when they are not in final position, but with the differences indicated above. Note however:

c   before *a, o, u, l* and *r* is like the *c* in "cut." Ex., *carte, cœur, cuisine, clarté, croire;*
            before *e* and *i* is like *s* in "see." Ex., *centre, cinéma*

ç   (c with cedilla) is like *s* in "see." Ex., *français, garçon*

ch   is like *sh* in "ship." Ex., *chéri, cheval.* But: *chr* is pronounced like English *kr.* Ex., *chrétien*

g   before *a, o, u, l, r* is like *g* in "go." Ex., *gare, goût, guerre, glace, grand;*

before *e* and *i*, is like the *s* sound in "measure." Ex., *genre, voyageur, Gigi*

gn   is like *ni* in "onion" or *ny* in "canyon." Ex., *oignon, soigner*

h   is not pronounced. Ex., *heure*

j   is like the *s* sound in "measure." Ex., *bonjour, joie*

l   is always "light" (as explained above) when it is pronounced as *l*. However, in the following combinations it is pronounced like the *y* in "yes": *-ail, -eil, -eille, -aille, -ille, -ill*. Ex., *chandail, vermeil, oreille, grisaille, vieillard*. But: in *mille, ville* the *l*'s are pronounced as *l*.

qu   before *a, e, i, o, u* is like *k*. Ex., *qui, quotidien;* with *oi* is like *kwa*. Ex., *quoi*

r   is made farther back in the throat than the English *r;* almost like a gargle. Ex., *rouge, rue*

s   is generally like the *s* in "see." Ex., *soir, estimer;* between vowels is like the *s* in "rose." Ex., *rose, vase*

w   (occurring only in foreign words) is generally pronounced *v*. Ex., *wagon;* the first letter in *whisky*, however, is pronounced *w*.

FINAL CONSONANTS

As a general rule, final consonants are silent. However, words ending in *c, f, l,* and *r* often do pronounce the final consonant. Ex.:

-c: parc, sac, trafic

-f: bref, chef, œuf

-l: moral, Noël, journal

-r: sur, erreur, manoir

There are several cases in which the final *r* is generally silent:

1) The infinite ending of *-er* verbs. Ex., *parler, aller, jouer*

2) Names of certain tradespeople. Ex., *le boucher, le boulanger, le plombier*

3) Nouns ending in *-er*. Ex., *verger, soulier, tablier*

There are many common words ending in *c, l* and *f* in which the final consonant is silent. Ex., *estomac, banc, blanc, gentil, pareil, clef*

4. SIMPLE VOWELS

a as in "ah!" or "father." Ex., *pâté, mâle, Jacques*

as in "cat." Ex., *ami, mal*

e as in "let." Ex., *belle, cher, cette*

as in "day," without the *y* sound at the end (as explained above). This occurs in monosyllables or words ending in *-er, -et* or *-ez*, and is the same sound as *é*. Ex., *les, des, laver, filet, allez*

as in "the" (the "mute" *e* between two single consonants or in monosyllabic words). Ex., *depuis, le, petit, tenir, besoin*

The unaccented *e* is silent ("mute") at the end of a word. Ex., *parle, femme, limonade*

é (*accent aigu*) as in "day," without the *y* sound at the end. Ex., *église, école, fâché, réalité*

è (*accent grave*) as in "let." Ex., *père, mètre, Agnès*

ê (*accent circonflexe*) as in "let." Ex., *tête, être*

i as in "machine." The letter *y*, when it acts as a vowel, is pronounced the same way. Ex., *machine, lycée, qui, bicyclette*

o (closed *o*) as in "go" (without the *w* sound at the end, as explained above). Ex., *tôt, mot, dos*

(open *o*) as in "north." Ex., *robe, alors, bonne, gosse*

u   has no equivalent in English. To approximate the sound, say *ee*, keep the tongue in the position of *ee* (with the tip of the tongue against the bottom teeth), and then round the lips. Ex., *lune, nuit, assure*

ai   as in "let." Ex., *mais, caisson, lait*

ei   as in "let." Ex., *reine, peine*

au   as in "go" (without the *w* sound at the end). Ex., *auprès, pauvre, eau, eau(x)*

eu   has no equivalent in English. To approximate the sound, place the tongue as if for *é,* but round the lips as for *o.* Ex., *deux, feu, peu, ceux*

œ   has no equivalent in English. It is more "open" than *eu.* To form the sound, place the tongue as if for the *e* of "let," but round the lips. This sound is usually followed by a consonant, as in *sœur, cœur*

oi   pronounced *wa.* Ex., *moi, voilà*

ou   as in "too." Ex., *nous, vous, cousin, rouge, amour*

5.   THE NASALIZED VOWELS

When the consonants *n* and *m* are preceded by a vowel, the sound is generally nasalized; that is, the airstream escapes partly through the nose. The four categories of nasalized vowels are as follows:

1. *an, am, en,* and *em* are like the *au* in the British *aunt* pronounced through the nose:

an	year
ample	ample
en	in

enveloppe	envelope
temps	time

2. *on* and *om* are like the vowel in *north* pronounced through the nose:

bon	good
tomber	to fall

3. *in, im, ein, eim, ain,* and *aim* are like the vowel in *at* pronounced through the nose:

fin	end
simple	simple
faim	hunger
plein	full

4. *un* and *um* are like the vowel in *burn* pronounced through the nose:

un	one
chacun	each one
humble	humble

Vowels are nasalized in the following cases:

1. When the *n* or *m* is the final consonant or one of the final consonants:

fin	end
pont	bridge

champ	field
temps	time

2. In the middle of a word, when the *n* or *m* is not followed by a vowel:

NASALIZED

chambre	room	*impossible*	impossible

NOT NASALIZED

inutile	useless	*inoccupé*	unoccupied
initial	initial	*imitation*	imitation

Note: *mm* and *nn* do not cause the nasalization of the preceding vowel:

flamme	flame	*innocent*	innocent
donner	to give	*immense*	immense

6. THE APOSTROPHE

Certain one-syllable words ending in a vowel drop ("elide") the vowel when they come before words beginning with a vowel sound.

This dropping of the vowel or "elision" is marked by an apostrophe. Common cases are:

1. The *a* of *la:*

je l'aime	I like her (or it)	*l'heure*	the hour
l'amande	the almond		

2. The vowel *e* in one-syllable words (*le, je, se, me, que,* etc.):

l'argent	the money	*j'habite*	I live
j'ai	I have		

3. the vowel *i* in *si* "if," when it comes before *il* "he" or *ils* "they":

s'il vous plaît   please ("if it pleases you")

4. *moi* and *toi* when they come before *en* are written *m'* and *t':*

Donnez-m'en   Give me some of it (of them).

5. A few words like *aujourd'hui* today, *entr'acte* interlude, etc.

7. THE DEFINITE ARTICLE

	SINGULAR	PLURAL
Masculine	*le*	*les*
Feminine	*la*	*les*

SINGULAR

le garçon	the boy
la fille	the girl

PLURAL

les garçons	the boys
les filles	the girls

1. *Le* and *la* become *l'* before words beginning with a vowel sound:
   This contraction takes place before most words beginning with *h* (this *h* is called "mute" *h*). There are a few words where this contraction does not occur (this *h* is called "aspirate" *h*):

l'ami	the friend	*l'heure*	the hour
le héros	the hero	*la hache*	the ax

2. Unlike English, the definite article is used in French before a noun used in a general sense, before titles, days of the week, parts of the body, etc.:

l'avion	the airplane
le dimanche	Sunday (or Sundays)
le Comte . . .	Count . . .
J'aime les livres.	I like books.
Le fer est utile.	Iron is useful.
L'avarice est un vice.	Avarice is a vice.
Je vais me laver les mains.	I'm going to wash my hands.

3. The definite article is used with names of languages, unless preceded by *en:*

Le français est difficile.	French is difficult.

But—

Elle raconte l' histoire en français.	She tells the story in French.

> Note: The article is usually omitted with the name of a language used immediately after the verb *parler:*

Elle parle français.	She speaks French.

4. Unlike English, the definite articles must be repeated before each noun they modify.

les portes et les fenêtres	the doors and windows

8. THE INDEFINITE ARTICLE

	SINGULAR	PLURAL
Masculine	*un*	*des*
Feminine	*une*	*des*

SINGULAR

un homme	a man
une femme	a woman

PLURAL

des hommes	men; some men; a few men
des femmes	women; some women; a few women

1. The indefinite article is omitted before an unmodified statement of profession, nationality, rank, etc.:

Je suis médecin.	I am a doctor.
Elle est américaine.	She is an American.
Il est capitaine.	He is a captain.

But, with an adjective:

C'est un bon médecin.   He is a good doctor.

2. The indefinite articles are repeated before each noun:

un homme et une femme   a man and a woman

9. THE POSSESSIVE

The possessive is expressed in the following way: State the thing possessed + *de* ("of ") + the possessor:

le livre de Marie	Mary's book ("the book of Mary")
le stylo de l'élève	the pupil's pen ("the pen of the pupil")

10. CONTRACTIONS

1. The preposition *de* "of" combines with the definite articles *le* and *les* as follows:

de + le = du:	*le livre du professeur*	the teacher's book
de + les = des:	*les stylos des élèves*	the pupils' pens

There is no contraction with *la* or *l'*.

2. The preposition *à* "to" combines with the articles *le* and *les* as follows:

à + le = au:	*Il parle au garçon.*	He's talking to the boy.

a + les =	*Il parle aux*	He's talking
aux:	*garçons.*	to the boys.

There is no contraction with *la* or *l'*.

11. GENDER

All English nouns take the articles *the* or *a(n)*. Adjectives modifying English nouns do not change their form. In French, however, all nouns show gender (*masculine* or *feminine*), and adjectives agree with nouns in gender and number (*singular* or *plural*).

Masculine nouns: Take the definite article *le* in the singular and *les* in the plural, and the indefinite article *un*. They are modified by the masculine form of an adjective.

le costume bleu	the blue suit
les costumes bleus	the blue suits

Feminine nouns: Take the definite article *la* in the singular and *les* in the plural, and the indefinite article *une*. They are modified by the feminine form of an adjective.

la robe bleue	the blue dress
les robes bleues	the blue dresses

The gender of each noun must be learned with the noun. The following tables describing which noun classes are masculine and which are feminine provide a general rule of thumb. There are a number of exceptions to each statement.

The following classes of nouns are generally masculine:

1. Nouns naming a male person. Ex., *le père* father, *le roi* king.
   But: *la sentinelle,* sentry.
2. Nouns ending in a consonant. Ex., *le parc* park, *le pont* bridge, *le tarif* rate, tariff.
   But: Nouns ending in *-ion* and *-son* are generally feminine. Ex., *l'action* action, *la conversation* conversation, *la raison* reason.
3. Nouns ending in any vowel except "mute" *e*. Ex., *le pari* bet, wager, *le vélo* bicycle, *le menu* menu
4. Nouns ending in *-ment, -age, -ege* (note that *-age* and *-ege* end in "mute" *e*). Ex., *le ménage* household, *le manège* riding school, *le document* document, *l'usage* usage.
5. Names of days, months, seasons, metals, colors, trees, shrubs. Ex.:

le jeudi	Thursday	*le bleu*	blue
(le) septembre	September	*le chêne*	oak
le printemps	spring	*l'olivier*	olive tree
l'or	gold	*le genêt*	broom (a
le plomb	lead		shrub)

6. The names of parts of speech when used as nouns. Ex., *le nom* noun, *le verbe* verb, *le participe* participle.
7. Decimal weights and measures. Ex., *le mètre* meter, *le litre* liter, *le kilogramme* kilogram. Note the contrast with a nondecimal measure: *la livre* pound.
8. The names of the cardinal points. Ex., *le nord* north, *l'est* east, *le sud* south, *l'ouest* west.

The following classes of nouns are generally feminine.

1. Nouns naming a female person. Ex., *la mère* mother, *la reine* queen.
   But: *le professeur* teacher (*m.* or *f.*)
2. Nouns ending in *-te, -son, -ion*. Ex., *la détente* détente, *la raison* reason, *la conversation* conversation.
   But: *le camion* truck, *l'avion* airplane, *le million* million
3. Names of qualities or states of being ending in: *-nce, -esse, -eur, -ude*.

la distance	distance
la gentillesse	niceness
la largeur	width
la douceur	sweetness

(But: *le bonheur* happiness, *le malheur* unhappiness, misfortune.)

la gratitude	gratitude

4. Most nouns ending in mute *e*. Ex., *la blague* joke, *la voiture* car.
   But: See exceptions mentioned in item 4, page 308, under nouns of masculine gender.
5. Names of moral qualities, sciences, and arts. Ex., moral qualities: *la bonté* kindness, *l'avarice* greed.
   science: *l'algèbre* algebra, *la chimie* chemistry.
   art: *la peinture* painting, *la musique* music.
   But: *l'art* (*m.*), art.
6. Most names of fruits. Ex., *la pomme* apple, *la cerise* cherry.
   But: *le pamplemousse* grapefruit, *le raisin* grapes.
7. Nouns ending in -té (very few exceptions). Ex.,

l'activité activity, *la générosité* generosity, *la proximité* proximity, *la priorité* priority.

12. PLURAL OF NOUNS

1. Most nouns add *-s* to form the plural:

la ville	the city	*les villes*	the cities
l'île	the island	*les îles*	the islands

2. Nouns ending in *-s*, *-x*, *-z* do not change:

le fils	the son	*les fils*	the sons
la voix	the voice	*les voix*	the voices
le nez	the nose	*les nez*	the noses

3. Nouns ending in *-au* or *-eu* add *-x:*

le chapeau	the hat	*les chapeaux*	the hats
l'eau	water	*les eaux*	waters
le jeu	the game	*les jeux*	the games

4. Most nouns ending in *-al* and *-ail* form the plural with *-aux.*

l'hôpital	the hospital	*les hôpitaux*	the hospitals
le travail	work	*les travaux*	works

SOME IRREGULAR PLURALS:

le ciel	the sky	*les cieux*	the heavens
l'œil	the eye	*les yeux*	the eyes
Madame	Madam, Mrs.	*Mesdames*	Madams

Mademoi-	Miss	*Mesdemoi-*	Misses
selle		*selles*	
Monsieur	Sir, Mr.	*Messieurs*	Sirs
le bon-	the fellow	*les bons-*	the fellows
homme		*hommes*	

13. FEMININE OF ADJECTIVES

1. The feminine of adjectives is normally formed by adding *-e* to the masculine singular, but if the masculine singular already ends in *-e*, the adjective has the same form in the feminine:

MASCULINE

| *un petit garçon* | a little boy |
| *un jeune homme* | a young man |

FEMININE

| *une petite fille* | a little girl |
| *une jeune femme* | a young woman |

2. Adjectives ending in *-er* change the *e* to *è* and then add *-e:*

étranger (*m.*)   *étrangère* (*f.*)   foreign

3. Most adjectives ending in *-eux* change this ending to *-euse:*

| *heureux* (*m.*) | *heureuse* (*f.*) | happy |
| *sérieux* (*m.*) | *sérieuse* (*f.*) | serious |

4. Some adjectives double the final consonant and add -e:

bon (*m.*)	*bonne* (*f.*)	good
ancien (*m.*)	*ancienne* (*f.*)	former, ancient
gentil (*m.*)	*gentille* (*f.*)	nice
gros (*m.*)	*grosse* (*f.*)	fat

5. Adjectives ending in -*eau* change the -*au* to -*lle:*

beau (*m.*)	*belle* (*f.*)	beautiful
nouveau (*m.*)	*nouvelle* (*f.*)	new

6. There are a number of irregular feminines:

actif (*m.*)	*active* (*f.*)	active
blanc (*m.*)	*blanche* (*f.*)	white
doux (*m.*)	*douce* (*f.*)	sweet, gentle, soft
faux (*m.*)	*fausse* (*f.*)	false
long (*m.*)	*longue* (*f.*)	long
vieux (*m.*)	*vieille* (*f.*)	old

14. Plural of Adjectives

1. The plural of adjectives is regularly formed by adding -*s* to the singular, but if the masculine singular ends in -*s* or -*x*, the masculine plural has the same form:

SINGULAR		PLURAL	
un petit garçon	a little boy	*deux petits garçons*	two little boys

une petite fille	a little girl	*deux petites filles*	two little girls
un mauvais garçon	a bad boy	*deux mauvais garçons*	two bad boys

2. Adjectives ending in -*au* add -*x:*

un nouveau livre	a new book	*des nouveaux livres*	new books

3. Adjectives ending in -*al* change to -*aux:*

un homme loyal	a loyal man	*des hommes loyaux*	loyal men

15. AGREEMENT OF ADJECTIVES

1. Adjectives agree with the nouns they modify in gender and number; that is, they are masculine if the noun is masculine, plural if the noun is plural, etc.:

Marie et sa sœur sont petites.	Mary and her sister are little.

2. An adjective that modifies nouns of different gender is in the masculine plural:

Marie et Jean sont petits.	Mary and John are little.

16. POSITION OF ADJECTIVES

1. Adjectives usually follow the noun:

un livre français	a French book
un homme intéressant	an interesting man
une idée excellente	an excellent idea

2. When they describe an inherent quality or when they form a set phrase, etc., they precede the noun:

une jeune fille	a young girl
le savant auteur	the learned author
une grande amitié	a close friendship
une éclatante victoire	a striking victory

3. The following common adjectives usually precede the nouns they modify:

autre	other	*jeune*	young
beau	beautiful	*joli*	pretty
bon	good	*long*	long
court	short	*mauvais*	bad
gentil	nice, pleasant	*nouveau*	new
grand	great, large, tall	*petit*	small, little
gros	big, fat	*vieux*	old

4. The following common adjectives differ in meaning depending on whether they come before or after the noun.

	BEFORE THE NOUN	AFTER THE NOUN
ancien	former	ancient
grand	great	tall
brave	worthy	brave
cher	dear (beloved)	dear (expensive)
pauvre	poor (wretched)	poor (indigent)
propre	own	clean
même	same	himself, herself, itself, very

5. The following adjectives have two forms for the masculine singular:

MASCULINE SINGULAR		FEMININE SINGULAR	
BEFORE A CONSONANT	BEFORE A VOWEL OR "MUTE" H		
beau	*bel*	*belle*	beautiful, fine, handsome
nouveau	*nouvel*	*nouvelle*	new
vieux	*vieil*	*vieille*	old

Examples:

un beau livre	a beautiful book
un bel arbre	a beautiful tree
une belle femme	a beautiful woman

17. COMPARISON OF ADJECTIVES

Most adjectives form the comparative and superlative by placing *plus* and *le plus* (*la plus*) before the adjective and using *que* where English uses "than":

POSITIVE

petit	small
grand	large

COMPARATIVE

plus petit que	smaller than
plus grand que	larger than

SUPERLATIVE

le plus petit	the smallest
le plus grand	the largest

Common exceptions:

POSITIVE

bon	good
mauvais	bad

COMPARATIVE

meilleur	better
plus mauvais *pire* }	worse

SUPERLATIVE

le meilleur	the best
le plus mauvais *le pire* }	the worst

18. POSSESSIVE ADJECTIVES

1. Possessive adjectives agree in gender and number with the thing possessed:

BEFORE SINGULAR NOUNS:		BEFORE PLURAL NOUNS:	
MASCULINE	FEMININE	MASCULINE AND FEMININE	
mon	*ma*	*mes*	my
ton	*ta*	*tes*	your (*fam.*)
son	*sa*	*ses*	his, her, its
notre	*notre*	*nos*	our
votre	*votre*	*vos*	your
leur	*leur*	*leurs*	their

Examples:

mon chien	my dog
sa mère	his (or her) mother
ma robe	my dress
votre livre	your book
leurs crayons	their pencils

2. Notice that these adjectives agree in gender not with the possessor as in English, but with the noun they modify. *Son, sa,* and *ses* may therefore mean "his," "her," or "its."

Jean parle à sa mère.	John is talking to his mother.
Marie parle à son père.	Mary is talking to her father.

3. Possessive adjectives are repeated before each noun they modify:

mon père et ma mère	my father and mother
leurs livres et leurs stylos	their books and pens

4. Before a feminine word beginning with a vowel or "mute" *h*, the forms *mon, ton, son* are used instead of *ma, ta, sa:*

son histoire	his story, his history
son école	his (or her) school

5. In speaking of parts of the body, the definite article is usually used instead of the possessive adjective (except where it might be ambiguous):

J'ai mal à la tête.	I have a headache.

19. POSSESSIVE PRONOUNS

MASCULINE		FEMININE		
SINGULAR	PLURAL	SINGULAR	PLURAL	
le mien	*les miens*	*la mienne*	*les miennes*	mine
le tien	*les tiens*	*la tienne*	*les tiennes*	yours (*fam.*)
le sien	*les siens*	*la sienne*	*les siennes*	his, hers, its
le nôtre	*les nôtres*	*la nôtre*	*les nôtres*	ours
le vôtre	*les vôtres*	*la vôtre*	*les vôtres*	yours
le leur	*les leurs*	*la leur*	*les leurs*	theirs

Examples:

Voici le mien.	Here's mine.
Laquelle est la vôtre?	Which is yours? (*fem. sing.*)
Apportez les vôtres; j'apporterai les miens.	Bring yours; I'll bring mine.

20. DEMONSTRATIVE ADJECTIVES

MASCULINE SINGULAR

ce (before a consonant)	*ce livre*	this (that) book
cet (before a vowel or "mute" *h*)	*cet arbre*	this (that) tree
	cet homme	this (that) man

FEMININE SINGULAR

cette	*cette femme*	this (that) woman

PLURAL

ces	*ces hommes*	these (those) men
	ces femmes	these (those) women

1. The demonstrative adjectives agree with the nouns they modify in gender and number. They must be repeated before each noun:

cet homme et cette femme	this man and this woman

2. The demonstrative adjective in French stands for both "this" and "that" (plural "these" and "those"). When it is necessary to distinguish between "this" and "that," *-ci* and *-là* are added to the noun.

Donnez-moi ce livre-ci.	Give me this book.
Voulez-vous cette robe-là?	Do you want that dress (over there)?
J'aime ce livre-ci mais je n'aime pas ce livre-là.	I like this book but I don't like that book.

21. DEMONSTRATIVE PRONOUNS

Masculine Singular	celui	this one, that one, the one
Feminine Singular	celle	this one, that one, the one
Masculine Plural	ceux	these, those, the ones
Feminine Plural	celles	these, those, the ones

Examples:

J'aime celui-ci.	I like this one.
Donne-moi celle de ton frère.	Give me your brother's (calculator (*la calculatrice*), for example).

22. Personal Pronouns

The forms of the pronouns will depend on how they are used in a sentence.

1. As the subject of a verb:

je	I
tu	you (*fam.*)
il	he, it
elle	she, it
on	we, one, people
nous	we
vous	you
ils	they
elles	they

a. *Vous* is the pronoun normally used in talking to one person or several people. *Tu* is the familiar form used only when addressing people you know very well (a member of one's family or a close friend; also children, pets, etc.).

b. *Il, elle, ils,* and *elles* are used as pronouns referring to things as well as to persons. They have the same number and gender as the nouns to which they refer. *Ils* is used to refer to nouns of different genders:

Où est le livre?	Where's the book?
Il est sur la table.	It's on the table.
Où est la lettre?	Where's the letter?
Elle est sur la table.	It's on the table.

| *Où sont les livres et les lettres?* | Where are the books and letters? |
| *Ils sont sur la table.* | They're on the table. |

2. As the direct object of a verb:

me	me
te	you (*fam.*)
le	him, it
la	her, it
nous	us
vous	you
les	them
en	some, any

3. As the indirect object of a verb:

me	to me
te	to you (*fam.*)
lui	to him, to her
nous	to us
vous	to you
leur	to them
y	to it, there

4. As the object of a preposition; disjunctive pronouns:

moi	I, me
toi	you (*fam.*)
soi	himself, herself, oneself, itself
lui	he, him
elle	she, her

nous	we, us
vous	you
eux	they, them (*masc.*)
elles	they, them (*fem.*)

5. As a reflexive pronoun:

me	myself
te	yourself (*fam.*)
se	himself, herself, itself, oneself
nous	ourselves
vous	yourself, yourselves
se	themselves

6. In affirmative requests and commands:

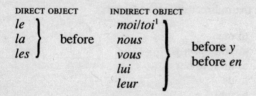

DIRECT OBJECT   INDIRECT OBJECT

le
la } before
les

moi/toi[1]
nous
vous } before *y*
lui   before *en*
leur

23. POSITION OF PRONOUNS

The direct and indirect pronoun objects generally precede the verb except in affirmative commands and requests.

---

[1] When *moi* or *toi* are used with *en*, they become *m'* and *t'* and precede *en*.

Examples: Donnez-*le-moi*.   BUT: Donnez-*m'en*.
          Lève-*toi*.   BUT: Va-t'en.

1. Position before a verb:

me
te
se   come before
nous
vous

le
la   before
les

lui   before y
leur   before en

Examples:

Il me le donne.	He gives it to me.
Il le lui donne.	He gives it to him (to her, to it).
Je l'y ai vu.	I saw him there.
Je leur en parlerai.	I'll speak to them about it.

2. Position after a verb:

le
la   come before
les

me (*moi*)
te (*toi*)
lui
vous
leur

before y before en

Examples:

Donnez-le-lui.	Give it to him.
Donnez-leur-en.	Give them some.
Allez-vous-en.	Go away. Get out of here.

3. In affirmative commands, both the direct and indirect object pronoun follow the verb, the direct preceding the indirect:

Donnez-moi le livre.	Give me the book.
Donnez-le-moi.	Give it to me.
Montrez-moi les pommes.	Show me the apples.
Montrez-les-moi.	Show them to me.
Écrivez-lui une lettre.	Write him a letter.
Écrivez-la-lui.	Write it to him.

4. The pronoun objects precede *voici* and *voilà:*

Où est le livre?	Where's the book?
Le voici.	Here it is.
Les voilà.	Here they are.

24. RELATIVE PRONOUNS

1. As the subject of a verb:

qui	who, which, that
ce qui	what, that which

Examples:

L'homme qui est là . . .	The man who is there . . .
Ce qui est bon . . .	What's good . . .

2. As the object of a verb:

que	whom, which, that
ce que	what, that which

Examples:

L'homme que tu vois . . .	The man who(m) you see . . .
Ce que je dis . . .	What I'm saying . . .

   3. As the object of a preposition:

qui (for a person)	whom
lequel (for a thing)	which

     Note: *dont* means whose, of whom, of which:

le problème dont je connais la solution . . .	The problem whose solution I know . . .
Le professeur dont je vous ai parlé . . .	The teacher about whom I talked to you . . .

25. INDEFINITE PRONOUNS

quelque chose	something
quelqu'un	someone
chacun	each (one)
on	one, people, they, etc.
ne . . . rien	nothing
ne . . . personne	no one

26. NOUNS USED AS INDIRECT OBJECTS

A noun used as an indirect object is always preceded by the preposition *à:*

| *Je donne un livre à la jeune fille.* | I'm giving the girl a book. |

27. REPETITION OF PREPOSITIONS

The prepositions *à* and *de* must be repeated before each of their objects:

| *Je parle au deputé et à son secrétaire.* | I'm speaking to the deputy and his secretary. |
| *Voici les cahiers de Jean et ceux de Marie.* | Here are John's and Mary's notebooks. |

28. THE PARTITIVE

1. When a noun is used in such a way as to express or imply quantity, it is preceded by the article with *de*. This construction very often translates the English "some" or "a few."

| *J'ai de l'argent.* | I have some money. |
| *Il a des amis.* | He has a few friends. |

In many cases, however, the article is used where we don't use "some" or "a few" in English:

| *A-t-il des amis ici?* | Does he have friends here? |

2. The article is omitted:

a. When an expression of quantity is used:

| *J'ai beaucoup d'argent.* | I have a lot of money. |

Combien de livres avez-vous?	How many books do you have?

Exceptions: *bien* much, many, and *la plupart* most, the majority:

bien des hommes	many men
la plupart des hommes	most men

   b. When the noun is preceded by an adjective:

J'ai acheté de belles cravates.	I bought some nice ties.

   c. When the sentence is negative:

Il n'a pas d'amis.	He has no friends.
Mon ami n'a pas d'argent.	My friend hasn't any money.

29. NEGATION

A sentence is made negative by placing *ne* before the verb and *pas* after it:

Je sais.	I know.
Je ne sais pas.	I don't know.
Je ne l'ai pas vu.	I haven't seen it.

Other negative expressions:

ne . . . guère	hardly
ne . . . point	not (at all) (literary)
ne . . . rien	nothing
ne . . . nul, nulle	no one, no

ne . . . jamais	never
ne . . . personne	nobody
ne . . . plus	no longer
ne . . . ni . . . ni	neither . . . nor
ne . . . que	only
ne . . . aucun, aucune	no one

30. WORD ORDER IN QUESTIONS

1. Questions with pronoun subjects:
   There are two ways of asking a question with a pronoun subject:

   a. Place the pronoun after the verb:

Parlez-vous français?	Do you speak French?

   b. Place *est-ce que* ("is it that") before the sentence:

Est-ce que je parle trop vite?	Am I talking too fast?
Est-ce que vous parlez français?	Do you speak French?

2. Questions with noun subjects:
   When a question begins with a noun, the pronoun is repeated after the verb:

Votre frère parle-t-il français?	Does your brother speak French?
Votre sœur a-t-elle quitté la maison?	Has your sister left the house?

3. Questions introduced by interrogative words: In questions which begin with an interrogative word (*quand, comment, où, pourquoi*), the order is usually interrogative word—noun subject—verb—personal pronoun:

Pourquoi votre ami a-t-il quitté Paris?	Why did your friend leave Paris?

31. ADVERBS

1. Most adverbs are formed from the adjectives by adding *-ment* to the feminine form:

froid	cold	*froidement*	coldly
certain	certain	*certainement*	certainly
naturel	natural	*naturellement*	naturally
facile	easy	*facilement*	easily

2. There are many irregular adverbs which must be learned separately:

vite	quickly	*mal*	badly

3. Adverbs are compared like adjectives (see pages 306–307):

POSITIVE	COMPARATIVE	SUPERLATIVE
loin far	*plus loin* farther	*le plus loin* the farthest
bien well	*mieux* better	*le mieux* the best
mal poorly	*pire* more poorly, worse	*le pire* the worst

4. Some common adverbs of place:

ici	here
là	there
à côté	at the side
de côté	aside
devant	before, in front of
derrière	behind
dessus	on top
dessous	underneath
dedans	inside
dehors	outside
partout	everywhere
nulle part	nowhere
loin	far
près	near
où	where
y	there
ailleurs	elsewhere
là-haut	up there
là-bas	over there

5. Some common adverbs of time:

aujourd' hui	today
demain	tomorrow
hier	yesterday
avant-hier	the day before yesterday
après-demain	the day after tomorrow
maintenant	now
alors	then
avant	before
autrefois	once, formerly
tôt	early
bientôt	soon
tard	late

souvent	often
ne . . . jamais	never
toujours	always, ever
longtemps	long, for a long time
encore	still, yet
ne . . . plus	no longer, no more
à nouveau	again

6. Adverbs of manner:

bien	well
mal	ill, badly
ainsi	thus, so
de même	similarly
autrement	otherwise
ensemble	together
fort	much, very
volontiers	willingly
surtout	above all, especially
exprès	on purpose, expressly

7. Adverbs of quantity or degree:

beaucoup	much, many
assez	enough
ne . . . guère	not much, scarcely
peu	little
plus	more
ne . . . plus	no more
moins	less
encore	more
bien	much, many
trop	too, too much, too many
tellement	so much, so many

32. THE INFINITIVE

The most common endings of the infinitive are:

I	*-er parler*	to speak	(The First Conjugation)
II	*-ir finir*	to finish	(The Second Conjugation)
III	*-re vendre*	to sell	(The Third Conjugation)

33. THE PAST PARTICIPLE

1. Forms:

	INFINITIVE	PAST PARTICIPLE
I	*parler*	*parl-é*
II	*finir*	*fin-i*
III	*perdre*	*perd-u*

2. Agreement:

a. When a verb is conjugated with *avoir*, the past participle agrees in gender and number with the preceding direct object:

La pièce que j'ai vue hier était mauvaise.	The play I saw yesterday was bad.
Avez-vous vu le livre qu'il a acheté?	Have you seen the book he bought?
Avez-vous donné la chemise à Charles?	Did you give the shirt to Charles?
Non, je l'ai donnée à Claire.	No, I gave it to Claire.

b. In the case of reflexive verbs the past participle agrees with the reflexive direct object:

Ils se sont levés.	They got up.
Elle s'est lavée.	She washed herself.

c. In the case of intransitive verbs conjugated with *être*, the past participle agrees with the subject:

Marie est arrivée hier.	Mary arrived yesterday.
Ils sont arrivés.	They arrived.
Nous sommes rentrés très tard.	We came back very late.

34. THE INDICATIVE

SIMPLE TENSES

1. The present tense of *-er* verbs is formed by the verb stem plus the endings *-e, -es, -e, -ons, -ez, -ent*. The endings of *-ir* verbs are *-is, -is, -it, -issons, -issez*, and *-issent*. *-Re* verbs take *-s, -s, -ons, -ez*, and *-ent*. This tense has several English translations:

je parle	I speak, I am speaking, I do speak
ils finissent	They finish, they are finishing, they do finish
je me lève	I get up, I'm getting up

2. The imperfect tense is formed by dropping the *-ont* of the present *nous* form and adding *-ais*,

-ais, -ait, -ions, -iez, -aient. It expresses a continued or habitual action in the past. It also indicates an action that was happening when something else happened:

Je me levais à sept heures.	I used to get up at seven o'clock.
Il dormait quand Jean est entré.	He was sleeping when John entered.
Il parlait souvent de cela.	He often spoke about that.

3. The future tense is formed by adding to the infinitive or future stem the endings *-ai, -as, -a, -ons, -ez, -ont*. It indicates a future action:

Je me lèverai tôt.	I'll get up early.
Il arrivera demain.	He'll arrive tomorrow.
Je le vendrai demain.	I'll sell it tomorrow.

4. The simple past tense (used only in formal written French) is formed by adding to the root the endings *-ai, -as, -a, -âmes, -âtes, -èrent* for *-er* verbs; the endings *-is, -is, -it, -îmes, -îtes, -irent* for *-ir* verbs; and for all other verbs either these last or *-us, -us, -ut, -ûmes, -ûtes, -urent*. It expresses an action begun and ended in the past.

Le roi fut tué.	The king was killed.
Les soldats entrèrent dans la ville.	The soldiers entered the city.

5. The past tense (present perfect) or *passé composé* is formed by adding the past participle to

the present indicative of *avoir* or, in a few cases, *être*. It is used to indicate a past action which has been completed.

Je me suis levé tôt.	I got up early.
Il ne m'a rien dit.	He didn't tell me anything.
J'ai fini mon travail.	I finished my work. I have finished my work.
L'avez-vous vu?	Have you seen him? Did you see him?
Ils sont arrivés.	They arrived.

6. The pluperfect or past perfect tense is formed by adding the past participle to the imperfect of *avoir* or, in a few cases, *être*. It translates the English past perfect:

Il l'avait fait.	He had done it.
Lorsque je suis revenu, il était parti.	When I came back, he had gone.

7. The past anterior tense is formed by adding the past participle to the simple past of *avoir* or, in a few cases, *être*. It is used for an event that happened just before another event. It is used mostly in literary style.

Après qu'il eut dîné, il sortit.	As soon as he had eaten, he went out.
Quand il eut fini il se leva.	When he had finished, he got up.

8. The future perfect tense is formed by adding the past participle to the future of *avoir* or, in a few

cases, *être*. It translates the English future perfect:

Il aura bientôt fini.	He will soon have finished.

Sometimes it indicates probability:

Il le lui aura sans doute dit.	No doubt he must have told him.
Il aura été malade.	He probably was sick.
Je me serai trompé.	I must have been mistaken.

9. The most common intransitive verbs that are conjugated with the verb *être* in the compound tenses are the following:
   aller, arriver, descendre, devenir, entrer, monter, mourir, naître, partir, rentrer, rester, retourner, revenir, sortir, tomber, venir.
   Examples:

Je suis venu.	I have come.
Il est arrivé.	He has arrived.
Nous sommes partis.	We have left.

10. Reflexive verbs are conjugated with the auxiliary *être* in the compound tenses:

Je me suis lavé les mains.	I have washed my hands.
Je me suis levé à sept heures ce matin.	I got up at seven o'clock this morning.
Elle s'est levée.	She got up.

CONDITIONAL

1. The conditional is formed by adding to the infinitive the endings *-ais*, *-ais*, *-ait*, *-ions*, *-iez*, *-aient*. It translates English "would" or "should":

Je le prendrais si j'étais à votre place.	I would take it if I were you.
Je ne ferais jamais une chose pareille.	I would never do such a thing.

2. The conditional perfect is formed by adding the past participle to the conditional of *avoir* or *être*. It translates the English "if I had" or "if I would have," etc.:

Si j'avais su, je n'y serais jamais allé.	If I had known, I would never have gone there.
Si j'avais eu assez d'argent, je l'aurais acheté.	If I had had the money, I would have bought it.

35. THE IMPERATIVE

1. The imperative of most verbs is generally formed from the present indicative tense. In the verbs of the first conjugation, however, the second person singular loses the final *s*:

donner	to give	*finir*	to finish
donne (*fam.*)	give	finis (*fam.*)	finish

donnez	give	*finissez*	finish
donnons	let us give	*finissons*	let us finish
vendre	to sell	*vendez*	sell
vends (*fam.*)	sell	*vendons*	let us sell

2. Imperatives of *être* and *avoir*:

être	to be	*avoir*	to have
sois (*fam.*)	be	*aie* (*fam.*)	have
soyez	be	*ayez*	have
soyons	let us be	*ayons*	let us have

36. VERBS FOLLOWED BY THE INFINITIVE

1. Some verbs are followed by the infinitive without a preceding preposition:

Je vais parler à Jean.	I am going to talk to John.
J' aime parler français.	I like to speak French.
Je ne sais pas danser.	I don't know how to dance.

2. Some verbs are followed by *à* plus the infinitive:

J' apprends à parler français.	I am learning to speak French.
Je l' aiderai à le faire.	I'll help him do it.

3. Some verbs are followed by *de* plus the infinitive:

Il leur a demandé de fermer la porte.	He asked them to shut the door.

37. THE SUBJUNCTIVE

The indicative makes a simple statement; the subjunctive indicates a certain attitude toward the statement—uncertainty, desire, emotion, etc. The subjunctive is used in subordinate clauses when the statement is unreal, doubtful, indefinite, subject to some condition, or is affected by will or emotion.

FORMS

1. Present Subjunctive:

   Drop the *-ent* of the third person plural present indicative and add *-e, -es, -e, -ions, -iez, -ient*. See the forms of the regular subjunctive in the Regular Verb Charts.
   The irregular verbs *avoir* and *être:*

que j' aie	*que je sois*
que tu aies	*que tu sois*
qu' il ait	*qu' il soit*
que nous ayons	*que nous soyons*
que vous ayez	*que vous soyez*
qu' ils aient	*qu' ils soient*

2. Imperfect Subjunctive:[1]

   Drop the ending of the first person singular of the past definite and add *-sse, -sses, -t, -ssions, -ssiez, -ssent*, putting a circumflex over the last vowel of the third person singular:

---

[1] The imperfect and the pluperfect subjunctive are not used today in conversational French. They do, however, appear in literature.

(THAT) I GAVE, MIGHT GIVE

que je donnasse
que tu donnasses
qu'il donnât
que nous donnassions
que vous donnassiez
qu'ils donnassent

(THAT) I FINISHED, MIGHT FINISH

que je finisse
que tu finisses
qu'il finît
que nous finissions
que vous finissiez
qu'ils finissent

(THAT) I SOLD, MIGHT SELL

que je vendisse
que tu vendisses
qu'il vendît
que nous vendissions
que vous vendissiez
qu'ils vendissent

3. Perfect Subjunctive:

   Add the past participle to the present subjunctive of *avoir* (or, in a few cases, *être*):
   avoir: que j'aie donné, que tu aies donné, etc.
   être: que je sois allé, que tu sois allé, etc.

4. Pluperfect Subjunctive:[1]

   Add the past participle to the imperfect subjunctive of *avoir* (or, in a few cases, *être*):

   avoir: que j'eusse donné, etc.
   être: que je fusse allé, etc.

---

[1] The imperfect and the pluperfect subjunctive are not used today in conversational French. They do, however, appear in literature.

USES

1. After verbs of command, request, permission, etc.:

Je tiens à ce que vous y alliez.	I insist on your going there.

2. After expressions of approval and disapproval, necessity, etc.:

Il n'est que juste que vous le lui disiez.	It's only fair that you tell him that.
Il faut que vous fassiez cela.	You have to do that.

3. After verbs of emotion (desire, regret, fear, joy, etc.):

Je voudrais bien que vous veniez avec nous.	I'd like you to come with us.
Je regrette que vous ne puissiez pas venir.	I'm sorry you can't come.

4. After expressions of doubt, uncertainty, denial:

Je doute que j'y aille.	I doubt that I'll go there.
Il est possible qu'il ne puisse pas venir.	It's possible that he may not be able to come.

5. In relative clauses with an indefinite antecedent:

Il me faut quelqu'un qui fasse cela.	I need someone to do that.

6. In adverbial clauses after certain conjunctions denoting purpose, time, concessions, etc.:

Je viendrai à moins qu'il ne pleuve.	I'll come unless it rains.
Asseyez-vous en attendant que ce soit prêt.	Sit down until it's ready.

7. In utterances expressing a wish or command:

Qu'ils s'en aillent!	Let them go away!
Dieu vous bénisse!	God bless you!
Vive la France!	Long live France!

VERB CHARTS

I. FORMS OF THE REGULAR VERBS

A. Classes I, II, III

Infinitive	Pres. & Past Participles	Present Indicative	Present Subjunctive†	Present Perfect	Past Subjunctive	Imperfect Indicative
-er ending parler to speak	parlant parlé	parl + e es e ons ez ent	parl + e es e ions iez ent	j'ai + parlé tu as il a nous avons vous avez ils ont	que j'aie + parlé que tu aies qu'il ait que nous ayons que vous ayez qu'ils aient	parl + ais ais ait ions iez aient
-ir ending finir to finish	finissant fini	fin + is is it issons issez issent	finiss + e es e ions iez ent	j'ai + fini tu as il a nous avons vous avez ils ont	que j'aie + fini que tu aies qu'il ait que nous ayons que vous ayez qu'ils aient	finiss + ais ais ait ions iez aient

Infinitive	Pres. & Past Participles	Present Indicative	Present Subjunctive†	Present Perfect	Past Subjunctive	Imperfect Indicative
-re ending	vendant	vend + s	vend + e	j'ai + vendu	que j'aie + vendu	vend + ais
vendre	vendu	s	es	tu as	que tu aies	ais
to sell		—	e	il a	qu'il ait	ait
		ons	ions	nous avons	que nous ayons	ions
		ez	iez	vous avez	que vous ayez	iez
		ent	ent	ils ont	qu'ils aient	aient

† Like the past subjunctive, the present subjunctive verb is always preceded by *que* or *qu'* + the appropriate pronoun, as in "*Il faut que je parte*" and "*Je veux qu'il quitte la maison.*"

Past Perfect	Future	Future Perfect	Conditional	Conditional Perfect	Imperative
j'avais + parlé tu avais il avait nous avions vous aviez ils avaient	parler + ai as a ons ez ont	j'aurai + parlé tu auras il aura nous aurons vous aurez ils auront	parler + ais ais ait ions iez aient	j'aurais + parlé tu aurais il aurait nous aurions vous auriez ils auraient	parle parlons parlez
j'avais + fini tu avais il avait nous avions vous aviez ils avaient	finir + ai as a ons ez ont	j'aurai + fini tu auras il aura nous aurons vous aurez ils auront	finir + ais ais ait ions iez aient	j'aurais + fini tu aurais il aurait nous aurions vous auriez ils auraient	finis finissons finissez
j'avais + vendu tu avais il avait nous avions vous aviez ils avaient	vendr + ai as a ons ez ont	j'aurai + vendu tu auras il aura nous aurons vous aurez ils auront	vendr + ais ais ait ions iez aient	j'aurais + vendu tu aurais il aurait nous aurions vous auriez ils auraient	vends vendons vendez

337

B. Verbs Ending in *-CER* AND *-GER*

Infinitive	Pres. & Past Participles	Present Indicative	Present Subjunctive[†]	Present Perfect	Past Subjunctive	Imperfect Indicative
placer[1] to place	*plaçant*[3] placé	place places place *plaçons* placez placent	place places place placions placiez placent	j'ai + placé tu as il a nous avons vous avez ils ont	que j'aie + placé que tu aies qu'il ait que nous ayons que vous ayez qu'ils aient	*plaçais* *plaçais* *plaçait* placions placiez *plaçaient*
manger[2] to eat	*mangeant* mangé	mange manges mange *mangeons* mangez mangent	mange manges mange mangions mangiez mangent	j'ai + mangé tu as il a nous avons vous avez ils ont	que j'aie + mangé que tu aies qu'il ait que nous ayons que vous ayez qu'ils aient	*mangeais* *mangeais* *mangeait* mangions mangiez *mangeaient*

[1] Similarly conjugated: *commencer, lancer, etc.*

[2] Similarly conjugated: *plonger, ranger, arranger, etc.*

[3] All spelling changes in verb forms will be italicized in this section.

Past Perfect	Future	Future Perfect	Conditional	Conditional Perfect	Imperative
j'avais + placé	placer + ai	j'aurai + placé	placer + ais	j'aurais + placé	
tu avais	as	tu auras	ais	tu aurais	place
il avait	a	il aura	ait	il aurait	
nous avions	ons	nous aurons	ions	nous aurions	*plaçons*
vous aviez	ez	vous aurez	iez	vous auriez	placez
ils avaient	ont	ils auront	aient	ils auraient	
j'avais + mangé	manger + ai	j'aurai + mangé	manger + ais	j'aurais + mangé	
tu avais	as	tu auras	ais	tu aurais	mange
il avait	a	il aura	ait	il aurait	
nous avions	ons	nous aurons	ions	nous aurions	*mangeons*
vous aviez	ez	vous aurez	iez	vous auriez	mangez
ils avaient	ont	ils auront	aient	ils auraient	

C. VERBS ENDING IN -ER WITH CHANGES IN THE STEM

Infinitive[1]	Pres. & Past Participles	Present Indicative	Present Subjunctive[†]	Present Perfect	Past Subjunctive	Imperfect Indicative
acheter[1] to buy	achetant acheté	achète achètes achète achetons achetez achètent	achète achètes achète achetions achetiez achètent	j'ai + acheté tu as il a nous avons vous avez ils ont	que j'aie + acheté que tu aies qu'il ait que nous ayons que vous ayez qu'ils aient	achet + ais ais ait ions iez aient
appeler[2] to call	appelant appelé	appelle appelles appelle appelons appelez appellent	appelle appelles appelle appelions appeliez appellent	j'ai + appelé tu as il a nous avons vous avez ils ont	que j'aie + appelé que tu aies qu'il ait que nous ayons que vous ayez qu'ils aient	appel + ais ais ait ions iez aient

340

payer[2][†] to pay	payant payé	*paie* *paies* *paie* payons payez *paient*	*paie* *paies* *paie* payions payiez *paient*	j'ai tu as il a nous avons vous avez ils ont + payé	que j'aie que tu aies qu'il ait que nous ayons que vous ayez qu'ils aient + payé	pay + ais ais ait ions iez aient
préférer[4] to prefer	préférant préféré	*préfère*[‡] *préfères* *préfère* préférons préférez *préfèrent*	*préfère* *préfères* *préfère* préférions préfériez *préfèrent*	j'ai tu as il a nous avons vous avez ils ont + préféré	que j'aie que tu aies qu'il ait que nous ayons que vous ayez qu'ils aient + préféré	préfér + ais ais ait ions iez aient

[1] Verbs like *acheter*: *mener, amener, amener, se promener, lever, se lever, élever*

[2] Verbs like *appeler*: *se rappeler, jeter*

[3] Verbs like *payer*: *essayer, employer, ennuyer, essuyer, nettoyer* (See note below.)

[4] Verbs like *préférer*: *espérer, répéter, célébrer, considérer, suggérer, protéger*

[†] Verbs ending in *-ayer* may use *i* or *y* in the present (except for *nous* and *vous* forms), the future, and the conditional, as in *payer, essayer*. Verbs ending in *-oyer, -uyer* change *y* to *i* (as in *essuyer, ennuyer, employer, nettoyer*). These changes are indicated by the use of italics.

[‡] Note the change from *é* to *è* in the *je, tu, il/elle/on,* and *ils* forms of verbs like *préférer*.

Past Perfect	Future	Future Perfect	Conditional		Conditional Perfect	Imperative
j'avais + acheté	*acheter* + ai	j'aurai + acheté	*achèter* + ais		j'aurais + acheté	
tu avais	as	tu auras	ais		tu aurais	*achète*
il avait	a	il aura	ait		il aurait	
nous avions	ons	nous aurons	ions		nous aurions	achetons
vous aviez	ez	vous aurez	iez		vous auriez	achetez
ils avaient	ont	ils auront	aient		ils auraient	
j'avais + appelé	*appeller* + ai	j'aurai + appelé	*appeller* + ais		j'aurais + appelé	
tu avais	as	tu auras	ais		tu aurais	*appelle*
il avait	a	il aura	ait		il aurait	
nous avions	ons	nous aurons	ions		nous aurions	appelons
vous aviez	ez	vous aurez	iez		vous auriez	appelez
ils avaient	ont	ils auront	aient		ils auraient	

payer				
j'avais + payé	*paier* or payer	+ ai	j'aurai + payé	*paier* or payer
tu avais		as	tu auras	
il avait		a	il aura	
nous avions		ons	nous aurons	
vous aviez		ez	vous aurez	
ils avaient		ont	ils auront	

préférer				
j'avais + préféré	préférer	+ ai	j'aurai + préféré	préfér
tu avais		as	tu auras	
il avait		a	il aura	
nous avions		ons	nous aurons	
vous aviez		ez	vous aurez	
ils avaient		ont	ils auront	

	paier or payer		j'aurais + payé	*paie*
		+ ais	j'aurais + payé	*paie*
		ais	tu aurais	payons
		ait	il aurait	payez
		ions	nous aurions	
		iez	vous auriez	
		aient	ils auraient	

	préfér		j'aurais + préféré	*préfère*
		+ ais	tu aurais	préférons
		ais	il aurait	préférez
		ait	nous aurions	
		ions	vous auriez	
		iez	ils auraient	
		aient		

D. VERBS ENDING IN -OIR

Infinitive	Pres. & Past Participles	Present Indicative	Present Subjunctive†	Present Perfect	Past Subjunctive	Imperfect Indicative
recevoir[1] to receive	recevant reçu	reçois reçois reçoit recevons recevez reçoivent	reçoive reçoives reçoive recevions receviez reçoivent	j'ai tu as il a nous avons vous avez ils ont + reçu	que j'aie que tu aies qu'il ait que nous ayons que vous ayez qu'ils aient + reçu	recev + ais ais ait ions iez aient

Future	Future Perfect	Conditional	Conditional Perfect	Imperative
recevr + ai as a ons ez ont	j'aurai tu auras il aura nous aurons vous aurez ils auront + reçu	recevr + ais ais ait ions iez aient	j'aurais tu aurais il aurait nous aurions vous auriez ils auraient + reçu	reçois recevons recevez

Past Perfect

j'avais tu avais il avait nous avions vous aviez ils avaient + reçu	

[1] Verbs like *recevoir*: *devoir* (*dois, doive, dû*).

E. Verbs Ending in -NDRE

Infinitive	Pres. & Past Participles	Present Indicative	Present Subjunctive	Present Perfect		Past Subjunctive		Imperfect Indicative	
craindre[1] to fear	craignant craint	crains crains craint craignons craignez craignent	craigne craignes craigne craignions craigniez craignent	j'ai tu as il a nous avons vous avez ils ont	+ craint	que j'aie que tu aies qu'il ait que nous ayons que vous ayez qu'ils aient	+ craint	craign	+ ais ais ait ions iez aient
éteindre[2] to extinguish	éteignant éteint	éteins éteins éteint éteignons éteignez éteignent	éteigne éteignes éteigne éteignions éteigniez éteignent	j'ai tu as il a nous avons vous avez ils ont	+ éteint	que j'aie que tu aies qu'il ait que nous ayons que vous ayez qu'ils aient	+ éteint	éteign	+ ais ais ait ions iez aient

[1] Verbs like craindre: plaindre, to pity. The reflexive form, se plaindre, means "to complain," and in the compound tenses is conjugated with être.
[2] Verbs like éteindre: peindre, to paint: teindre, to dye.

Past Perfect		Future		Future Perfect		Conditional		Conditional Perfect		Imperative
j'avais	+ *craint*	craindr	+ ai	j'aurai	+ *craint*	craindr	+ ais	j'aurais	+ *craint*	
tu avais			as	tu auras			ais	tu aurais		*crains*
il avait			a	il aura			ait	il aurait		
nous avions			ons	nous aurons			ions	nous aurions		*craignons*
vous aviez			ez	vous aurez			iez	vous auriez		*craignez*
ils avaient			ont	ils auront			aient	ils auraient		
j'avais	+ *éteint*	éteindr	+ ai	j'aurai	+ *éteint*	éteindr	+ ais	j'aurais	+ *éteint*	
tu avais			as	tu auras			ais	tu aurais		*éteins*
il avait			a	il aura			ait	il aurait		
nous avions			ons	nous aurons			ions	nous aurions		*éteignons*
vous aviez			ez	vous aurez			iez	vous auriez		*éteignez*
ils avaient			ont	ils auront			aient	ils auraient		

F. COMPOUND TENSES OF VERBS CONJUGATED WITH ÊTRE

Present Perfect	Past Subjunctive	Past Perfect	Future Perfect	Conditional Perfect
je suis allé(e)	que je sois allé(e)	j'étais allé(e)	je serai allé(e)	je serais allé(e)
tu es allé(e)	que tu sois allé(e)	tu étais allé(e)	tu seras allé(e)	tu serais allé(e)
il est allé	qu'il soit allé	il était allé	il sera allé	il serait allé
elle est allée	qu'elle soit allée	elle était allée	elle sera allée	elle serait allée
nous sommes allé(e)s	que nous soyons allé(e)s	nous étions allé(e)s	nous serons allé(e)s	nous serions allé(e)s
vous êtes allé(e)(s)	que vous soyez allé(e)(s)	vous étiez allé(e)(s)	vous serez allé(e)(s)	vous seriez allé(e)(s)
ils sont allés	qu'ils soient allés	ils étaient allés	ils seront allés	ils seraient allés
elles sont allées	qu'elles soient allées	elles étaient allées	elles seront allées	elles seraient allées

G. Compound Tenses of Reflexive Verbs (All Reflexive Verbs Are Conjugated With *ÊTRE*)

Present Perfect	Past Subjunctive	Past Perfect	Future Perfect	Conditional Perfect
je me suis levé(e)	que je me sois levé(e)	je m'étais levé(e)	je me serai levé(e)	je me serais levé(e)
tu t'es levé(e)	que tu te sois levé(e)	tu t'étais levé(e)	tu te seras levé(e)	tu te serais levé(e)
il s'est levé	qu'il se soit levé	il s'était levé	il se sera levé	il se serait levé
elle s'est levée	qu'elle se soit levée	elle s'était levée	elle se sera levée	elle se serait levée
nous nous sommes levé(e)s	que nous nous soyons levé(e)s	nous nous étions levé(e)s	nous nous serons levé(e)s	nous nous serions levé(e)s
vous vous êtes levé(e)(s)	que vous vous soyez levé(e)(s)	vous vous étiez levé(e)(s)	vous vous serez levé(e)(s)	vous vous seriez levé(e)(s)
ils se sont levés	qu'ils se soient levés	ils s'étaient levés	ils se seront levés	ils se seraient levés
elles se sont levées	qu'elles se soient levées	elles s'étaient levées	elles se seront levées	elles se seraient levées

H. Infrequently Used and "Literary" Tenses (Classes I, II, III)

Past Definite[1†]		Past Anterior[2]		Imperfect Subjunctive[3]	
parlai	perdis	eus parlé	eus perdu	parlasse	perdisse
parlas	perdis	eus parlé	eus perdu	parlasses	perdisses
parla	perdit	eut parlé	eut perdu	parlât	perdît
parlâmes	perdîmes	eûmes parlé	eûmes perdu	parlassions	perdissions
parlâtes	perdîtes	eûtes parlé	eûtes perdu	parlassiez	perdissiez
parlèrent	perdirent	eurent parlé	eurent perdu	parlassent	perdissent

finis		eus fini		finisse	
finis		eus fini		finisses	
finit		eut fini		finît	
finîmes		eûmes fini		finissions	
finîtes		eûtes fini		finissiez	
finirent		eurent fini		finissent	

[1] Used in formal narrative only. In informal conversation and writing, use the present perfect (*j'ai parlé*, etc.)

[2] Used in literary style only, after *quand, lorsque, après que, dès que* for an event that happened just before another event expressed in the past definite. Example: *Après qu'il eut dîné, il sortit.* As soon as he had eaten, he went out.

[3] "That I spoke," "that I might speak," etc. This tense is infrequently found in ordinary conversation, but is used fairly often in literary works.

† All other regular verbs use either the *-er*, *-ir*, or *-re* endings, depending upon the conjugation to which they belong. The past definite forms of irregular verbs must be memorized.

349

Past Perfect Subjunctive[4]

que j'eusse parlé	que j'eusse fini	que j'eusse perdu
que tu eusses parlé	que tu eusses fini	que tu eusses perdu
qu'il eût parlé	qu'il eût fini	qu'il eût perdu
que nous eussions parlé	que nous eussions fini	que nous eussions perdu
que vous eussiez parlé	que vous eussiez fini	que vous eussiez perdu
qu'ils eussent parlé	qu'ils eussent fini	qu'ils eussent perdu

[4] "That I had spoken," "that I might have spoken," etc. A predominantly literary tense.

II. FREQUENTLY USED IRREGULAR VERBS

The correct auxiliary verb is indicated in parentheses below each verb.
For compound tenses, use the appropriate form of the auxiliary verb + past participle.

Infinitive	Pres. & Past Participles	Present Indicative	Present Subjunctive	Imperfect Indicative	Future	Conditional	Imperative
acquérir to acquire (*avoir*)	acquérant acquis	acquiers acquiers acquiert acquérons acquérez acquièrent	acquière acquières acquière acquérions acquériez acquièrent	acquér + ais ais ait ions iez aient	acquerr + ai as a ons ez ont	acquerr + ais ais ait ions iez aient	acquiers acquérons acquérez
aller to go (*être*)	allant allé(e)(s)	vais vas va allons allez vont	aille ailles aille allions alliez aillent	all + ais ais ait ions iez aient	ir + ai as a ons ez ont	ir + ais ais ait ions iez aient	va allons allez

Infinitive	Pres. & Past Participles	Present Indicative	Present Subjunctive	Imperfect Indicative	Future	Conditional	Imperative
(s')asseoir[†] to sit (down) (*être*)	asseyant assis(e)(s)	assieds assieds assied asseyons asseyez asseyent	asseye asseyes asseye asseyions asseyiez asseyent	assey + ais ais ait ions iez aient	asseyer *or* assiér *or* assoir + ai as a ons ez ont	asseyer *or* assiér *or* assoir + ais ais ait ions iez aient	assieds-toi asseyons-nous asseyez-vous
avoir to have (*avoir*)	ayant eu	ai as a avons avez ont	aie aies ait ayons ayez aient	av + ais ais ait ions iez aient	aur + ai as a ons ez ont	aur + ais ais ait ions iez aient	aie ayons ayez
battre to beat (*avoir*)	battant battu	bats bats bat battons battez battent	batte battes batte battions battiez battent	batt + ais ais ait ions iez aient	battr + ai as a ons ez ont	battr + ais ais ait ions iez aient	bats battons battez

† There is a variant form of the conjugation of *s'asseoir* based on the present participle *assoyant* and first person singular *assois*, but this is rather archaic and is rarely used. There are also two variant forms for the future stem: *assiér-* and *assoir-*. *Assiér-* is frequently used.

				buv	+ ais	boir	+ ai	conclur	+ ais		bois

boire to drink (*avoir*)	buvant bu	bois bois boit buvons buvez boivent	boive boives boive buvions buviez boivent	buv	+ ais ais ait ions iez aient	boir	+ ai as a ons ez ont	boir	+ ais ais ait ions iez aient		bois buvons buvez
conclure to conclude (*avoir*)	concluant conclu	conclus conclus conclut concluons concluez concluent	conclue conclues conclue concluions concluiez concluent	conclu	+ ais ais ait ions iez aient	conclur	+ ai as a ons ez ont	conclur	+ ais ais ait ions iez aient		conclus concluons concluez

Infinitive	Pres. & Past Participles	Present Indicative	Present Subjunctive	Imperfect Indicative	Future	Conditional	Imperative
conduire to drive to lead (*avoir*)	conduisant conduit	conduis conduis conduit conduisons conduisez conduisent	conduise conduises conduise conduisions conduisiez conduisent	conduis + ais ais ait ions iez aient	conduir + ai as a ons ez ont	conduir + ais ais ait ions iez aient	conduis conduisons conduisez
connaître to know (*avoir*)	connaissant connu	connais connais connaît connaissons connaissez connaissent	connaisse connaisses connaisse connaissions connaissiez connaissent	connaiss + ais ais ait ions iez aient	connaîtr + ai as a ons ez ont	connaîtr + ais ais ait ions iez aient	connais connaissons connaissez
courir to run (*avoir*)	courant couru	cours cours court courons courez courent	coure coures coure courions couriez courent	cour + ais ais ait ions iez aient	courr + ai as a ons ez ont	courr + ais ais ait ions iez aient	cours courons courez

		Present	Pres. Subjunctive	Imperfect	Future	Conditional	Imperative
croire to believe (*avoir*)	croyant cru	crois crois croit croyons croyez croient	croie croies croie croyions croyiez croient	croy +ais ais ait ions iez aient	croir +ai as a ons ez ont	croir +ais ais ait ions iez aient	crois croyons croyez
cueillir to gather to pick (*avoir*)	cueillant cueilli	cueille cueilles cueille cueillons cueillez cueillent	cueille cueilles cueille cueillions cueilliez cueillent	cueill +ais ais ait ions iez aient	cueiller +ai as a ons ez ont	cueiller +ais ais ait ions iez aient	cueille cueillons cueillez
devoir to owe to ought (*avoir*)	devant dû	dois dois doit devons devez doivent	doive doives doive devions deviez doivent	dev +ais ais ait ions iez aient	devr +ai as a ons ez ont	devr +ais ais ait ions iez aient	*not used*
dire to say to tell (*avoir*)	disant dit	dis dis dit disons dites disent	dise dises dise disions disiez disent	dis +ais ais ait ions iez aient	dir +ai as a ons ez ont	dir +ais ais ait ions iez aient	dis disons dites

Infinitive	Pres. & Past Participles	Present Indicative	Present Subjunctive	Imperfect Indicative	Future	Conditional	Imperative
dormir to sleep (*avoir*)	dormant dormi	dors dors dort dormons dormez dorment	dorme dormes dorme dormions dormiez dorment	dorm + ais ais ait ions iez aient	dormir + ai as a ons ez ont	dormir + ais ais ait ions iez aient	dors dormons dormez
écrire to write (*avoir*)	écrivant écrit	écris écris écrit écrivons écrivez écrivent	écrive écrives écrive écrivions écriviez écrivent	écriv + ais ais ait ions iez aient	écrir + ai as a ons ez ont	écrir + ais ais ait ions iez aient	écris écrivons écrivez
envoyer to send (*avoir*)	envoyant envoyé	envoie envoies envoie envoyons envoyez envoient	envoie envoies envoie envoyions envoyiez envoient	envoy + ais ais ait ions iez aient	enverr + ai as a ons ez ont	enverr + ais ais ait ions iez aient	envoie envoyons envoyez
être to be (*avoir*)	étant été	suis es est sommes êtes sont	sois sois soit soyons soyez soient	ét + ais ais ait ions iez aient	ser + ai as a ons ez ont	ser + ais ais ait ions iez aient	sois soyons soyez

		Present	Pres. Subj.	Imperfect	Future	Conditional	Imperative
faillir† to fail (*avoir*)	faillant failli	not used	not used	not used	fer + ai as a ons ez ont	fer + ais ais ait ions iez aient	not used
faire to do to make (*avoir*)	faisant fait	fais fais fait faisons faites font	fasse fasses fasse fassions fassiez fassent	fais + ais ais ait ions iez aient	fer + ai as a ons ez ont	fer + ais ais ait ions iez aient	fais faisons faites
falloir to be necessary, must (used only with *il*) (*avoir*)	*no pres. part.* fallu	il faut	il faille	il fallait	il faudra	il faudrait	
fuir to flee (*avoir*)	fuyant fui	fuis fuis fuit fuyons fuyez fuient	fuie fuies fuie fuyions fuyiez fuient	fuy + ais ais ait ions iez aient	fuir + ai as a ons ez ont	fuir + ais ais ait ions iez aient	fuis fuyons fuyez

† Used in expressions such as *Il a failli tomber. He nearly fell* (lit., he failed to fall).

357

Infinitive	Pres. & Past Participles	Present Indicative	Present Subjunctive	Imperfect Indicative	Future	Conditional	Imperative
haïr to hate (*avoir*)	haïssant haï	hais hais hait haïssons haïssez haïssent	haïsse haïsses haïsse haïssions haïssiez haïssent	haïss + ais ais ait ions iez aient	haïr + ai as a ons ez ont	haïr + ais ais ait ions iez aient	hais haïssons haïssez
lire to read (*avoir*)	lisant lu	lis lis lit lisons lisez lisent	lise lises lise lisions lisiez lisent	lis + ais ais ait ions iez aient	lir + ai as a ons ez ont	lir + ais ais ait ions iez aient	lis lisons lisez
mettre to put to place (*avoir*)	mettant mis	mets mets met mettons mettez mettent	mette mettes mette mettions mettiez mettent	mett + ais ais ait ions iez aient	mettr + ai as a ons ez ont	mettr + ais ais ait ions iez aient	mets mettons mettez
mourir to die (*être*)	mourant mort(e)(s)	meurs meurs meurt mourons mourez meurent	meure meures meure mourions mouriez meurent	mour + ais ais ait ions iez aient	mourr + ai as a ons ez ont	mourr + ais ais ait ions iez aient	meurs mourons mourez

358

Infinitive	Participles	Present	Pres. Subj.	Imperfect	Future	Conditional	Imperative
mouvoir† to move (*avoir*)	mouvant mû	meus meus meut mouvons mouvez meuvent	meuve meuves meuve mouvions mouviez meuvent	mouv + ais ais ait ions iez aient	mouvr + ai as a ons ez ont	mouvr + ais ais ait ions iez aient	meus mouvons mouvez
naître to be born (*être*)	naissant né(e)(s)	nais nais naît naissons naissez naissent	naisse naisses naisse naissions naissiez naissent	naiss + ais ais ait ions iez aient	naîtr + ai as a ons ez ont	naîtr + ais ais ait ions iez aient	nais naissons naissez
ouvrir to open (*avoir*)	ouvrant ouvert	ouvre ouvres ouvre ouvrons ouvrez ouvrent	ouvre ouvres ouvre ouvrions ouvriez ouvrent	ouvr + ais ais ait ions iez aient	ouvrir + ai as a ons ez ont	ouvrir + ais ais ait ions iez aient	ouvre ouvrons ouvrez

† *Mouvoir* is seldom used except in compounds like *émouvoir*, to move (emotionally).

Infinitive	Pres. & Past Participles	Present Indicative	Present Subjunctive	Imperfect Indicative	Future	Conditional	Imperative
partir to leave to depart (*être*)	partant parti(e)(s)	pars pars part partons partez partent	parte partes parte partions partiez partent	part + ais ais ait ions iez aient	partir + ai as a ons ez ont	partir + ais ais ait ions iez aient	pars partons partez
plaire to please (to be pleasing to) (*avoir*)	plaisant plu	plais plais plaît plaisons plaisez plaisent	plaise plaises plaise plaisions plaisiez plaisent	plais + ais ais ait ions iez aient	plair + ai as a ons ez ont	plair + ais ais ait ions iez aient	plais plaisons plaisez
pleuvoir to rain (used only with *il*) (*avoir*)	pleuvant plu	il pleut	il pleuve	il pleuvait	il pleuvra	il pleuvrait	*not used*

Infinitive	Participles	Present	Pres. Subjunctive	Imperfect stem		Future stem		Conditional stem		Imperative
pouvoir† to be able, can (*avoir*)	pouvant pu	peux (puis)† peux peut pouvons pouvez peuvent	puisse puisses puisse puissions puissiez puissent	pouv	+ ais ais ait ions iez aient	pourr	+ ai as a ons ez ont	pourr	+ ais ais ait ions iez aient	*not used*
prendre to take (*avoir*)	prenant pris	prends prends prend prenons prenez prennent	prenne prennes prenne prenions preniez prennent	pren	+ ais ais ait ions iez aient	prendr	+ ai as a ons ez ont	prendr	+ ais ais ait ions iez aient	prends prenons prenez
résoudre to resolve (*avoir*)	résolvant résolu	résous résous résout résolvons résolvez résolvent	résolve résolves résolve résolvions résolviez résolvent	résolv	+ ais ais ait ions iez aient	résoudr	+ ai as a ons ez ont	résoudr	+ ais ais ait ions iez aient	résous résolvons résolvez

† The interrogative of *pouvoir* in the first person singular is always *Puis-je?*

Infinitive	Pres. & Past Participles	Present Indicative	Present Subjunctive	Imperfect Indicative	Future	Conditional	Imperative
rire to laugh (*avoir*)	riant ri	ris ris rit rions riez rient	rie ries rie riions riiez rient	ri + ais ais ait ions iez aient	rir + ai as a ons ez ont	rir + ais ais ait ions iez aient	ris rions riez
savoir to know (*avoir*)	sachant su	sais sais sait savons savez savent	sache saches sache sachions sachiez sachent	sav + ais ais ait ions iez aient	saur + ai as a ons ez ont	saur + ais ais ait ions iez aient	sache sachons sachez
suffire to be enough, to suffice (*avoir*)	suffisant suffi	suffis suffis suffit suffisons suffisez suffisent	suffise suffises suffise suffisions suffisiez suffisent	suffis + ais ais ait ions iez aient	suffir + ai as a ons ez ont	suffir + ais ais ait ions iez aient	suffis suffisons suffisez

Infinitive (aux.)	Participles	Present	Subjunctive	Imperfect	Future	Conditional	Imperative
suivre to follow (*avoir*)	suivant suivi	suis suis suit suivons suivez suivent	suive suives suive suivions suiviez suivent	suiv + ais ais ait ions iez aient	suivr + ai as a ons ez ont	suivr + ais ais ait ions iez aient	suis suivons suivez
(se)taire to be quiet, to say nothing (*être*)	taisant tu(e)(s)	tais tais tait taisons taisez taisent	taise taises taise taisions taisiez taisent	tais + ais ais ait ions iez aient	tair + ai as a ons ez ont	tair + ais ais ait ions iez aient	tais-toi taisons-nous taisez-vous
tenir to hold, to keep (*avoir*)	tenant tenu	tiens tiens tient tenons tenez tiennent	tienne tiennes tienne tenions teniez tiennent	ten + ais ais ait ions iez aient	tiendr + ai as a ons ez ont	tiendr + ais ais ait ions iez aient	tiens tenons tenez
vaincre to conquer (*avoir*)	vainquant vaincu	vaincs vaincs vainc vainquons vainquez vainquent	vainque vainques vainque vainquions vainquiez vainquent	vainqu + ais ais ait ions iez aient	vaincr + ai as a ons ez ont	vaincr + ais ais ait ions iez aient	vaincs vainquons vainquez

Infinitive	Pres. & Past Participles	Present Indicative	Present Subjunctive	Imperfect Indicative	Future	Conditional	Imperative
valoir to be worth (*avoir*)	valant valu	vaux vaux vaut valons valez valent	vaille vailles vaille valions valiez vaillent	val + ais ais ait ions iez aient	vaudr + ai as a ons ez ont	vaudr + ais ais ait ions iez aient	vaux† valons valez
venir to come (*être*)	venant venu(e)(s)	viens viens vient venons venez viennent	vienne viennes vienne venions veniez viennent	ven + ais ais ait ions iez aient	viendr + ai as a ons ez ont	viendr + ais ais ait ions iez aient	viens venons venez
vivre to live (*avoir*)	vivant vécu	vis vis vit vivons vivez vivent	vive vives vive vivions viviez vivent	viv + ais ais ait ions iez aient	vivr + ai as a ons ez ont	vivr + ais ais ait ions iez aient	vis vivons vivez
voir to see (*avoir*)	voyant vu	vois vois voit voyons voyez voient	voie voies voie voyions voyiez voient	voy + ais ais ait ions iez aient	verr + ai as a ons ez ont	verr + ais ais ait ions iez aient	vois voyons voyez

† The imperative of *valoir* is not often used.

LETTER WRITING

1. FORMAL INVITATIONS AND ACCEPTANCES

FORMAL INVITATIONS

Monsieur et Madame de Montour vous prient de leur faire l'honneur d'assister à un cocktail, donné en l'honneur de leur fille Marie-José, le dimanche huit avril à neuf heures du soir.

M et Mme de Montour
35 avenue Hoche
Paris xvième.

R.S.V.P.

Mr. and Mrs. de Montour request the pleasure of your presence at a cocktail reception given in honor of their daughter, Marie-José, on Sunday evening, April eighth, at nine o'clock.

Mr. and Mrs. de Montour
35 avenue Hoche
Paris xvième.

R.S.V.P.

R.S.V.P. stands for *Répondez s'il vous plaît*. Please answer.

NOTE OF ACCEPTANCE

Monsieur et Madame du Panier vous remercient de votre aimable invitation à laquelle ils se feront un plaisir de se rendre.

Mr. and Mrs. du Panier thank you for your kind invitation and will be delighted to come.

2.   FORMAL THANK-YOU NOTES

le 14 mars 2005

Chère Madame,

Je tiens à vous remercier de l'aimable attention que vous avez eue en m'envoyant le charmant présent que j'ai reçu. Ce tableau me fait d'autant plus plaisir qu'il est ravissant dans le cadre de mon studio.

Je vous prie de croire à l'expression de mes sentiments de sincère amitié.

Renée Beaujoly

March 14, 2005

Dear Mrs. Duparc,

I should like to thank you for the delightful present you sent me. The picture was all the more welcome because it fits in so beautifully with the other things in my studio.

Thank you ever so much.

Sincerely yours,
Renée Beaujoly

3. BUSINESS LETTERS

Roger Beaumont
2, rue Chalgrin
Paris
75003

le 6 novembre 2005
Monsieur le Rédacteur en Chef
"Vu"
3, Blvd. des Capucines
Paris

Monsieur,
  Je vous envoie ci-inclus un chèque de €110, mon-
tant de ma souscription pour un abonnement d'un an
à votre publication.
  Veuillez agréer, Monsieur, mes salutations distin-
guées.

Roger Beaumont

Ci-joint un chèque

2, rue Chalgrin
Paris
November 6, 2005

Editor-in-Chief
"Vu"
3, Blvd. des Capucines
Paris

Gentlemen:
  Enclosed please find a check for 110 euros to cover
a year's subscription to your magazine.

Sincerely yours,
Roger Beaumont

Enc.

Dupuis Aîné
3, rue du Quatre-Septembre
Paris

> *le 30 septembre 2005*
> *Vermont et Cie*
> *2, rue Marat*
> *Bordeaux*
> *Gironde*

Monsieur,
    En réponse à votre lettre du dix courant, je tiens à vous confirmer que la marchandise en question vous a été expédiée le treize août par colis postal.
    Veuillez agréer, Monsieur, mes salutations distinguées,

> *Henri Tournaire*

db/ht

> 3, rue Quatre-September
> Paris
> September 30, 2005

Vermont and Co.
2, rue Marat
Bordeaux
Gironde

Gentlemen:

    In reply to your letter of the tenth of this month, I wish to confirm that the merchandise was mailed to you parcel post on August 13.

> Sincerely yours,
> Henri Tournaire

db/ht

4. INFORMAL LETTERS

le 5 mars 2002

Mon cher Jacques,

Ta dernière lettre m'a fait grand plaisir.

Tout d'abord laisse-moi t'annoncer une bonne nouvelle: je compte venir passer une quinzaine de jours à Paris en début avril et je me réjouis d'avance à l'idée de te revoir ainsi que les tiens qui je l'espère, se portent bien.

Colette vient avec moi et se fait une grande joie à l'idée de connaître enfin ta femme. Les affaires marchent bien en ce moment, espérons que ça continuera. Tâche de ne pas avoir trop de malades au mois d'avril, enfin il est vrai que ces choses-là ne se commandent pas.

Toute ma famille se porte bien, heureusement.

J'ai pris l'apéritif avec Dumont l'autre jour, qui m'a demandé de tes nouvelles. Son affaire marche très bien.

J'allais presque oublier le plus important, peux-tu me réserver une chambre au Grand Hôtel pour le cinq avril, je t'en saurais fort gré.

J'espère avoir le plaisir de te lire très bientôt.

Mes meilleurs respects à ta femme.

En toute amitié,
André

March 5, 2002

Dear Jack,

I was very happy to receive your last letter.

First of all, I've some good news for you. I expect to spend two weeks in Paris at the beginning of April and I'm looking forward to the prospect of seeing you and your family, all of whom I hope are well.

Colette's coming with me; she's delighted to be able at last to meet your wife. Business is pretty good right now. Let's hope it will keep up. Try not to get too many patients during the month of April, though I suppose that's a little difficult to arrange.

Fortunately, my family is doing well.

I had cocktails with Dumont the other day and he asked about you. His business is going well.

I almost forgot the most important thing. Can you reserve a room for me at the Grand Hotel for April the fifth? You'll be doing me a great favor.

I hope to hear from you soon. My best regards to your wife.

Your friend,
Andrew

Paris, le 3 avril 2005

Ma chérie,

J'ai bien reçu ta lettre du trente et je suis heureuse de savoir que ta fille est tout à fait remise.

Rien de bien nouveau ici, sauf que Pierre me donne beaucoup de mal, enfin toi aussi tu as un fils de cet âge-là, et tu sais ce que je veux dire!

L'autre jour, j'ai rencontré Mme Michaud dans la rue, Dieu qu'elle a vieilli! Elle est méconnaissable!

Nous avons vu ton mari l'autre soir, il est venu dîner à la maison; il se porte bien et il lui tarde de te voir de retour.

Tu as bien de la veine d'être à la montagne pour encore un mois. Que fais-tu de beau toute la journée à Chamonix? Y a-t-il encore beaucoup de monde là-bas? Il paraît que les Villenèque sont là. A Paris tout le monde parle des prochaines fiançailles de leur fille.

Nous sommes allés à une soirée l'autre soir chez les Clergeaud, cette femme ne sait pas recevoir, je m'y suis ennuyée à mourir.

Voilà à peu près tous les derniers potins de Paris, tu

vois que je te tiens bien au courant, tâche d'en faire autant.

Embrasse bien Françoise pour moi.

> *Meilleurs baisers de ton amie,*
> *Monique*

Paris, April 3, 2005

Darling,

I received your letter of the thirtieth and I'm happy to learn that your daughter has completely recovered.

Nothing new here, except that Peter is giving me a lot of trouble. You have a son of the same age, so you know what I mean.

The other day I ran into Mrs. Michaud in the street. My, how she's aged! She's unrecognizable!

We saw your husband the other night—he had dinner at our house. He's well and is looking forward to your coming home.

You're lucky to be staying in the mountains for another month! What do you do all day long in Chamonix? Is it still very crowded? It seems that the de Villenèques are there. In Paris, the future engagement of their daughter is the talk of the town.

The other evening we went to a party given by the Clergeauds. She doesn't know how to entertain and I was bored to death.

That's about all of the latest Paris gossip. You see how well I keep you posted—try to do the same.

Give my love to Frances.

> Love,
> Monique

5. FORMS OF SALUTATIONS AND COMPLIMENTARY CLOSINGS

SALUTATIONS

FORMAL

Monsieur l'Abbé,	Dear Reverend:
Monsieur le Député,	Dear Congressman:
Monsieur le Maire,	Dear Mayor (Smith):
Cher Professeur,	Dear Professor (Smith):
Cher Maître, (Mon cher Maître),	Dear Mr. (Smith): (Lawyers are addressed as "Maître" in France.)
Monsieur,	Dear Sir:
Madame,	Dear Madam:
Messieurs,	Gentlemen:
Cher Monsieur Varnoux,	My dear Mr. Varnoux:
Chère Madame Gignoux,	My dear Mrs. Gignoux:

INFORMAL

Mon cher Roger,	Dear Roger,
Ma chère Denise,	Dear Denise,
Chéri,	Darling (*m.*),
Chérie,	Darling (*f.*),
Mon chéri,	My darling (*m.*),
Ma chérie,	My darling (*f.*),

COMPLIMENTARY CLOSINGS

FORMAL

1. *Agréez, je vous prie, l'expression de mes salutations les plus distinguées.*

("Please accept the expression of my most distinguished greetings.") Very truly yours.

2. *Veuillez agréer l'expression de mes salutations distinguées.*
("Will you please accept the expression of my distinguished greetings.") Very truly yours.

3. *Veuillez agréer, Monsieur, mes salutations empressées.*
("Sir, please accept my eager greetings.") Yours truly.

4. *Veuillez agréer, Monsieur, mes sincères salutations.*
("Sir, please accept my sincere greetings.") Yours truly.

5. *Agréez, Monsieur, mes salutations distinguées.*
("Sir, accept my distinguished greetings.") Yours truly.

6. *Votre tout dévoué.*
("Your very devoted.") Yours truly.

1. *Je vous prie de croire à l'expression de mes sentiments de sincère amitié.*
("Please believe in my feelings of sincere friendship.") Very sincerely.

2. *Meilleures amitiés.*
("Best regards.") Sincerely yours.

3. *Amicalement.*
("Kindly.") Sincerely yours.

4. *Mes pensées affectueuses* (or *amicales*).
("My affectionate *or* friendly thoughts.") Sincerely.

5. *En toute amitié.*
Your friend. ("In all friendship.")

6. *Je te serre la main.*
("I shake your hand.") Sincerely.

7. *Affectueusement.*
   Affectionately.
8. *Très affectueusement.*
   ("Very affectionately.") Affectionately yours.
9. *Je vous prie de bien vouloir transmettre mes respects à Madame votre mère.*
   Please give my regards to your mother.
10. *Transmets mes respects à ta famille.*
    Give my regards to your family.
11. *Rappelle-moi au bon souvenir de ta famille.*
    Remember me to your family.
12. *Embrasse tout le monde pour moi.*
    ("Kiss everybody for me.") Give my love to everybody.
13. *Je t'embrasse bien fort.*
    Millions de baisers. } Love.
14. *Cordialement.*
    Cordially.
15. *Bien à vous.*
    Yours truly.

6. Form of the Envelope

Vermont et Cie.
5, rue Daunou
75002 Paris

> Maison Dupuis Aîné
> 2, cours de l'Intendance
> 41200 Romorantin

Jean Alexandre
6, rue Voltaire
37270 Montlouis

Monsieur Robert Marcatour
c/o de M.P. Lambert
2, rue du Ranelagh
75016 Paris

E-MAIL AND INTERNET RESOURCES

1. SAMPLE E-MAIL

à: *azizam@yahoo.com*
de: *elianep@livinglanguage.com*
objet: *Apprendre le français*
cc: *jenb@livinglanguage.com*

Salut Aziza:
Comme promis, je t'envoie les informations (en pièces jointes) concernant notre voyage.
N'hésite pas à les faire suivre aux parents.
J'espère que tu vas bien, ainsi que toute ta famille.
Bises,
Eliane
PS: J'ai reçu les photos que tu m'a envoyées la semaine dernière. Elles sont super! J'ai téléchargé la plus belle—ta fille—sur mon écran . . .

Hello Aziza:
As promised, I am sending you the info (in the attachment) about our trip.
Don't hesitate to forward them to your parents.
I hope you are well, and your family too.
Love,
Eliane
PS: I've received the pictures that you sent me last week. They're great! I've downloaded the most beautiful—your daughter—onto my screen . . .

2. IMPORTANT E-MAIL VOCABULARY AND EXPRESSIONS

address book	*le carnet d'adresses*
e-mail address	*l'adresse e-mail*
password	*le mot de passe*
account ID	*le compte*
to read a message	*lire un message*
mailbox	*la boîte aux lettres*
spell check	*orthographe*
to send	*envoyer*
to insert signature	*insérer la signature*
to read	*lire*
to write	*écrire*
to answer	*répondre*
keep/mark as new	*marquer comme non lu*
add to address book	*ajouter au carnet d'adresses*

3. INTERNET RESOURCES

The following are resources for students of French that are available on the internet.

http://www.french-linguistics.co.uk/dictionary/
A dictionary from French into English and from English into French.

http://www.francemonthly.com
A travel site (and more) that will give you great ideas about where to travel. Beautiful pictures, and lots of cultural material.

http://www.yahoo.fr
Yahoo France. A good way to increase your French vocabulary and learn about French life.

http://www.lemonde.fr
Le Monde. A serious daily newspaper covering international and national news, as well as culture, sports, science, and more.

http://www.monde-diplomatique.fr
A monthly version of the same.

http://www.courrierinternational.com
Le Courrier International. A weekly newspaper that collects material from international press sources and translates it in French. A good way to practice French while getting an international perspective on the news.

http://www.paroles.net
A site that provides the lyrics for most French songs. A great way to practice and learn French, especially if you get the CDs and sing along.

INDEX

Take Your **Language Skills** to the **Next Level!**

Go *Beyond the Basics* with this acclaimed new series, developed by the experts at LIVING LANGUAGE®

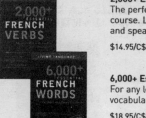

2,000+ Essential French Verbs
The perfect companion book to any language
course. Learn the forms, master the tenses,
and speak fluently!

$14.95/C$22.95 • ISBN: 1-4000-2053-0

6,000+ Essential French Words
For any level, a simple and effective way to expand
vocabulary and achieve fluency.

$18.95/C$26.95 • ISBN: 1-4000-2091-3

Drive Time French
A hands-free language course for learning
on the road!

4 CDs or Cassettes/Listener's Guide
$21.95/C$29.95 • ISBN: 1-4000-2182-0 (CD Package)
1-4000-2185-5 (Cassette Package)

French For Travelers
An essential language program for leisure
and business travelers.

2 CDs/Phrasebook • $19.95/C$27.95 • ISBN: 1-4000-1487-5

In-Flight French
A essential one-hour program aimed at
helping travelers learn enough to get by in
every travel situation.

CD/Audioscript • $13.95/C$21.00 • ISBN: 0-609-81066-9

Ultimate French: Beginner-Intermediate
Our most comprehensive program for serious
language learners, businesspeople, and
anyone planning to spend time abroad.

8 CDs/Coursebook • $79.95/C$110.00 • ISBN: 1-4000-2105-7

Ultimate French: Advanced
Ideal for serious language learners who would like
to develop native-sounding conversational skills.

8 CDs/Coursebook • $79.95/C$120.00 • ISBN: 1-4000-2057-3